The Play of the Gods

To the memory of my parents
András Östör and Magdaléna Östör (née Gallus)

New Edition

The Play of the Gods

Locality, Ideology, Structure, and Time
in the Festivals of a Bengali Town

Ákos Östör

Chronicle Books
An imprint of DC Publishers
New Delhi
2004

First edition publised by University of Chicago Press, 1980.

Chronicle Books is an imprint of DC Publishers

Distributed by
Orient Longman Limited
Bangalore Bhopal Bhubaneshwar Chandigarh
Chennai Ernakulam Guwahati Hyderabad Jaipur
Kolkata Lucknow Mumbai New Delhi Patna

ISBN 81-8028-013-6

Typeset by Eleven Arts, New Delhi
Printed in India by Pauls Press, New Delhi
Published by DC Publishers
D-27 NDSE Part II, New Delhi 110 049

Contents

Acknowledgments

Fieldwork for this study was carried out in the town of Vishnupur, West Bengal, from 1967 to 1969.

I received indispensable help, intellectual stimulation, and treasured friendship from many people in the course of my graduate studies at the University of Chicago, my years of research in India, and the intervening and subsequent periods of reflection, discussion, teaching, and writing at the University of Chicago and the University of Minnesota, the Institute for Advanced Study, and Harvard University.

I was introduced to anthropology through the core program at the University of Chicago under Paul Friedrich, Milton Singer, Nur Yalman, and Melford Spiro. Bernard Cohn followed my work from the very beginning, through my experiences in the field, to particular result. As advisor and friend he has influenced me far beyond this one piece of work. David Schneider, Clifford Geertz, Louis Dumont, and Edward Dimock have read parts of the typescript at various stages; their commentary and the resulting discussion have helped shape my thinking. Milton Singer, Victor Turner, and McKim Marriott have commented and given me cause for reflection. I discussed many details with Ralph and Marta Nicholas, who also suggested stylistic improvements. Lina

Fruzzetti, my wife, is the *śakti* of this study. Without her support and critical contributions the task would not have been accomplished.

In India I received polite and courteous consideration from officials. In Calcutta many friends, colleagues, and acquaintances encouraged me in my attempts to understand Bengali society. Sri Tarun Mitra in particular has contributed his expertise most unselfishly. Above all, I am indebted to the people of Vishnupur. Through the painful and rewarding process of fieldwork, their friendship, laughter, and sorrow have shaped my understanding. As I write about other aspects of my research I will have an opportunity to remember those who have helped me in specific ways, and so here I will mention only those who were influential in my experience of Durgāpūjā, Śiva's gājan. To them and to the many, many more who have contributed in planned or chance encounters, I offer my thanks and the fruit of my labors. Sir Maniklal Singha introduced me to the town and gave generously from his vast store of local knowledge. Sri Haridas Bhattacharya, Sri Kalipada Chakrabarti, Sri Bhaskar Mahapatra, Sri Girija Sankar Ghor, Sri Gopalchandra Bidh, Sri Rabilachan Khar, Sri Ratan Tanti, the Bābu Sāhib, Sri Phakir Narayan Karmakar, Sri Rabi Kamar, Sri Tulsi Das Bauri, Sri Gopal Das Bauri, Sri Bharat Majhi, and their caste brothers, relatives, and households enriched my stay in Vishnupur in inestimable measure.

My two years in India was funded from grants and fellowships by the American Institute of Indian Studies and the National Science Foundation. The dissertation on which this book is based was written between 1969 and 1970, while I was holding a University of Chicago fellowship. In 1971 we returned to West Bengal for further fieldwork on matters other than pūjās and festivals. I began rewriting the thesis during a membership year at the Princeton Institute of Advanced Study (1973–74) and completed it during a term's leave granted by Harvard University.

The transcription of Bengali words follows the scheme suggested by Dimock and Inden (1967). Earlier versions of pūjā, Durgāpūjā, and Śibergājan were published in *Eastern Anthropologist* (reprinted as a monograph of the Ethnographic and Folk Culture Society, Lucknow), and the *Journal of the Anthropological Society of India*.

Finally, I would like to thank the University of Chicago Press for passing on the comments of an anonymous reviewer of the manuscript who made many excellent suggestions that I incorporated in the text.

Captions

Durgāpūjā

Picture 1 The rājā's goddess: Mrinmoyī Debī (Śiva is above, the ten forms of Durgā are painted on the wall, the permanent ghat is in front of the Āsura).

Picture 2 The rājā's image maker at work (the ṣolaānā image at the Bāsaṇṭi Durgāpūjā).

Picture 3 The belbaraṇ pūjā of Choṭoṭhākurānī (note the two nabapatrikas, silver and gold paṭs, the painted paṭs, two small and two large ghats).

Picture 4 Ghātpūjā (note the maṅgal patra, nabapatrika, the paṭs and the Brāhmaṇ's attire and gestures).

Picture 5 Bāsaṇṭi Durgāpūjā: procession from the pond to the temple (nabapatrika, ghats, pūjā vessels are carried to the temple).

Picture 6 Life is given to the deities (note the Bhattacharya's gesture and the Tantrik's manuscript, the offerings and the sālāgram sila near the ghat).

Picture 7 Immersion procession of Bāsaṇṭi Debī.

Picture 8 Immersion of the rājā's goddess.

Śiva's gājan

Picture 9 Taking the sacred thread: Ṣaṛeśvar gājan (note the bhaktas' attire and equipment; the agradhānī Brāhmaṇ is in the middle).

Picture 10 Śiva liṅga (the śaktipaṭ surrounds the liṅga, priests sit on both sides, Bhairab's clay horses are in the back, the bhaktas' flower offerings and beṭs rest on the image).

Picture 11 Suryaarghya: offerings to the sun (Rātgājan of Buṛo Śibtalā: paṭ, pāṭbhakta and agradhānī in the middle of the field).

Picture 12 Rātgājan trance and Ṣaṛeśvar gājan (the chalunibhakta is in the right foreground, the pāṭbhakta is about to fall into trance).

Picture 13 Pāṭā pūjā in the Dvarakeśvar river.

Picture 14 Dingājan at Boltalā Śiva gājan (sannyāsībhakta recites, flanked by the pāṭbhakta and rajbhakta).

Picture 15 Dingājan of Buṛo Śibtalā gājan (the sāddhu stands on a chair, sannyāsībhakta recites flanked by the pāṭbhakta and agradhānī).

Picture 16 Immersion of the sacred thread at Buṛo Śibtalā gājan.

The Play of the Gods

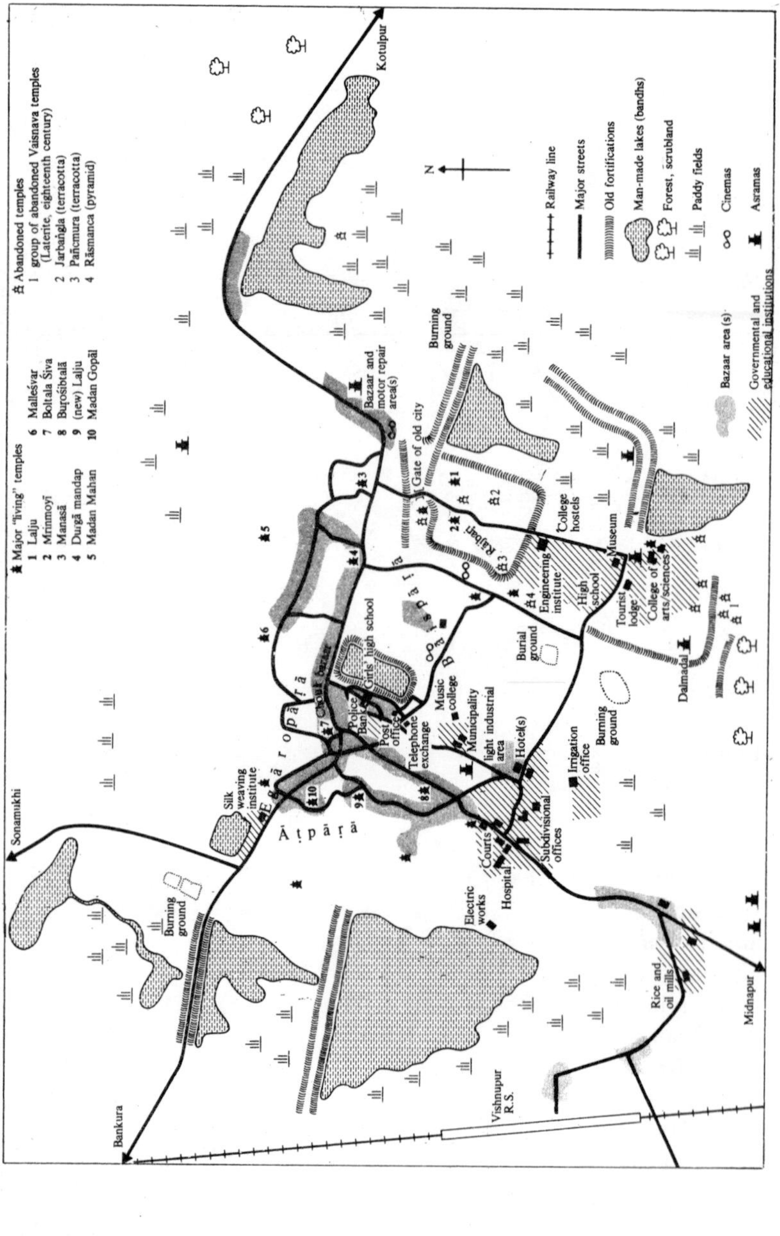

Figure 1. Sketch map of Vishupur.

Introduction

Paths to *The Play of the Gods*

What is in the study of a society different from one's own? Why do some of us feel compelled to stray far from home and find new homes? In my own case these are difficult questions to answer, considering they may not be relevant at all. Which is my own society? Hungary, Austria, Australia, the United States, India or the Sudan—all of which, at various times, I left and returned to, adopted and was adopted by, and to which I feel deeply attached and grateful. They are all my societies, encountered at different times in different ways but they are always with me. For me the process began early, with my birth and early childhood during World War II, in Hungary and Austria, with vivid memories of armies—Hungarian, German, Soviet, and American.

My first brief visit to Calcutta was a 1957 stopover of a few hours at Dum Dum Airport on the way to Australia, a journey occasioned by the Hu Revolution of 1956 and our subsequent emigration. I came back in 1965 and stayed several weeks. This time I was on my way to the United States for graduate studies in Anthropology. I returned to Calcutta and Bengal with my wife, Lina Fruzzetti (herself of Eritrean and Italian parentage) for my dissertation and post-doctoral research between 1967 and 1969 and 1971 and 1973. In the 1970's we worked in the Sudan but in the 1980's we were back in India just about every year, including, for me, a longer stay in Benares and shorter ones in Bengal, filming and doing ethnography in both places.

My focus shifted from ritual and myth to kinship/politics/economics, and to visual images and film. A common thread over the years has been a commitment to modes of understanding and interpretation rather than surveys, quantification, and empiricism, although I have never experienced a formative or even telling opposition between scientific and interpretive anthropologies, only differing approaches to the problems at hand. Nevertheless, I did not take an explicitly and formally quantitative approach to any problem, and at the same time, I never lost sight of the empirical nature of my work. My starting point has always been ideology and local practice, hence an interpretive as well as empirical turn were indicated from the beginning. To this day my concern remains with ideas in relation to action in a context, not chronology and local history or abstraction and theory out of space and time. Nor was I drawn to the empiricism of rural sociology, micro-economics, or the minutiae of anthropological village studies with their paradoxically broad and unexamined categories. I attempted to see the whole, revealed and realized in a place, the hierarchy of locality and time from village to nation, domain to domain and level to level, near and distant, anchored in a particular place at a particular moment. Hence, Vishnupur and the surrounding villages in Bengal and the old city of Benares served as the territories of my labor with shorter stays in Delhi and Calcutta and travels all over India.

Such an effort at balancing the particular and the general, the ideational and the empirical is in no way more limited than the approaches followed by history, political science, or sociology. Archives, statistics, questionnaires, surveys, and interviews do not yield better data than anthropology with its insistence on immersion in particular places. In any case, all the methods of the social sciences and humanities can be and are used in particular disciplines and do not in themselves set insuperable boundaries.

Being there, at the grass roots, does give anthropology an advantage since it provides an opportunity to pursue detailed and finely drawn connections between different domains of human experience such as family, politics, religion, and economics. The links can be pursued in place and time through the hierarchy of levels in social life.

Why Vishnupur? Studying Bengali at the University of Chicago

I read Benoy Ghosh's vivid and lively account of Vishnupur and Mallabhum in his *Cultural History of Bengal*. Edward Dimock and Sibnarayan Ray in Chicago and Calcutta have suggested that the town would be ideal for the kind of field study I envisioned. I knew I wanted to be in a town rather than a village, since most anthropologists worked in villages at the time. But it was my first visit in 1967 that convinced me to stay. I had already visited towns the length and breath of Bengal from Midnapur to Krishnanagar and in the end Lina and I decided to settle in Vishnupur. Manik Lal Singha found a small house for us at the edge of town near the old laterite temples, next to the garden of the Ramakrishna Asram. Manikbabu proved to be of great help during the next several months. The scale of Vishnupur was important to me: the town grew out of a series of settlements around a royal court and temples, and became an administrative and market center. Even today it can boast distinct localities and a widely known indigenous history. Vishnupur was far from the timeless social structure and hide-bound tradition that was once ascribed to rural India. I did not end up writing the social history of the town, though I planned to write it at one point. But I felt called upon to deal with history as it was lived in the present. There were a great many social practices with diverse forms of organization in Vishnupur and despite the size and complexity I felt I could encompass the entire town, even if selectively, in a study. It seemed to me that Vishnupur was experienced by its inhabitants as a totality, both as an idea and a fact and I quickly learned to follow the lead of townspeople.

Finally, both Lina and I liked Vishnupur and we never questioned the more ineffable reasons for our choice. I am certain we could have studied in any of the dozen other towns I visited on that trip in 1967 and at any time we could have moved to another place had the necessity arisen. But Vishnupur it was and remained.

Foremost in my mind was working with indigenous categories: the terms, concepts, ideas in and through which people act. Relations among domains formed by such ideas and actions proved to be the kernel of my approach. The configuration of domains is given by categories in structure, event, locality, and time. The search for cultural categories (which are, for anthropologists, ethnographic ones, elicited through the dialectic of field work) necessitates a comparison among societies. Comparison implies a recognition of the differences between kinds of societies, without the construction of a full fledged classificatory or typological scheme as an end in itself.

Here I refer to an awareness of the terms and scale of comparison, a knowledge of what is being compared with what, and in which context, Hence my concern with limits, boundaries, systems, structures, and configurations among categories and domains; Bengal, India, and the West; colonial, industrial, contemporary and other societies. I do not want to reify method and theory here—methods are merely the way I go about my work as an anthropologist, something visible and accountable, so that others who wish to follow may come to similar or different conclusions. I give enough detail for someone else to reformulate my accounts, to confirm or challenge the analysis and/or interpretation I give. Both the logic and narrative I offer are open to scrutiny, acceptance, or doubt. Similarly, theories are made up of informed guesses, hypotheses or other likely stories in a context: anything that would make something of ethnographic work, and would not leave my findings on the same scale and level as I encountered them.

Why ritual? I was interested in rituals and myths, and the logic of categories within the indigenous forms of culture. The anthropological reference includes ideas and practices, although of what kind, and within what boundaries has been a matter of controversy. The ideas of Lévi-Strauss, Turner, Geertz and Schneider were just beginning to make an impact in America in the mid 1960's and the University of Chicago was the place to be. I came to Chicago to study anthropology in 1965, having taken a BA and MA in history at the University of Melbourne in Australia. In Chicago I encountered not only structuralism in linguistics and anthropology but also British social anthropology, American cultural anthropology and the works of a whole host of contemporary anthropologists in the course of the rigorous graduate instruction given by Paul Friedrich, Nur Yalman, Milton Singer, Clifford Geertz, Bernard Cohn, Melford Spiro, McKim Mariott, David Schneider, Robert McCormick Adams, Leslie Freeman, Pedro Armillas, and Charles Merbs during the six academic quarters of 1965–66 and 1966–67, before I went to the field. Victor Turner came to Chicago later and I joined his and Terry Turner's seminar on ritual upon returning from the field in 1969. Hence an interest in cultural accounts, narrative and exegesis, ritual as a cultural system, thick description and interpretation, was wedded to the structuralism of Dumont and Lévi-Strauss, especially the Dumont of the superb critical pieces in *Contributions to Indian Sociology*. The theoretical background I took to the field alerted me to the reciprocity between my own ideas, observations, and experiences, and indigenous accounts including the practice and ideology of participants in rituals and the internal logic and organization of the performances.

In writing *The Play of the Gods* I faced the problems of dealing with structure and event, indigenous logic and process, cultural categories and everyday life. All these considerations played themselves out in contexts, localities and times (which I put, at the time, in theoretical terms of synchrony and diachrony, structure and process). But the elements of the study came from ethnography—observed action, social relations, and indigenous categories. I looked for patterns in a local context and perceived a structure of relationships, a set of principles, and values which I interpreted in the light of people's concerns. These are also the concerns manifested in daily events, relations among social groups, ritual practices, ultimate ends, and the means of living. Concepts and categories issue from performance and practice, encounters with participants during events, and later, detailed discussions with selected informants.

We were in India almost two years with most of the time spent in Vishnupur and the surrounding region. In time I saw the links between the indigenous history of the town, social organization, settlement and population patterns, deities, rituals and festivals. The units of the town are historical and correspond to the organization and performance of rituals. Out of all this material came an analysis of structure and the further attempt to interpret the structure in the variant practices and ideas of townspeople. The book made use of the similarity of structure underlying the performance of different rituals and myths, in texts as well as practice.

Later, Lina and I pursued complementary approaches in the study of what went under "kinship" and "caste" in the anthropology of the day. For us these were not separate domains as witnessed by our awkward, hyphenated English gloss on Bengali actualities: kinship-caste-marriage. This study turned around the concept of "person" with indigenous accounts of birth, marriage, death, and the ancestors. Once again the analysis rested on materials gathered from observation, practice, and discussion, interpreted through local cultural categories such as seed and earth, male and female, relatives, descent lines and marriage alliances.

Culture and Power

We returned to India in 1971 and stayed again for almost two years. Lina carried out research which resulted in her doctoral dissertation and the book *The Gift of a Virgin*. The research on the person led to a number of articles we wrote jointly for *Contributions to Indian Sociology*, which, together with articles based on Lina's work among Hindu and Muslim women and published in various journals, were later collected in a book we called *Kinship and Ritual in Bengal*. In 1976 we organized a conference at Harvard University on the category of the person in kinship/caste/marriage. We edited the revised proceedings with Steve Barrett and called it *Concepts of Person*.

The second period of field work concerned domains of relationship usually subsumed in anthropological writings under the rubics of politics, economics, kinship, caste, and religion. In fact, I dealt with local considerations clustering around *itihasa* (history and legend); *jatra-pūraṇa-pūjā* (theater, myth, ritual), *bazaar* (market) and *andolan* (revolution). These categories and practices (and the arenas in which they occur) seemed related to me both in sets of ideas and actions and also through an indigenous logic or mode of knowledge. Not that Western sociological categories had to be dismissed: to accomplish the "indigenous" aspect of the task it would have been enough to write the book in Bengali. Rather, I saw the need to develop a dialectic between Bengali cultural and Western sociological categories in order to make sense of what I saw, heard, and read in Vishnupur, Calcutta, and elsewhere in India. Itihasa did not oppose society to ideology and history (not even in terms of the more fashionable pairings of history and theory, history and society, or society and theory), nor did it oppose the present to the past. Rather itihasa suggested something closer to Collingwood's idea of the past encapsulated in the present, the living, continuing, presence of the past connecting different times (not necessarily chronological) to contemporary life. Past practices, truths, and events become contemporaneous with present concerns this way, but even further itihasa suggested to me a way into the analysis and interpretation of my ethnographic materials. Thus each of the four sets of Bengali terms (above) has become a chapter in a book (*Culture and Power*) where I looked into the configuration of local cultural domains, starting with the living realities of thought and action in the bazaars of Vishnupur, the Naxalite uprising and local movements, the myths, rites and theatrical performances of Manasā the Snake Goddess.

I turned to these matters because, in the USA, myth and rite were still considered to be more ideological, symbolic and "superstructural" than, for example, economics. I was convinced this was not the case:

economy and religion were equally symbolic to me, equally a part and made up of every day life, with all the elements of structure, event, time and place the term "culture" implies. I found that politics and economics can be approached the way I have dealt with sacred festivals, the latter being neither more nor less real or fundamental than the former.

I found a configuration of categories around symbols, practices, ideas, and events in each complex. I saw these as domains, not in terms of a priori definitions of social science (genealogical kinship, production, and distribution of goods and services, worship of supernatural beings, authority and power) but in terms of Bengali cultural forms, with sets of relationships and structures understood through Bengali categories.

These domains were distinct from yet linked to each other. Pūjā was something in of itself (not just a reflection of productive forces or power relations) a set of related elements, but it was also linked to bazaar, itihasa, and andolan. So too with the other domains: bazaar had a pūjā element and form and so did andolan. The complex whole was made up of relational and comparative processes, in interpretation as in fieldwork, the actuality of what I was trying to comprehend parallel to the problems and attempts of understanding Vishnupur, Bengal, and India.

The bazaar I found to be as much a set of related cultural concepts as the daily activities of buying/selling and supplying and distributing produce and other goods and services. The whole construct included categories of person (with links to the domains of kinship/caste/marriage and ritual); time-based processes (the rhythms of season and exchange); concepts of mediation, hierarchy in a structure (spatially and temporally linking more and more expansive mediations among bazaars in terms of indigenous ideas of power and ability, superiority and dependence).

Andolan was a local notion of change, not revolution in the Western sense (though often extended to cover that term as well) but transformation in the sense of a cycle, the restoration of *dharma* (sacred law, or proper order). *Bhakti* (devotion) was also relevant since the great devotional movements of Vaiṣṇava and Shaiva saints were also called *andolan*. It may have seemed invidious to extend *andolan* to the movement started in Naxalbari (variously called by Indians, in English, revolution, uprising, rebellion or agitation). But the Naxalites' own analysis, in terms of axiomatic Marxist-Leninist formulations were too narrow and neglected the cultural categories and ideologies of the villagers.

They also ignored the links among domains as cultural forms. Having followed the latter I saw the devotional dimension of the Naxalite movement with its characteristic features of andolan. One reason for the failure of the Naxalite movement was its single minded insistence on what it considered to be the "correct analysis" of village life in Bengal.

The domains of politics, economy, kinship, caste and the like did not turn out to be objective, God given compartments in which Vishnupur and Bengali realties could be easily sorted and contained. I realized that having been led to pūjā, andolan, bazaar, and itihasa, I was dealing with cultural forms, living realities in words and actions, always linked to something empirical and practiced by people in a context. I used the analytical term "cultural form" for these realities to highlight the interplay between social science and indigenous cultural categories and the necessity for both analysis and interpretation to proceed hand in hand in a dialectical fashion. These cultural forms (not just their scientific, objective equivalents) had a shape, pattern, past, internal divisions, links, and articulating principles.

I was intrigued by the ways the elements of pūjā came together in a recognizable whole, linked to other forms yet not determined by any obvious outside factors in the local schema. In what ways were these wholes distinct yet related? How did they articulate with each other? What processes of understanding and generalization did they call upon in daily life? Did they come together in larger, overarching structures, or even a single master scheme? What could be meant by constructing such a scheme? For whom, when and where? Are the larger articulations themselves relational and situational, with shared elements but no overall coherence? Are the satisfying, elegant structures too distant and austere (even if resting on or implied by the cultural logic)? Or are we faced with shifting, context bound constructs, which tolerate tension, disarticulation or even contradiction? What does it tell us to look for and find coherence or the lack of it? Surely, the processes of disciplinary interrogation are related to real life phenomena and the results partially present in both the approach and theory as well as the reality investigated. In part recognized and brought out by the anthropologist, in part by the people, to yield meanings, with the cultural construction being carried out on all sides.

I was striving for some kind of structural, interpretive, and cultural category based answers to these questions in the place of determination of any sort privileging single factor, genetic explanations—be they economic, political, religious, or historical. Indigenous cultural forms and outside scientific categories seemed equally called for: the work of anthropology is necessarily comparative, dialectical, both in the field and in analysis, and refers to continuities and changes, the reciprocal play of categories in particular and general contexts. Much of this thinking found its way into *Culture and Power*, with the descriptive subtitle of "Legend, Ritual, Bazaar, and Rebellion in a Bengali Society".

Issues Raised by *The Play of the Gods*

Over the years many questions have been addressed to me about the book: in reviews, books and articles, seminars, and discussions in general. Much praise and some blame has also followed in the wake of publication. Rather than embark on an item by item accounting I shall group the most interesting and critical questions under a few broad headings and attempt to deal with them as best I can.

History. Is history missing from *The Play of the Gods*? History moves only in certain ways, so the critique goes, and it is determined by large, impersonal forces, the general shaping the particular, the former being unavailable from within a particular time and place. People living through an era are not aware of the determining forces which can only be glimpsed at over the long term, and always with hindsight. Hence any account privileging the participants in events and advocating a synchronic, systemic look at people's own views and actions is bound to be myopic, at best incomplete, at worst misleading.

The assumption here is that people do not know why they act the way they do (or at least they are not aware of the *real* causes of their actions). The same argument works equally well for other agendas of hidden causes such as the more extreme, single factor genetic (causal and ontological) explanations found in some Marxist, positivist, psychological, feminist, functionalist, psychoanalytical, and modernization theories of history and society. Alternatively, the real (or underlying) story has to be pieced together from long term trends: population movements and demography, statistics and incomes, taxation and prices, production and consumption figures; in other words quantified data producing genetic, causal explanations of secular trends which involves state power, political economy, and class.

Immediately we are faced with a problem: what is history and how do we know "it"? What are "our" views (social scientists' assumptions often contradict each other) and how do we determine these? What other views are there? If "theirs" ((whoever *they* are) do not count, then whose? Not that objectivity is impossible, rather that it is a construct, the result of working through many versions, comparisons placed in contexts on levels and scales of organization and complexity which have to be determined, not assumed or ascribed. On the surface of it "our" views are no better than "theirs" since ours are equally embedded in our day to day lives. Marxist, functionalist, psychoanalytic and like theories do not account for this problem because they offer a way out only through an axiomatic leap which merely provides a general expectation about the way the world works. Once the leap is taken, selective facts seem to fall into place: selective advisedly, because the theory highlights those aspects of life that are singled out by it.

Marx's famous dictum that men enter into relations not of their own making is fraught with problems: aside from the gendered talk, who is to separate what human beings choose and what they are given, what categories of understanding and practice are appropriate in which context? From anthropology we can demonstrate that a particular case does or does not come out according to the expectations of general theory. Indeed, the very division into participants' views and the objective reality already condemns any understanding to be at best selective, partial and incomplete.[1]

Objectivity. Does *The Play of the Gods* provide an "objective" account? To call on an objective history or sociology with axiomatic theories and set categories of analysis is to miss much of what is routinely the anthropologist's work. I do not deny the significance and value of Marxist, psychoanalytical, functional and other quests, but these do not answer the questions I ask in *The Play of the Gods.* Such questions are ignored or not even raised in many contemporary works since assumptions rule them out or reduce them to epiphenomena, all in the name of some theory purporting to deal with objective reality. Such theories exempt themselves from being ideological by axiomatic claims to some scientific method or another and cannot account for their own cultural (or ideological) construction. They also exempt the pursuit of *their* methods from being similarly determined as they claim for their opponents. Thus, what is meaningful and of value to people at a particular time are denied significance and are replaced by general theory which the particulars do not demonstrate, but at best selectively illustrate. Either we throw out much of *The*

[1]I have considered these questions in greater detail in later works, especially *Culture and Power* and *Vessels of Time.*

Play of the Gods as unimportant and peripheral, or we have to provide a theory for the empirical and conceptual materials it provides. We can do the latter in the light of long term trends and secular factors but that will merely encapsulate and then dismiss, or at best relegate pūjās, symbols, and exegeses to secondary significance. If causal, genetic factors are called upon to "produce" or "express" culture, the latter being an idiom for the expression of something deeper, more real and determinant, then what is being proposed is a parallel albeit more general level of analysis to that on which my own work is situated. However the two approaches are not exclusive alternatives and cannot replace each other: their provenance is different. Questions of meaning cannot be resolved by genetic explanations and by the consideration of factors outside the reach of participants.

Indigenous Categories. Some would protest that all attempts to render "insider" accounts are bound to fail. Arguments range from the impossibility of reaching a truly "native point of view" and the inevitable conflation of natives' and anthropologists' models, to the more recent trouble with defining indigenous categories, the necessity of dialogics, the implications of knowledge, rhetoric and power, and the contamination of all social constructs by the observer's categories and ideologies. How can we construct an indigenous level without being compromised by the very acts of observation and writing, and the social, economic contexts of disciplinary practice? Furthermore, spatial allusions exclude time and change, and create false expectations of pure domains with set boundaries.

The simple answer would be that if we cannot get a pristine inside reality it does not mean we have to settle for none at all. Similarly, if we cannot get unqualified, guaranteed objectivity it does not mean we can't strive for a measure of it in relation to other (e.g. indigenous) requirements. On the other hand, if we restrict ourselves to unquestionably inside accounts alone, then we may be tempted to rely on ritual and narrative texts, informants' verbatim reports, presumably uncontaminated by social scientific interpolations. Seeking such textual validation will only produce a timeless India where meanings are permanently fixed on the leaves of manuscripts, the reels of audio-visual tape recorders, and the pages of transcription.

Change is undeniable but even admitting that we have participants' accounts which refer to ritual texts and sacred narratives. The latter themselves are found in living contexts that go beyond mere mystification, false consciousness, and failed explanation. My account of gājan and Durgāpūjā, relying on participants' knowledge, cannot be dismissed on the grounds of failing to provide the kinds of generalization claimed by theories of hidden agendas. Rituals, pūjās, symbols can be explained to the extent causal and genetic accounts would disprove them. If *līlā*, *māyā*, *bhakti* and other indigenous categories are of no use then does power, production, and exploitation provide the true explanation for rituals and festivals? I do not claim to have the last word but I do claim that I work with items, facts, and values which are to be woven into any anthropological account because they are what people are concerned with in their daily lives.

To privilege some putatively objective factor of state power or economic production in opposition to a cultural account is in effect to ideologize the case, and to impose a Euro-centric point of view even when aiming at Indian conditions. The world thus presented is a Euro-American one derived from post-Enlightenment history: the nation state, race, and imperial rule. On the other hand it can be argued that if indigenous accounts are available at all, they are bound to be so internal as to be meaningless to any outsider. The impossibility of translation is a radical stance that has merit. At worst we can go on compiling local texts based on dialogues with informants, reproduce old manuscripts with exegetical additions and explanatory notes, hoping to represent the voices of insiders. But we need not leave it at that: we can attempt to make something of these materials in relation to actions and practices, indeed the very reality of people's lives across the domains of social life. The crucial movement is to admit a whole class of evidence and attempt to work through it in relation to other materials without deciding in advance that because they have to do with, say ritual, they are subordinate to say, political economy. The difficulty is to locate the reciprocal relations between ritual and economy (and a hundred other things) without placing them in a hierarchy of domains and ideologies which would axiomatically account for the links between them.

Locality. Vishnupur may be fascinating but *The Play of the Gods* does not tell us much about the world beyond Vishnupur. This objection takes the locality of the study and buries it under discrete, substantive boundaries. The argument is spatially biased in a different way: data have to be widened and quantified to be representative. Regional surveys and statistical aggregates persuade. One should provide percentages and regional variations about objects used, exegeses given, events and practices observed: as if numbers can account for questions of relationship and meaning!

The particulars I am talking about are not local history or the small world of a country town in opposition to regional, urban, and national levels. Nor is it a quest for the unique, a chronicle of discrete events and elements concerning notable individuals and families, quaint myths and other curiosities. Vishnupur is still a part of Mughal, British, and independent India with connections to the wider world in different directions, on different levels, at different times. The smaller scale does not make it any less complex or easier to deal with, but it is a factor, since it cannot be derived from a more general case. All we have to do here is to be aware of level, scale, and aspect in exegesis, comparison, interpretation, and take account of relationships and contexts. I have in fact used materials from sources outside Vishnupur. There is no virtue in just being local and the pūjās I considered are not isolated from the rest of Bengal and India, nor do they form a detachable modular world.

My aim has been to study a system and a structure in a locality, to probe deep into the relationships of a particular case and to show how diverse elements come together. Elsewhere in Indian different elements may come together in different ways but the cases would be comparable. In this fashion we can discuss all-India, regional and local levels, aspects of ideology and practice, historical changes and cultural as well as analytic constructs of all kinds. I was not after the content and substance, nor the correct, authentic version of rituals, myths, and symbols. If structures are revealed as a result of the analysis then we may note how histories are encapsulated in the present, variations form a system, and cultural forms are living realities. Then we may go on to discuss plurality, change and transformation in society and culture.

State Power and Culture. The most extensive and thoughtful commentary on *The Play of the Gods* was by Hitesh Sanyal, the Bengali anthropologist and historian whose untimely death occasions my dedication. His argument concerns both history and political economy. Studying bhakti, pūjā, and līlā is all very well, he writes, but we should be aware of the political power and purpose behind religion. Bhakti (devotion) is weak in this region of Bengal and constitutes resistance to the centralizing effort of the Malla kings and their Mughal overlords throughout the pre-colonial period. Local people seized on religion to retain their independence. The same impulse can be seen in the nationalist, anti-British movements in the area during more recent times.

My response is: may be so, but something has to be there before it can be made use of, both to resist and to extend political power. What is that thing?—especially if "religion" (a problematic term for me for reasons discussed in the book) is already designated to be an idiom for more basic realities, power for instance. How are cultural forms and ideologies (bhakti and otherwise) constituted, how do they work, and what do they mean? A modified, more sophisticated Marxist analysis would look at the Vaiṣṇava movement from the sixteenth century on as an ideological veil covering the real, underlying struggle for power: the kings building temples and sponsoring rituals to assert control over the resisting people. But what guarantees this explanation other than the axiomatic "theory" underlying it? Maybe an "objective" theory (such as historical materialism) tells us so, but for whom, when, under what conditions, in which contexts and ontologies? It is a likely story and bears undeniable and partial truth. But as a theory it axiomatically asserts the way the world works and explains only what falls within its purview. The distinctive shape and structure of Vaiṣṇava worship and devotion (or the *śakta* rites of the Malla kings for that matter), the sacred in relation to society are not explained, merely explained away. How do local people resist? How does bhakti articulate with pūjā, bazaar, *rajniti* and the like? How do the kings manipulate the same cultural form over two centuries in order to centralize political power and draw the smaller, more distant or recalcitrant rulers into the center? Two opposite results from the same "religious" ontology may be the way the dialectic works (literally a *deus ex machina* here) but the process should be demonstrated for each particular case.

At the very least we ought to investigate the processes and phenomena in question and avoid turning them into epiphenomena, idioms, and settle for deriving them from general principles. Maybe the rituals and myths discussed in *The Play of the Gods* were only one way for the Malla kings to extend their power. But what is "power" here? What are its limits and meanings: is it the same everywhere regardless of place and time? Is it religious, political, and economic at the same time? Are these the same or different kinds of power? If the same, then why is religion eclipsed by politics or economics? How does it become only a vehicle for the exercise of political power? If not the same, then why are they not distinguished in analysis? It seems to me that power itself is a cultural category, the cultural context forming a limit to the provenance of power. The pūjā structure (relations of deity, ritualist, worshiper), the process, form and meaning of worship, the Brāhmaṇ-Ksatriya relation are all factors here and cannot be lumped together in a single variable. The articulation of domains in a region is another kind of limit. The political-economic dimension cannot be abstracted and invested with some a priori significance. After all power is nothing by itself: it is given form by rituals, myths, symbols and values as well as religious, political, and economic institutions. It is true that the elements I listed above are not of equal value: inequalities and hierarchies characterize the entire system, just as bhakti, pūjā, *śakti*, and other principles do. I have discussed these matters at greater length in *Culture and Power*. Nothing is more mystified these days than "power" (except perhaps "production"): looking for something behind bhakti, śakti, gājan, and Durgāpūjā as the real determinant is to ignore the context and expect everything else to fall into place where "power" can sort it all out. If culture masks power then power is the most "cultural" category, but without the benefit of analysis, the outcome having been determined before the conclusion of the investigation. Power too has to be culturally constituted and interpreted. If the cultural context makes no difference to the critic then it does to those who live and experience it.

Universal and Particular. Arguing for indigenous, local configurations of society and culture is not to replace the wider view: the local has no aprior virtue. Further, indigenous and local are not the same, nor are they on the same scale and level. Nevertheless either one can be of all-India significance, as has been argued by many, beginning with Srinivas in his pioneering study of the Coorgs.

What I call for is an interpretive and analytic strategy that deals with the dialectic, tension, and harmony of universal and particular, inside and outside, local and national. This argument goes against drawing too sharp a contrast between emic and etic, objective and subjective as identifiable substantive alternatives (with different methods and theories, opposing science to the humanities). I would like to contribute to approaches that deal with tension, reciprocity, interplay, and articulation, utilizing relational, linking categories. In the Vishnupur (as in any other) region we can contemplate the encounter between India and the West in the light of history, as well as locality, nation, and the world. These analytic and interpretive tasks are all relevant and can be constructed in Indian and Western terms. The procedures are no less valid than those of other disciplines, if anything more so, given the relevance of anthropology to the task at hand.

Cultural Chauvinism. Books like *The Play of the Gods*, I have been told, can easily feed nostalgia or worse: cultural chauvinism and self congratulation. In the hands of some contemporary political practitioners symbolic and structural accounts may reinforce the status quo, as indeed may all anthropology. Left and right radicalism can coopt ethnographic works under both colonial and post-colonial regimes. Such works, we are told, underplay the potential for change, revolutionary and otherwise, and celebrate "tradition," continuity, and stability. For example, no matter how badly off they are, women, the poor, and low caste people still may respect their superiors, offer pūjās to the gods, recite sacred texts, so "tradition" can claim consent and consensus. It takes a small step then to argue that things are not too bad after all. It is irritating to see the worst traits of Indians: fatalism, resignation, fortitude which feed into permanence and stagnation, being complemented by foreigners. The need of the hour is change and the old ways are tied to inequalities and inequities. Even if an interpretive work does not set out to do all this, the tendency in India is toward self glorification and indulgence, to be self congratulatory toward a culture which is ancient, resilient, and triumphant over invaders, thus contributing to reactionary traditionalism and revivalistic politics.

My response has to be, as in the case of Hitesh Sanyal's critique, that in part the objections may well be true, but the attempt to understand something is not necessarily to approve it. The cultural is not a replacement for other accounts: the more variations in theory and method are pursued the better. My own is not a "totalizing" or "historicist" approach and while I have been made aware of the potential (and to me unpalatable) use of my work I must pursue its appointed tasks as outlined above no matter where they lead, because they are basically sound. Some safeguards are built into the work itself in terms of method, analysis, context, and interpretive practice. I have to look at what there is around me, and avoid privileging the more as against less attractive aspects of contemporary Indian society. The problem is how to assess differences and variations and not merely celebrate selected features of culture.

Nor is the "indigenous" a mere replica of what "informants say," a translation of conversations, myths, *maṅgalas*, and other ritual texts, because it does not consist of reporting local terms alone. Rather it is built of local materials and applied to local practices on a comparative scale. I do not agree with the formula: to each informant his or her model. In constituting indigenous categoires and suing them comparatively to account for differences and variations we add something to "what people say," and do not leave the latter the way we found it.

Of course we rely, in the first instance, on what people say and do, what we see them do and hear them say, and what we find out from other sources: historical, ethnographic, contemporary. We synthesize, compare, arrange and rearrange, apply and take from many sources, eventually coming up with something new. Our "indigenous models" cannot be the creation of any single person we "talk" to in the locality, unless that person has also subjected his/her findings to a similar process of model building. So we have a responsibility to be careful with what we do, keeping track of what we compare and in whose terms, how we establish categoires and attempt to disentangle layers of meaning.

Here I note that the approach I pursue has at least the promise of accomplishing what most others neglect: once differences are acknowledged I try to account for both continuity and change and responses to change. What does the ongoing process of transformation mean for India's present and future? Is India becoming something different or just a pale reflection of Europe and America? The cultural dimension suggests the answers to the question of difference even in a prosperous, modernized, future India. Indian society will have changed in different ways with different results because the contexts and especially the cultures are different.

At one point, however, an author has to let go of the work and allow it to wander where it will. Other books have made stranger bdfellows than mine and so far I have no cause for alarm. I may regret from time to time that I cannot guide the reception of a book or film of mine, but that may be for the better. At most one can time the process of publication and stop if conditions warrant. Obviously one does not publish detailed sociopolitical information in an area at a time of insurgency or counter-insurgency. I chose to pursue a particular path if only because there were so many others dealing with economics, politics, modernization and development.

The More Things Change. India as a timeless, eternal, static society is the image of colonial, imperial, even neocolonial projects: denying change and history is to contribute to domination and hegemony.

However this charge cannot be hung on *The Play of the Gods*, because the book's emphasis on structure is purely ideational, belonging to the sphere of cultural logic in the sense discussed above. There is structure and structure: clearly the Vishnupur study demonstrates dynamism and renewal in this particular Indian society. Continuity is not necessarily static or stagnant. Rituals change and texts are reinterpreted in new contexts but changes may not be visible as they occur. Social systems may change through the action of individuals: performance changes rituals in bazaars, temples, and households, myths and other texts are neglected or reintroduced. The book does not hide the ongoing processes of transformation, although it concentrates on structural relations. Further, it seems to me, history is always particular: generalizations are based on comparison implicit or otherwise. Historical accounts are constituted in abstraction, through reflection eventually influencing contemporary perceptions, in turn contributing to change. In being acted upon structures are also produced: history has to be in terms of something, not disembodied spirits. History is often invoked these days (as function, structure, political economy, psychology or teleology) as if it was some noxious or blessed cloud wafting over the social system.

Exegetical Conundrums. A final and serious objection would question the reliance on exegesis. In using exegesis a la Turner the voices of anthropologist and informant are inevitably conflated: indigenous ideologies ought to be separated from secondary or tertiary interpretations. Cultural accounts, such as those given in *The Play of the Gods*, are not dialogical enough: it should be clearer who speaks where. Exegeses can not be individualized and even if inside views can be stated they are reproduced through the author's voice.

The complaint makes more sense with hindsight: the emergence of more insistent postmodern claims about the impossibility of "culture". A more extreme position would hold that we can only render the words of our informants: abstraction such as "model," "structure," even "society" are misleading and illegitimate. Nevertheless, if I choose to give an interpretation then I cannot stop at merely replicating informants' speech. Since my study transcends a purely individualistic, idiosyncratic level, it has to contend with questions of culture. Even so to be asked to separate the voices of informant and analyst in such a radical manner is a strange request since the critics have already posited the impossibility of reaching a truly "native" level and we all know that there is no point outside of any culture from which we can speak. We are always situated partially within and partially without that which we would describe, hence the need to specify contexts and frameworks through which we speak. The anthropologist and his/her culture are always implicated: a process I described clearly enough in the book, especially in the Appendix on field work. The exegetical material is separated as far as possible, noting ritual specialist or participant accounts. Beyond that, however, it is clear that I am writing both the exegetical and interpretive accounts. The expectation that our own assumptions can be concisely stated and separated so that at some point they no longer complicate the interpretive process, allowing us to forget about them after fessing up to them, seems to me dubious and I have yet to see a convincing example. Establishing categories of analysis and interpretation is not a question of voice or dialogue, nor that of statistics or a census of how many people agree with this or that definition of a term. No survey or aggregation of numbers can decide what are the significant categories because the latter are always complex, public, collective constructions that have to be constituted out of terms, symbols, practices, as the *The Play of the Gods* in fact demonstrates. One example is the treatment of pūjā as both a category and a set of variant terms that occur in different contexts and apply to different practices described in the course of detailed analytical and interpretive accounts.

If an examination of variations is called for (and the indigenous model is deemed to be too monolithic) then there still has to be something which is being varied: just posting variations in abstraction is not enough. The current obsession with "contestation" among cultural variants as a way of fashioning culture falls into the same trap: what is being contested still has to be stated in a context since there cannot be contestation just for the sake of it. Categories and processes still have to be constituted and analyzed in cultural terms. Besides, a concern with system and structure is legitimate, without thereby denying individuality, history, and much else which is preserved in any given human situation and could be equally legitimately emphasized. So we speak of, say, the ancient Greeks and Greek society and mean a structural construction. Similarly, current efforts to prove that the British "invented" the caste system and much else besides that used to be regarded "Indian" is equally misguided since they beg the question of what is yielded by culture through time, from what and from whose point of view. Origins do not determine the outcome and effect of social processes, nor do they predict the nature and characteristics of the result. Ontology is a poor indicator of meaning. Where the discrete features originate even if it can be stated is less important than the way in which elements come together in a system. Ascribing colonial origins belies the complex British-Indian interaction, nor can we accept a supine colonial India upon which the British impose invented social systems at will.

Chapter One

The City of the Gods

The Goddess Durgā and the Lord Śiva are divinities of a sacred Indian tradition vast in space and time. They are also deities of a small Bengali town where their rites are part of the people's daily lives. They live in the myths of the past and in the idle talk of the bazaar. They are powerful, majestic deities who rule the heavens, and they are a loving couple devoted to their divine children. They dwell on the high peaks of the Himalayas and in the humble temples of rural towns. They are timeless, capable of taking any form, and yet they appear at the annual festivals of villagers, manifesting themselves in the clay and straw images men prepare for them. They are creators, rulers, and destroyers of the world. Their cosmic dance dissolves and recreates the world, drawing a veil of illusion in front of all creatures, dazzling men with wealth, diversity, and desire. They also give men the ability to tear the veil asunder and to achieve the liberation of a soul oppressed by the cycle of rebirths. Together Śiva and Durgā provide the elements and the very possibility of action. Separately they rule the different aspects of life. They create an order for living that defines things animate and inanimate, social and natural, fate and the frame of time, the ideals and obstacles of everyday life. They allow themselves to be desired, and they reward their followers. They reveal themselves in human form to their devotees. If aroused to anger by a transgression of the rules, they strike the offender with all their power. They command the agents of sorrow, disease, and misfortune. They bring joy and righteousness as well as social turmoil and disintegration: theirs is the play of the gods.

The Problematics of the Study

This work concerns the implications of Śiva and Durgā in Bengal—in symbol and society, ideology and action, structure and event, myths and rituals. Above all I want to clarify the meanings created for people by the activities surrounding the gods. For in the organization, performance, and meaning of festivals for the gods we find the world, as the people know it, structured, interpreted, and expressed through ritual action. We gain perspective on men through the eyes of the gods and through other men, constructing an indigenous understanding for society and constituting an internal view of the ends and meaning of life. No theological paradox should follow, since we are firmly grounded in the sociocultural context of life in a Bengali town. Even the seeming generalities of my opening sentences are a living reality for the people whose festivals I propose to analyze. But I want to study this "reality" in terms of the indigenous culture that defines and interprets experience. To glimpse these terms and experiences, let us follow the progress of a townsman through the festival of the Goddess Durgā.

As the autumn festival of the goddess approaches, Benoi G. of Vishnupur informs his relatives that this year he is responsible for the worship of the ancestral deity. In order to have the rituals performed, he also calls on the priest (*kulapurohit*) of his line (*baṇgśa*) to officiate at the festival. This has been the custom for generations, ever since the image of the goddess was installed as the deity (*kuladebatā*) of Benoi Bābu's ancestors.[1] The office of priesthood was inherited by the descendants of the original priest, just as men and women of the succeeding generations come back to the ancestral temple to witness the annual ceremonies. Many new lines have been created since the consecration of the goddess; some have died out, others have moved away, and some have set up their own deities. But those who are left, male heads of households who themselves head a line in their own name, alternate among themselves the duty of arranging the many details of the performance.

The priest is to be given gifts for his assistance, and the items he lists as necessary for the rituals must be acquired in just the prescribed proportions (there are various colored powders, spices, oils and scents, earthenware vessels, many small objects, food items for the offering, and so on). The clay image of the goddess must be commissioned: a man of the carpenter caste builds the image year after year, as his ancestors had done in the past. A man of the garland maker caste decorates the image; the potter brings new cooking pots and vessels for the rituals; the low-caste men gather flowers for the ceremonies and provide labor, carrying water and other things. The sweeper cleans the temple yard, and musician caste drummers and flutists are asked to play at the ceremonies. The barber is asked to assure the purity of the participants in the rituals by paring nails and shaving beards. Heads of households must make gifts during this joyous season: new clothing for the family, food for relatives and friends, and charity for the poor. Entertainment also must be provided; theatrical performances of sacred stories, the recitation of myths, and the singing of devotional songs are much valued by the whole neighborhood. Food deliveries must be ensured, and the cooking of ritual offerings and of ceremonial feasts is to be supervised. Finally, the married daughters of the family are to be invited, with the permission of their in-laws, preferably attended by their husbands and brought home by a male member of the household. Though it is a light-hearted time, filled with joy and happiness for all, Benoi Bābu knows that every detail must fit the rules, for the power of the goddess is awesome and is quickly provoked by mistakes and omissions. On the other hand, the goddess is also a mother to her devotees, and the household regards her with love and affection. In her turn a well-pleased goddess will bestow favors and blessings on the whole line.

The festival begins with the first invocations of the goddess on the sixth lunar day of the full moon according to the Bengali calendar (see Appendix 3). Benoi Bābu does not eat the whole day; he bathes and wears new clothes. Then he joins the priest in a resolution to perform all the rites of the festival on behalf of the line. He asks the goddess to stay in his house during the festival, to enjoy herself, to forgive any unwitting transgressions, and to give her blessings freely. And so it goes through the separate and cumulative, as well as the daily repeated rituals of the festival. In the course of succeeding rituals the goddess is invoked in trees, sacred vessels, and finally in a clay image. Processions bring her to the temple, where she is welcomed and served with refreshing, purifying, and ceremonial objects. Then she is asked to manifest herself in the image and to partake of all oblations, sacrifices, and cooked food offerings given to her. When the offerings are given and accepted, she is asked to rest till the next set of rituals. These performances follow each other morning, noon, and night. The next day the goddess is worshiped in the image of her creation: in the different things in the world as classified through and attributed to her power, and in the basic principles expressing diversity and plurality through gestures, objects, and recitations. The culminating moment comes at night, when the goddess is said to appear to her most fervent devotees, but the blessing of a sight of her face at that instant is not for all participants. The following day sees the sharing of sanctified food among the worshipers. That evening people parade around town in their new clothing, visiting the celebrations of other families and community groups, expressing respect to the gods, and passing judgment on the artistry of the display.

The final day is joyous and sorrowful at the same time. The goddess departs amid the last offerings and prayers asking her to return in another year. Women perform rituals of farewell, elders embrace, and men greet each other; young people touch the elders' feet in respect. Then comes the merriment of the immersion procession. Youths smear colored powder on each other, boys tease girls, and the young play jokes on the old. The goddess is immersed in the river and bade to depart as she came, through the waters, which will carry her to the Ganges and beyond, to her abode in the sacred mountains.

The festival of Durgā is performed all over Bengal. Rituals vary from place to place and group to group, but the scheme given above embraces most instances.[2] Extraordinary expenditures are made at festival time in this already impoverished country. A whole month is devoted to the goddess, from the initial recitation of myths to the disassembling of temporary temples and images. Durgā is the Bengali goddess par excellence. She is mother above all others—the mother of a family, a town, and a country. She is the principle of power that creates the world and constitutes action in daily life. She lives among the people but comes to the festival with specific, contextual meaning. Bengalis speak of her festival as Durgāpūjā (the *pūjā* of Durgā) or Saradatsab (the autumn festival). Pūjā shall concern us fundamentally in this work.

Pūjā is men's expression of respect for the gods—an event, an idiom of action, and a symbol. As a symbol it expresses relationships deemed proper among men, among gods, and between the two. As an idiom it states how one must act and how these actions relate to others outside the scope of the festival. Pūjā is a part of the social order, which it also defines in a particular domain. Pūjā is elaborated in a series of ideologies, sects, forms, and meanings, but it rests on a single fundamental structure. Therefore I shall also be concerned with the general problems of analyzing symbols in society.

There are many pūjās and many gods. Pūjās can be rich with pomp and circumstance, or they may be performed by a single person with no paraphernalia. Pūjās may have a whole town and region as participants, or they may mark events in the life cycle (for a general schematic study of pūjās, see Östör 1978*b*). Families, households, sects, neighborhood groups, castes, voluntary associations, and political, charitable, and occupational groups perform pūjās of various kinds, on various occasions, for various purposes. It follows that the concomitants of pūjā are not only social segments but also ideologies, basic notions of space, time, and locality, and notions of what life is all about and how it should be lived. Pūjā, then, is a complex whole that touches every aspect of the participant's life. Another aspect of pūjā is time. Baṇgśa (line) rituals may go back hundreds of years in the essentials of their pūjās. Different castes observe ancient variations on a basic performance. Equally ancient notions of community cut across caste boundaries in ritual. The now impoverished kings of the area still perform a royal form of the Durgāpūjā, an expression of the region as a society in ritual action.

Any attempt to generate an anthropological analysis out of indigenous concepts resting on the activities surrounding the gods is bound to depart in some ways from current disciplinary practice. Events such as those in Durgāpūjā have been variously described and interpreted by anthropologists in general and by South Asianists in particular. Some would find my narrative a basis for the functional analysis of religion in the caste system. Others would recognize that the rituals create social solidarity as well as expressing the stratification and diversification of groups. These structural-functional features are not incompatible, but they call attention to aspects of the festival from different points of view. In a different vein, some may regard the festival as an indigenous dramatic form that expresses significant underlying tensions in society, which are in turn resolved through symbolic action, triumphantly reasserting a hierarchy already noted in other aspects of society. Other approaches may focus on religion and may distinguish the ritual from social processes, assimilating local features to great traditional ones and defining in this manner the sacred in general and Hinduism in particular. Yet others may find "ritual value," "mythic charter," "social force," "expression of power," or "symbolic interaction" in the various facets of the festival. Finally, some may find data for folk, local level, or practical religion, concentrating on the relation between general dogma and particular practices.[3] Would these be true of all rituals? Is there a general category of action—"ritual"—that can be interpreted at will, in any mode, in all possible contexts?

Let us now follow our actor through the performance of a different ritual, the festival of Śiva, complementary to the Durgāpūjā in terms of the importance awarded to it by townsmen and of the status of Śiva himself: Durgā's husband, lover, preceptor, and the male god par excellence.

In the spring the town prepares for the festival of Śiva, known as Śiva's *gājan*. The gājan also consists of pūjās, some similar to, others different from those of Durgā. If it is significant that social segments such as localities, castes, families, and voluntary groups perform the Durgāpūjā, then we must immediately notice that there are only three central performances of the gājan in the town. The pomp and ceremony of other festivals are replaced by simplicity, and multiplicity and plurality give way to unity and singularity. The myriad details of Durgāpūjā seem to distill to a few offerings and a single group of devotees.

Together with the people of his neighborhood who decide to perform gājan, Benoi G. goes to be shaved in the temple yard by the barber (*nāpit*) the day before the festival. He fasts the whole day, but in the evening he goes with the other *bhakta*s (adepts, devotees) to the temple to eat sacred food previously offered to the gods (*habisanna,* "the best food"). He is now in a pure state, and from now on he cannot stay at home or touch and use ordinary objects. At night he puts on a red loincloth and wears a string of beads, the distinctive dress of Śiva's devotees. He gathers the objects devotees need: a cane, a water jug, and a basket for offerings (fruits, sandalwood, incense, and flowers). Devotees sleep in the temple that night. The next morning they set out barefoot for the great temple of Śiva some miles out of town. Calling the names of Śiva they make their way, collecting flowers and fruits from the gardens and fields along the road. No one interferes with their approved, holy scavenging.

The group consists of men from all castes. Brāhmaṇ priests are waiting for the small groups appearing from all directions. The first ritual takes place at the edge of the river that curves around the foot of the hill on which the temple stands. The priests confer the sacred thread, normally worn only by the twice-born, on all devotees. Having renounced their own social identity, the devotees take on the identity of Śiva himself. Now they are ready for the works of devotion that must be carried out. One after the other they perform the pūjās of Śiva in the central temple and those of other deities in the smaller temples and shrines scattered around the hill. They are allowed to touch, bathe, and worship the gods with their own hands, acts normally reserved for Brāhmaṇs. They follow this cycle, mornings and evenings, on each day of the festival.

Bhaktas also take part in a series of cumulative rituals that build up to the climax of the festival on the fifth day. They fast from sunrise to sunset, and at night they may eat only uncooked food, fruits, puffed rice, soaked pulses, and milk. The second day Durgā is invoked in a sacred vessel and is brought to Śiva's temple: a secret performance at night to bring the god and the goddess together. The next day, in an analogous manner, the devotees bring a particular manifestation of Śiva to the same temple. The following day they go in procession to offer their respects to the local king as the owner of the land on which the temples stand. The fifth day the gājan of the night is performed: devotees dance in procession around Śiva's temple, engaging in such ascetic practices as rolling on the ground, falling in trance, and celebrating the power of the Great Lord in other ways pleasing to him. Power is generated out of the union between Śiva and Durgā, and in rejoicing in it the climax of the festival is reached. The following afternoon the same procession is repeated as gājan of the day, attended by fire walking and other ordeals. The power acquired by devotees through the festival allows them to endure the last two days. The final day is a reversal of the first: the sacred thread is immersed, and the devotees return to everyday life. In the last communal act the devotees partake of a feast of cooked rice and fish.

Much of the gājan resonates with Durgāpūjā. There are the gods themselves, offerings and pūjās, myths, temples and priests. Other actions of the gājan seem to contrast it with the Durgāpūjā in the most fundamental ways. Can we say about the gājan all that we said about Durgāpūjā? Do we find here the same analytic possibilities? Can we still speak of ritual value, solidarity, and a symbolic expression of social relations? To the extent to which these things are a part of Durgāpūjā they are also a part of gājan. With some ingenuity, the same approaches can be applied to the gājan as well. If so, then there is no way to understand the seeming opposition of the two performances, and there is no way to understand diversity. This might imply that we are faced with some kind of unvarying "ritual truth."

Trying a different tack, our alternative theorists may ask, Is not the gājan a rite of reversal, acting to reinstate the social configuration of Durgāpūjā by trying out an egalitarian alternative to social hierarchy and settling for hierarchy in the end? Does the gājan symbolize tensions, fission, and fusion in Bengali society? Is anything resolved through the form and symbols of the festival? All of these possibilities have been suggested by anthropological approaches to rituals and myths (see note 3, and especially Douglas 1966; Turner 1969; Nicholas 1967).

The same polarity of religion and society that I suggested, on others' behalf, for a possible approach to Durgāpūjā may be suggested for the gājan as well (in a recast form of the question above). And yet the problem of meaning remains: the meanings for the actors, the systemic construction of the festivals themselves, the differences and similarities, processes of symbolism, and the actions of the performance itself would still be left where they were—not understood, but merely explained away. And there are further problems: the many gods and their different actions, the various levels of manifestations, the concepts expressed by symbols in a coherent, systemic manner—What are these all about? Then there are the different things symbols mean in different contexts, in changed statuses and roles, in the relations among different fields of action such as "caste," "kinship" or even "religion," "economics," and "politics." Then there are the problems of symbolic differentiation, unification, and classification and the principles for setting things apart or bringing them together.

There seems to be an inexhaustible series of questions about these festivals. But a basic problem of meaning underlies them all. This, in even more general terms, is the problem of how ideas relate to action, how processes of symbolization are to be understood, how meanings are generated, how ideologies relate to underlying structures. More specifically, there is the question of boundaries and their definition in whatever terms, of whichever domain. The festivals themselves remain: Do they designate something or are they just an idiom for the expression of social, political, and economic "realities" (Östör, n.d.)? Why do people devote so much attention, time, and effort to pūjās? What do festivals mean? Are they systematic, self-congruent, capable of generating separate meanings? Are they, in other words, a domain in their own right? If so, in what ways is this true, and what kinds of system and structure do they exhibit? Can we analyze them as a totality just as we would analyze "caste," for example? Are other domains related to and expressed by festivals, rituals, and myths?

One of my interests in studying these festivals, then, is the extent to which we can realize a culturally constituted domain through analyzing ritual action as the total social fact. If we study festivals as wholes, we may find an initial answer to our questions of domain boundaries and the generation of meaning in ritual not exhausted by kinship, religion, politics, and economics. Therefore I shall be concerned with all these questions, directly or indirectly, in general or in particular. But I do not pretend to answer them once and for all: they strike at the very core of a continuing anthropological and indeed social-scientific endeavor. Rather, I plan to present a particular context for these problems and suggest a particular approach in that context.

Of Religion and Other Matters

In anthropological studies of India it has become customary to start with social relations, then move on to religion, festivals, and ritual cycles. The final burden of sociological analyses has been the claim that "religious" matters mark group boundaries, castes, subcastes, and sects. A variant of this approach has been to attempt to show how local religious practices conform to or diverge from the great Indian tradition; how the little community articulates with the larger one, how regional variations fit into an all-India whole.[4]

In this work the usual approach is inverted. My aim is to study the festivals themselves, without postulating a direction from society to religion. I take seriously the actions and objects as well as the performances, ideologies, and exegeses of the festivals. Thus I am interested in the festival itself, not merely as a dramatic form or a symbolic expression of social processes, but also as a cultural system of symbols that is structured in certain ways, that articulates the expression of certain meanings not expressed elsewhere, and that determines the way other domains such as caste, kinship, and economics are related to and participate in rituals and festivals.

My argument is that festivals are a legitimate form of analysis. I am concerned with the actors in the ritual process, how they orient themselves to the ritual as object, activity, symbol, and so on. In those moments the actor faces a totality, a universe in itself, aspects of which we may recognize to be society, "ultimate reality," or anything else. The question is what these categories are in indigenous cultural terms. Thus we are led to the ideologies of festival participants, and beyond that to the system of meanings that ideologies and actions express. In the festivals themselves we see society realized in a certain way that may not be the same as "caste," "kinship," or "politics." If festivals, rituals, and myths are a domain in specific, structural terms, then other domains are articulated and expressed through festivals in these terms. Thus we do not expect the contents of caste and politics to be expressed in festivals; rather, we expect to find the meanings of the festival itself and the ways other domains are related to these meanings through the performance of the festival. Such a focus may yield a view different from but as legitimate as that which would start from markets, family, or other institutions as systems of social relations. Taking festivals to be a totality, we are also viewing other aspects of society through ritual performance. In doing this, however, we are studying cultural constructs, systems of symbols, not individual psychology or even mentalistic processes of thought.

The issue is whether we can study widely different experiences, in different societies with differing cultures, in terms of a general language whose definitions (and components of definitions) are held constant while the data are selected from different contexts in terms of that general language. This is the case when social scientists speak of the religion of India, Egypt, or Burma. Serious problems of inclusion arise with this procedure: is something constituting "religion" in one case also part of the problem examined in another? More specifically, one thing is meant by religion in one case and something quite different in another.[5] Such a general language for "religion" (as adopted by social science) is inadequate for my purposes and incompatible with my approach. "Religion" in this sense acts as an order of reality in terms of which different cultures are compared. But in the course of this other orders of reality may be violated. What is then compared is only the extent to which different cultures approximate the requirements of "religion." As a result, a preconceived grid is imposed on aspects of culture in different societies, and internal domains are cut off where the grid ends. The same problem arises in other fields. In a different context Schneider (1965, 1972) has argued that an anthropological notion of "genealogy" forms a kinship grid in terms of which indigenous "kinship systems" are discovered and defined. The situation is similar in economic anthropology also, where much discussion is devoted to what should be included under "economics." Should the subject be restricted to the "allocation of scarce resources to alternative ends," or should it be extended to cover all exchange and prestation in indigenous terms?

In both cases, kinship and economics, a priori frameworks are applied to particular social facts in particular societies. The results are typologies: "families" joint, extended, or nuclear; "kinship systems" of various types; terminologies of "kin relations" skewed, ramaged, and bifurcating; functional or dysfunctional values in "economic" systems, economies with or without "markets," and so on. Common to all these instances is the imposition of a general grid of terms and concepts on different cultures.[6] What is being compared "cross-culturally" in these cases is not the cultural variations themselves but rather aspects of culture preselected in terms of a general language, a measuring stick supposedly universal in its applicability, which we just "know" to be true. Thus we "know" what religion, kinship, and economics are, and we proceed to find variant realizations of basic forms in different cultures. But what we find is not something "out there"; rather, it is something in our own minds, as social scientists—distortions of semantic fields, as Lévi-Strauss has remarked of totemism.

I suggest that general concepts are helpful only in and through specific cultural contexts; when they are imposed from outside as categories with predetermined institutional meaning, they will be so general as to be useless—devoid of any specific explanatory power or any meaning.[7] For perspectives based on a mixture of Western social experience and social science schematization, I aim to substitute an indigenous cultural perspective.[8]

To deny that there is a cultural form and a symbolic meaning in the actions and categories of our devotee in the Durgā and Śiva festivals would raise many difficulties. But what sort of reality are we studying in these festivals? Whose reality and whose society? Where do the terms of the discussion come from? Whose are they? The anthropologist himself is subject to the constraints of his own society, ideology, and hierarchy of domains (with an emphasis on the "economic"). Yet terms are themselves related to each other; they form and are formed by their contexts, thus yielding the possibility of systemic analysis and the pursuit of structure and meaning.

I mean to take the festivals seriously, both in observing action and in heeding the concerns of actors. There are social morphology, ideology, and action as well as meaning for the actors in the performances we study. The central question to be answered is, What are these ideas and practices all about: what do they accomplish, and what do they mean? A whole order of reality is to be understood in and around these questions. Ideologies do not merely mark the boundaries of social groups; they utilize basic constructions of reality—terms in which one ought to lead one's life, meanings of categories (gods, saints, men, and so forth), and different levels of relationships among groups, things, concepts, and symbols.

In this endeavor it should be clear that the approach I have taken has been influenced by recent works, most notably those of Dumont, Geertz, Lévi-Strauss, Schneider, and Turner. Where others may see only differences and even contradiction in these contributions, I note a convergence in the study of ideology, symbol, and meaning in social relations. Even allowing for some obvious differences, I base my own departure on this insight and will develop my own theories and interpretations on its realization.[9]

Analysis does involve abstraction and separation into levels from existential situations, freezing and dissolving reality into constituent elements as we encounter it. But the crucial questions are on what basis and in what terms these operations are carried out, what categories are used, and to what end they are applied. For the anthropologist the basis must be a social one, whereas for the historian of religion it may be theological and for the philosopher ontological. Mauss's rule still applies, though with some added difficulties. Mauss held that we give a sociological answer to a problem of social analysis when we discover *what* is done and *who* does it. This axiom has usually been honored in terms of a supposedly culture-proof sociological language. If our problem is ritual, then we look at who is who and who does what in terms of family and kinship, political and economic institutions, status and role, and so forth. In other words, we fit the particular case into a general terminology: chiefs, fathers, priests, merchants, and so on. But who *is* who? In whose terms, and with what meanings?

The proper starting point is indigenous experience and category. We cannot pretend to know, before the fact, what these concepts and actions are, though we may well be prepared by previous work for at least a suggestion of them. Fieldwork and research in relationships are the key to this seeming paradox. It is reasonable to assume that things may be different in Bengal from what they are in Hungary, Australia, or America. At least we cannot assume they are the same, for then we would make the universal part of our analysis without any way to avoid imposing a conceptual and meaningful schema on an as yet unexamined and unanalyzed reality.

Several processes are involved here. One is recognizing the precise structures, functions, meanings, and contexts of ourselves (as members of societies) and our categories. Then there is the related construction of the realities, situations, and experience to which these concepts refer. These reciprocal processes may be crafted and pursued differently in Bengal; yet, to crown the edifice, they are related to our schemes of concept and experience. Complicated though this is, it yields us a dialectic through which "our" categories are transformed into "theirs" and vice versa. This is not a single-minded opposition of "native" and "anthropological" models. The dialectic we refer to takes place in the West as well as in Bengal, and through fieldwork the two are, in turn, dialectically related. Thus one society becomes comprehensible in terms of another. This is indeed fieldwork most parsimoniously defined for the purposes of our endeavor (here I note a convergence with the recent work of Roy Wagner [1975]).

Yet is there some cheating involved here? Once when Schneider outlined his cultural account of American kinship someone countered that, culture or no culture, we all know the stuff of kinship: we always begin with mothers and children. So too, we might add, we know the stuff of religion: gods and spirits, rituals and priests. Further, the objection could run, although structure, culture, symbol, and category may be nice ideological embellishments, we all proceed the same way on the ground, through assumption, hypothesis, investigation, proof, verification, and refutation. Yet looking for priests, temples, and supernatural spirits would indeed be cheating. We start with ourselves, our society, history, and experience. But we also see other people—townsmen of Vishnupur in this case—and note their words, activities, and recurrent relationships. We do not work in a vacuum: although we have ideas of kinship and religion (of our own society as well as of others already reported in some or other terms), we need not go to mothers and priests, especially when we do not know who and what they are.

The Plan of the Study

In chapter 2 I shall narrate the actions and ideologies connected with Durgāpūjā. In separating the narrative and exegesis of action, I follow Victor Turner's pioneering studies of Ndembu symbolism. Let me add that "exegesis" does not correspond to the "native" model, and that the narrative of action is not exclusively an "observer's" model. These are inevitably mixed up in both the narratives and my exegeses. My practice here is heuristic and is determined by convenience of presentation. The exegeses I present are also "ideological" in the sense that they belong to indigenous ideologies that are a part of the universe within which I aim to find relationships among constituent units, systems, and structures and which I interpret as part of both analysis and understanding. Chapter 2 closes with a provisional analysis to which I return in chapter 4.

Chapter 3 presents the narrative and exegesis of Śiva's gājan, with a provisional analysis. In chapter 4 I shall undertake the tasks of analysis and interpretation, combining structural and cultural approaches in the process. I return to the problem of religion, myth, and ritual, India and the West, sacred and nonsacred, hierarchy and equivalence, ideology and structure, indigenous and analytical models, reality and abstraction.

I may note here why I selected the rājā's pūjā and one of the ābārgājans from among the many different kinds of Durgāpūjās and gājans I have witnessed.[10] The rājā's goddess, the Mrinmoyī (earthen) Debī of Vishnupur, is unquestionably the most elaborate observance of Durgāpūjā in the town. It is not the most opulent by any means, but in view of its significance for the town my concentration on its performance is justified. Beyond these considerations is the structural position of the king in the system of festivals and rituals, which I discuss in chapter 4.

There are many other Durgāpūjās and Debīpūjās that I have not considered here, but I expect to remedy this situation in future studies of the Goddess Kālī, the complex of Bhūmidebatās (deities of the earth) and Vaiṣṇava deities. However, the autumn festival of the Goddess Durgā is a totality in itself and an appropriate subject for anthropological analysis.

There are many variants of the gājan festival: of these I selected the performance in the Madhab ganja section of the town. The temple here is that of Buṛo Śiva (the Old One), and while it is not the most spectacular gājan, it is the only one that boasts its own resident *sāddhu* (renouncer, holy man) who received initiation (*dīkṣā*) from an older sāddhu who revived this ancient festival after it had lapsed in the late nineteenth century.

The ābārgājan performances are homogeneous, but the Ṣāṛeśvar gājan, the largest and most ceremonial performance, is somewhat different. Again I hope that my presentation will reveal the gājan for the universe it is, and I defer a comparative study of the gājan in relation to the gājans of other deities such as Manasā (the goddess of snakes) for a later time.

In referring to caste I base my remarks on the structural explication of the system in Dumont's *Homo Hierarchicus*. This account of encompassing/encompassed relations has considerable powers of explanation and interpretation.[11] However, though the initial derivation of hierarchy and its form is given by the pure and impure relationship, I shall have occasion to derive the same principle from other relationships and find it in other forms. Similarly, I shall use indigenous terms such as *śakti* and *bhakti* (and many others) both as ethnographic categories, whose meaning I shall elucidate, and as principles that can be applied in interpreting and understanding my data. In this way I try to encompass indigenous terms as ideological devices, categories, and instruments of analytical and hermeneutic processes.

It is evident that I stress what Geertz called generalization within a case rather than making a series of regional comparisons.[12] Yet I have not shirked the task of generalizing within boundaries from locality to abstract universals. I am convinced that this sort of endeavor should precede "all-India" generalizations that, in the absence of detailed regional studies, would inevitably degenerate into a facile enlargement of local contents, entities, and substances into those of all South Asia, thus abdicating any possibility of truly comparative, relational understanding.

Starting from indigenous ideologies and the living realities we encounter in fieldwork, I shall break down general categories such as pūjā and *parab* into more particular ones, and in the process I shall give full play to the dialectic of indigenous action, category, and principle (from both internal and external directions). Thus I shall move from pūjā to *jajmān, jāti, kriyā, debatā,* and *bhakti,* and to *puruṣa* and *prakriti* as well. But I shall also have opportunity to separate and bring together the elements of systems on different levels of action and abstraction.

The Pūjā of Durgā in Myth and Legend

The forms of the goddess are countless, her manifestations infinite. She is known under many names and labels, but Durgā is the most used. Durgā is the aspect of the goddess that includes all her characteristics—

the most universal manifestation, synonymous with Debī.[13] Speaking of the many different aspects of the goddess, townspeople often remark "they are all Durgā, they are all her forms (*rūp*)." In the widest sense, Durgā is the mother of all living things, creator par excellence. Her other characteristics are related to this most inclusive role. Among these are power and victory, protection and grace, rule, knowledge, love, and peace. She means different things in different situations. First of all she is Ādi (Āddā), the origin of all things. She is *śakti,* creative power. She is the savior of the gods and the killer of demons. She maintains a balance among the different forces of cosmic play (*līlā* and *nitya*). Finally, she presides over human life and worldly affairs; she can be approached with the troubles of everyday life. For human beings, Mā, mother, is perhaps the most significant aspect of the goddess. A multiplicity of meanings are grouped hierarchically under the symbol of motherhood, just as a series of goddesses are arranged in a hierarchical order under Durgā herself. There are no easy correspondences in this scheme: no single characteristic correlates with a single concrete aspect of the goddess. Each manifestation has multiple meanings, depending on the situation in which the goddess appears and the locality where she manifests herself. (I shall come back to this problem of hierarchy and the multivocal meaning of categories, terms, and symbols.)

The goddess appears in many myths and legends. Some myths come from the śāstras, sacred books in general. People do not differentiate the older and more recent texts: *śāstra* is an inclusive term referring to the contribution of the renouncer, the saint, and the seer to the rest of society, usually in the form of prescriptive and exegetical writings. Almost anything can be *śāstrik* (of the śāstras): Vedas, Epics, Purāṇas, and Upapurāṇas. Versions of the same myth about Durgā and Śiva may appear in several classes of texts. Some of these are of local significance, written by people in this part of Bengal, but these too come under the general term śāstra. Other myths tell the legendary history of the town, king, social groups (jāti and baṇgśa), temples, sects, and individual devotees. All these narratives, regardless of source, constitute a unity. In this sense the origin or history of texts themselves is less significant than the relationships they reveal. Narratives as texts of verbal or written kinds are of the greatest significance, raising problems of analysis beyond *Quellenforschung.*[14]

The two most widely known myths of the goddess link belief and ritual. Two major pūjās of Durgā feature in these myths: Bāsanṭipūjā and Saradiyapūjā. The former takes place in the spring, the latter in the autumn. The spring worship is also known as the pūjā of Bāsanṭi Debī, the goddess of the spring. The autumn (saradiya) worship is the pūjā of

Mahiṣamardinī (the killer of the buffalo demon). In this pūjā the season is not emphasized; rather, the more abstract features of the goddess are glorified. The myths give the circumstance of these divisions.

Rāvan, the demon king of Laṇka, was a fervent devotee of the goddess, and he gave men the model for the worship of Durgā as the goddess of spring. Rāvan established the Bāsaṇṭipūjā, and at one time that was the only annual pūjā of the goddess. Once a year people used to worship Durgā in this special way, with all the elaborate rituals, just as Rāvan taught them, the same way the rituals are still performed today. But when Rāma (the incarnation of Viṣṇu in the world of the Rāmāyana) came into conflict with Rāvan, he had to seek the help and grace of the goddess. In order to defeat Rāvan, Rāma performed the pūjā when he was in trouble, without waiting for the proper time of the annual pūjā. He did the pūjā in the autumn, and later this pūjā became the most popular ritual of the goddess. The people regard it as the pūjā of the Bengalis, the one pūjā they all share. This pūjā is Akāl Badhan, an "invocation out of time," referring to the coming of the goddess in an unusual way, answering Rāma's call, even though the time was not proper for the annual pūjā. Rāvan was a great Brāhmaṇ, a *sādhak* (one who goes through ascetic, ritual practices and thus gains unusual powers). For his acts of devotion the goddess granted him many boons that made him victorious in all encounters with gods, demons, and men. When Rāvan abducted Sīta (Rāma's wife) Rāma could not defeat him while the goddess helped Rāvan. So Rāma wanted to perform the pūjā, but the goddess instructed him to ask Rāvan to do it for him, Rāvan being the most accomplished ritualist (*paṇḍit*). Neither the goddess nor the priest could refuse Rāma's wish because of his great devotion (*bhakti*). Rāvan performed the pūjā even though he knew that the aim (*kalpa*) of the worship was to grant Rāma victory. Rāma pleased the goddess when he showed no hesitation to offer his own eye to her on discovering that there were only one hundred and seven lotus flowers instead of the sacred (and required) number of one hundred and eight.

Rāma and Rāvan showed different aspects of bhakti, and their acts form one of the most popular series of myths in West Bengal. I shall return to this paradox, since it has implications not only for the concept of devotion, but also for the concepts of divinity, priestly office, and the role of worshiper. In the myths Rāvan performs the pūjā because he is a Brāhmaṇ, one with the greatest knowledge, and so cannot deny the request to perform a pūjā. The goddess still favors him, but she complies with Rāma's wish to kill Rāvan (*Rāvanbodh*), since Rāma incorporates this aim into the pūjā. People enjoy elaborating Rāvan's part in the myth, for Rāvan achieves his own aim, paradoxically enough, by dying at the hands of the supreme God, the incarnation of Viṣṇu. Rāvan's devotion is the path of force and fighting, one of the many ways of eliciting the favor and attention of the gods.

In these pūjās the goddess is represented as the victorious ruler, the protector of her devotees. The iconography links the image to the purāṇic myths of the goddess who slew the demon.

Everyone knows these myths as part of the Caṇḍīpāṭ (the account of the doings of Caṇḍī, the fighting aspect of Durgā). This account forms part of the Markandiya Purāṇ, but it is best known as a separate book about the Goddess Durgā, even though the name Durgā is rarely used in the narrative. (For the Purāṇas in general, see Hazra 1963).

The first pūjās of the goddess were performed by Rāma (among the gods) and Surat Rājā (among men). Durgā is the ultimate form of the goddess, hence the Caṇḍī is the story of Durgā. In the Caṇḍī the goddess appears as the killer of the most terrible demon, Mahiṣāsur, the demon who terrified all the gods. The first myth recounts the origin of the goddess "who was not born." When brahman, the Immense Being, conceived of creation, the goddess (Āddā Śakti, the original power) personified its power of desire. With Viṣṇu she formed a motionless unity: she separated herself from the male deity, also conceived in relation to her as an aspect of brahman, giving him the power of action. In this way she allowed Viṣṇu to defeat the demons who were threatening the creator god Brahmā (the demons having sprung from the dirt that fell from Viṣṇu's ears). The myth creates a continuity between the original manifestation of the goddess and her later roles, under different names, in different situations, exhibiting a different complex of attributes in each case.

The myth that concerns us most directly is that of the buffalo demon. The goddess appears on the scene in this, as in the previous myth, out of "nowhere," answering a need that no other creature can fulfill.

When the powerful demon Mahiṣāsur (the demon in the shape of a buffalo) received boons from Śiva as a reward for his devotion and ascetism, even the gods were unable to withstand him. The incredible *āsura* conquered all the worlds and drove the gods from heaven. At a loss, the gods went to Brahmā, Viṣṇu, and Maheśvār (Śiva) in turn, but even the greatest among the gods could not help them. In consternation all the gods sat together. Then Śiva rose in great anger, and in his wrath an intense light emanated from his body. This light merged with the energy of the great gods in the assembly, and from it issued the form of Mahādebī, Durgā herself. She came to save the gods just as she did at the time of creation. The gods gave her their own weapons, and she rode off on a lion (given by Himalaya) to battle the demons. She defeated army after army of demons, killing famous subjects of the Great Buffalo. She assumed different forms at will to deal with different demons. Her anger became a series of manifestations of herself; Caṇḍikā, Cāmuṇḍā, and Ambika are all forms of the goddess in different situations. Finally she killed the āsura himself and received the adulation of the gods. She disappeared then, reminding them of her promise that she would come whenever called: she would answer those who perform her annual pūjā. Many other myths of Durgā are incorporated into other parts of the Markandiya Purāṇ: these are also recited by the people of Vishnupur on occasion. These myths and the situations they refer to are elaborated in Upapurāṇas and Bratakathās.[15]

In the Mahiṣamardinī legend the goddess manifests herself to the gods out of Parvatī's form, suggesting that she is the Āddā, the Mahā Māyā (the Great Illusion) who is also Śiva's consort through the ages. As Śiva's consort she is Gaurī, Parvatī, and Satī. Śiva was given Satī when Brahmā and the other gods decided that his ascetism was endangering the world. But Satī killed herself when her father, Daksa, spurned and abused Śiva because of his unconventional practices, insulting him at the great sacrifice Daksa offered to become the universal king. Śiva took Satī's body and roamed all over the earth causing destruction and death. The gods were terrified at this threat of total dissolution and begged Viṣṇu to stop Śiva. Viṣṇu followed Śiva, cutting the body of the goddess into pieces with his *cakra* (discus). Parts of the dismembered body scattered all over North India; these places became centers for the worship of the goddess, the fifty-one *pīthasthān*s. The goddess came back to Śiva in a different form, as the daughter of Himalaya, Parvatī. Most of the popular myths have to do with the love, quarrels, and the pūjās of Śiva and Parvatī. In this family context the goddess is also called Durgā. Debī in this case is synonymous with Durgā, Durgā being the most encompassing aspect of the goddess: all other names relate to particular aspects in particular relations to Śiva, other gods, or specific situations. Gaurī is the virgin aspect of the goddess, trying to seduce Śiva from his ascetic, yogic practices.

The three aspects of the goddess, hierarchically arranged under Ādi, the all-encompassing form, correspond to the three qualities, or *guṇ, sattva, raja, tama* (truth, power/force, worldly life). The three goddesses are Mahā Sarasvatī, Mahā Lakṣmī, and Mahā Kālī. These aspects combine into different relationships on the level of kinship. As Satī the goddess revealed to Śiva her Ten Great Forms, the Das Mahābiddya (ten objects of transcendental knowledge), one of which is Tārā, another is Kālī. Śiva opposed his consort's desire to go to Daksa Rājā's sacrifice because he was not invited. Satī assumed ten different forms to show Śiva her real nature, her power, and the extent of her rule over all creation. Śiva was overawed and allowed her to go. At the sacrifice she vindicated him and entered into a new cycle of creation.

Kālī, the destructive aspect of the goddess, is also linked with Rāma and the Rāvan myth. Here an āsura's son, Mahi-Rāvan, is the incarnate god's opponent. The demon king is killed by Indra, but before dying he receives the boon of a son from the gods. The posthumous son grows up battling the gods and defeats Indra. He captures Rāma and his brother Lakṣman and prepares to sacrifice them to the goddess. On Hanumān's advice the gods and Rāma perform Kālīpūjā, and the goddess promises to deliver them from danger. When the moment of sacrifice comes, Hanumān asks Mahi-Rāvan to demonstrate the pose Rāma should take, then he cuts off the demon's head. This moment is also portrayed in some of the annual Kālīpūjās, Mahi-Rāvan kneeling in front of the black goddess. The most popular image of Kālī is related to a different myth. Kālī, the destroyer of all evil, begins a mad dance of victory after her triumph. The whole world is threatened with destruction, for the earth cannot withstand the joy of the goddess. The gods approach Śiva in terror; only he can intercede with Kālī, the power of destruction. Śiva throws himself at the feet of the whirling goddess, but it takes her some time to realize that Śiva is under her feet, and stopping suddenly she puts her tongue out in shame. Most Kālīpūjā images show Śiva under the goddess's feet, the goddess dancing with garlands of skulls around her neck, naked, with a bright red tongue and drops of blood spattering from the severed heads of her enemies.

The autumn worship of the goddess brings Durgā among men in yet another way, in everyday life, beyond cosmology, creation, and cosmogony. The most pervasive myth of Durgāpūjā is one in which the goddess comes to the dwelling of her father once a year to spend some time with her father's kin. She brings her children, leaving her husband's house, and stays with her parents during the annual pūjā—her own pūjā. Colored lithographs and pictures on calendars illustrate her arrival at the landing ground in the river, alighting from a boat with her sons and daughters. Many households display such pictures, the cheap paper prints properly framed and decorated with flowers. The myth is linked to the rituals of the householder. Wherever the pūjā is performed at home, in the "room of the lord" or the temple of the household deity, the women of the house perform special rites welcoming and bidding farewell to the goddess as if she were the daughter of the house. The householder who performs the pūjā regards the goddess as his own daughter who was given away in marriage and returns every year to the people who share her blood. This aspect of Durgā is missing from the major public rituals, where the royal and martial element is emphasized. Sarasvatī and Lakṣmī become her daughters, bringing wealth and knowledge with them into the householder's world. Sons Kārtik and Gaṇeś complete the picture of the householder. Gaṇeś is the son of Śiva and Durgā. His pūjā prefaces all pūjās: after the initial purification Gaṇeś must be invoked as the guru of all beings, the god of fortune and wisdom. When Parvatī invited guests for Gaṇeś's *annaprasan* (the ceremony of eating cooked rice for the first time), she neglected to invite Saturn (Sanī), the most malevolent deity. Sanī came nonetheless and cast a baleful glance on the infant, and at that instant the child's head disappeared. In the uproar Śiva instructed Naṇdi, his helper, to bring the first head he could find, so Gaṇeś came to have the head of an elephant. Kārtik is the ideal of all girls; he is a handsome warrior, a bachelor, and a great lover. Gaṇeś is everybody's friend in need.

There are countless legends about Durgā's married life, her strife with Śiva, her problems with children and parents, her petulance, her neglect by Śiva. (These stories are often told in relation to *brata*s, life-cycle rituals, and women's pūjās; see Fruzzetti 1975). Śiva appears as the mad *yogi* (ascetic) who wanders around inauspicious places, burning grounds, and the haunts of ghosts, or else is forever steeped in meditation, oblivious to the world. At other times he appears as the chaser of village girls, the seducer of married women, the foolish, lazy wanderer always ready for an adventure, never content to stay at home. Durgā, on the other hand, is the faithful and devoted wife, forever complaining about her husband, reproaching him for his infidelities, upbraiding him for his unconventional ways, always wanting to be loved, always trying to distract Śiva from his ascetic practices. At other times Durgā is the perfect *yogini* (female ascetic), bent on gaining Śiva's mercy through ritual practices and meditation—asking Śiva the rules of the renouncer's way of life, begging for instruction in his worship, trying to propitiate him and gain boons from him, eliciting the paths of pūjā and meditation that can be followed by virtuous men to gain Śiva's favor and to receive liberation from the world of illusion. These characteristics may appear paradoxical, but they occur on different levels of symbolism, in different fields of action. Myths of Durgāpūjā in their kinship and marriage aspects are paralleled by myths of the divine consorts in a family relationship. The *nabapatrika* (the Nine Durgās, represented by nine plants) in the Durgāpūjā is worshiped as a symbol of the goddess; it is bathed and invoked before the main rituals begin. It is dressed in a sāri, and it is married, according to a myth, to Gaṇeś. When Gaṇeś complained that the gods did not want him to marry, a banana tree was dressed up as a girl and married to him; only later did the unfortunate god discover the trick. The nabapatrika stands next to Gaṇeś, its popular name being kala bou (the banana wife). The kala bou is the recipient of the women's rituals in the householders' pūjā. It also features in the rājā's pūjā, where the sāri worn by nabapatrika is worn, in turn, by the female and male members of the king's family on the final day of the worship. Here also it stands for the goddess herself, representing the special relation between king and goddess.

Other pūjās of Durgā in the ritual cycle of the year relate to different myths about the killing of various āsuras. The pūjās of the goddess as Jāgaddhatrī and Gandheśvarī commemorate her as the victor over Jarāsur and Gandhāsur. In the former she appears as the originator and savior of the world. In the latter she is also the protector of a social group, the Gadhabaniks, traders in spices and oils. Similarly, persons of castes such as Jele (fishermen) and Śaṅkari (conch-shell carvers) tell myths linking their jātis to Durgā in special ways.

The legends of Sankattarinī and Bipadtarinī relate the goddess to situations, as the deliverer from danger. In the former manifestation she saves the Paṅdavas from their pursuers when the mother, Kunti, prays to Durgā as she conceals the fugitives in a tree. Temples of Sankattarinī are regarded as the locality where this incident took place. The pūjā of Bipadtarinī, a brata of the women, is followed or preceded by the telling of a legend: how the goddess saved a queen. The legend in Vishnupur is told about the Malla kings, but it is a well-known one with printed versions all over Bengal. The rānī had a low-caste Muci friend who ate beef every now and then. The rānī was horrified to learn this but, immediately curious, she wanted to see the meat. The Muci girl feared the pious Hindu king and did not care to comply. When she finally did, the queen was betrayed, and the king rushed in to kill her. The rānī prayed to Durgā, and when the king tore her clothes to see what she was hiding, all he could find were red jaba flowers. Both these pūjās are mainly women's rites, performed to gain the boon of the goddess for the family. Similar legends abound in the region about the goddess and her timely intervention on behalf of her devotees. Myths of the king's Durgā temple and the Goddess Mrinmoyī also abound in the town; these involve not only the royal lines but also devotees from the whole region. Other myths bring the goddess into contact with saints and ritualists who passed through the town (among them Rāmakṛṣṇa). In these there is a combination of general themes and a variety of particular, local events. The whole cycle of myths around the king and the goddess is paralleled by cycles of myths from neighboring kingdoms.

Some of the myths recounted above are general, without any reference to the region. But some are related to localities in the town and the kingdom, others to the people of this area. Still others relate to situations well known by townsmen. All these myths tell something about Durgā from different points of view. They must be regarded as a totality, for only then do the links among the separate levels of the symbolism become significant. Here the town and the people are our frame of reference, rather than history, texts, and sacred books. The myths are variations on a theme: we seek the principles that determine the theme. What we try to understand are the relations among symbolic units brought together by myths and rites through the circumstances of time, events, persons, and groups in the complex and varied cultural system of Vishnupur town and of the people who experience that system as a reality.

Goddess, King, and Priest

The most elaborate sequence of rites takes place in the Debī Mandīr of the king. This temple is in the *mandap* style, with arches and columns on one side, the other three sides being walled up. But inside there is a permanent image—a remarkable one. The rājā's Mrinmoyī Debī stands within a smaller temple inside the mandap. She is the ten-armed goddess, shown in the pose of killing the buffalo demon. She is inside a roofed enclosure, her children mounted on its outer wall, all represented in the round. Śiva and his attendants, also represented by sculptures, occupy the upper frame of the roof. The Ten Forms of Great Knowledge are painted on the wall of this smaller altar.

The pūjā is much changed today from what it was under the Malla kings. The rājā still has a significance in the ritual life of the town, since his pūjā is the model for the community pūjās. It is still regarded as the primary pūjā of Vishnupur. What can be observed today is recognizably royal, but it is shorn of the pomp and magnificence that marked these occasions in the past. Certain rituals are left out or abbreviated nowadays, and the full range of jātis no longer officiates at the temple during the festival. In the past there were a large number of subcastes, specially named and endowed with land, just for the purpose of performing certain specialized duties in different festivals. No longer does the temple retain its full complement of servant jātis. These named groups are still present in the town; they act as endogamous subcastes (they have separated from the jātis of their origin; they marry within the group, they worship and eat separately, and they are regarded as different by the other subsections of the caste). Despite all this, the rājā's Durgāpūjā is still a spectacular occasion and is so regarded by the townspeople.

The rājā's pūjā unifies and defines the town as a single unit, and the town is encompassed by the king's goddess. This is clear not only from contemporary ideology but also from legend. There is a conception of oneness in the idea of the goddess and the town, just as there is an idea of multiplicity and variation in the plurality of goddesses and the units within the town. This is, of course, not a causal connection, but a parallel that occurs in many other contexts as well. The rājā's Debī has played a significant role in the history of the town. Everybody knows this history, everyone acknowledges the place of the goddess in the town. Despite the uniqueness of the rājā's Durgāpūjā, it includes the basic elements that are common to all pūjās.

The rājā's pūjā tells us most about the whole system because it is a model for other Durgāpūjās in the town; it is the most encompassing of all pūjās.

The Malla kings established the settlement in Vishnupur on the express intervention of the goddess. According to lengendary accounts widely known in the town, the kings ruled from Laugrām, not far from the present police station of Vishnupur. The circumstances of their coming to Vishnupur were unusual and, in the judgment of the people, supernatural (*aloukik*).[16]

One of the kings (according to some accounts it was Jagat Malla, nineteenth in the line of Malla kings, who flourished about the tenth century A.D.) was hunting in the jungle near the present site of the Durgā temple. Catching sight of a heron on a treetop, he dispatched his hunting hawk, hoping for a quick kill. To his amazement, however, the heron struck the hawk dead. The king realized that the hand of a divinity must be behind such an unusual event. He then heard sounds from the direction of the tree, and from these noises (according to Tantric practice) he identified the divinity as the Goddess Durgā. Revealing herself to him, the goddess commanded him to establish her worship in this place and to remove his capital from Laugrām so that all his subjects might worship and serve her. The goddess would then take up her residence under that very tree. She further instructed him that her image lay buried in the earth under the tree and that he must install this image and begin its worship.

Some versions of the legend state that only the head of the goddess lay buried in the earth, and the king had the body constructed later. Some say that the block of stone that was to yield the head lay under the tree and the body had to be made out of earth. The goddess came to be called Mrinmoyī, the One from the Earth. This same deity is now enshrined in the temple that bears the inscription: "The Goddess Durgā (Mrinmoyī) / The Debī of Mallabhum / Her Worship Established in A.D. 994." The temple was built in the twentieth century; previously the goddess rested on a mud platform in a mud hut. It is said that she did not like elaborate buildings but preferred simplicity and open places, breaking the roof at each attempt to build a proper temple. Finally the present one was built when the goddess consented to the wish of a great *bhakta* (devotee); but in a vision (*sapna,* also meaning dream) she specified that the tree on which the heron sat should not be harmed. The bhakta had to show his powers once more when the building reached the lowest branch, and every time the masons wanted to proceed the walls would fall down the next day. The devotee, however, forced the deity to lift the branches clear of the proposed height of the temple, thus demonstrating his great devotion. Some identify this bhakta with an ancestor of the present king's priest.

The way ritualists are organized corresponds to the spatial arrangement of pūjās in the town. Different kinds of priests relate to different segmentary divisions. There are ritualists who serve the whole town (in the context of the rājā's or the community pūjās). Others serve only one of the segments, the polar opposites being most clearly defined. Priests serving Brāhmaṇs usually do not perform the pūjās of the low castes, and low-caste ritualists cannot perform pūjās in Brāhmaṇ temples. The priest as a category of office raises a question independent of these considerations. For this we must turn to the discussion of the relations among the categories that designate the structure of pūjā.

The priest and the king stand in a special relation to the goddess, as well as to each other. Several legends throw light on these relationships. The first king of the Malla dynasty ascended the throne of a small jungle kingdom (the extent of a group of villages) sometime in the seventh century A.D. The circumstances of this accession were miraculous. His father was a Rājput prince who, caught in the "fever of pilgrimage" to the shrine of Jagannath in Puri, abandoned his pregnant wife in the jungle when her labor began. The mother died and the newborn was picked up by a Bagdi jāti woman who was gathering firewood in the jungle. The boy grew up among the low-caste earthworkers ("tribals," according to the legend), the Nicu jāti Bagdis. Hence he became known as the Bagdi rājā; in fact, the kings of the dynasty are often called the Bagdi rājās by the people of the region. The Bagdis themselves are still associated with the royal line in many ways, an attribute that makes them and the Majhis who are similarly related to the kings the highest among the low. The boy's father had left a Rājput sword and a scroll attesting the boy's origin with his abandoned wife. A Brāhmaṇ priest noted that the royal child was different from the rest of the Bagdi boys and took him away to his house, together with the kingly insignia. Many portents foretold the future kingship of the boy. He brought home golden nuggets he found in a riverbed; he fished out golden insignia from the river; a huge cobra was seen standing over him shielding him from the sun when he fell asleep in the forest herding cows (much to the horror of his adoptive father, who searched the whole area in despair when the boy did not return home on time). When the king died and the Brāhmaṇ was invited to the funeral feast (*śrāddha*), he took the boy with him. To everyone's amazement, the dead king's elephant lifted the boy from the rows of spectators and placed him gently on the throne.[17]

A different version states that the boy's wrestling ability attracted the notice of the king (at the annual Ind Parab, the royal rite of raising Indra's flag). Undefeated in wrestling, the youth received a small fief from which he set out to conquer the whole kingdom. He appointed his Brāhmaṇ benefactor to the office of the king's priest. The present priests of the rājā claim descent from this Brāhmaṇ. The first king was Ādi Malla, the original Malla. The area was known as Mallabhum, the land of the wrestlers, but there is no agreement among Bengali scholars on the derivation of this word (for a summary, see Banerji 1968 and Mitra 1953). According to the legends, the kings were Saiva at this time, worshipers of Śiva; only three centuries later did the goddess first reveal herself to Jagat Malla, thus introducing Debī worship to the area. The earliest temples still extant and datable are all Śiva temples, yet they cannot be placed earlier than the eleventh or twelfth century (even this evidence is far from conclusive).

There are many myths about the relations between king, goddess, and priest. As a result of Jagat Malla's hunting trip the settlement of Vishnupur was established and developed. The king received a special boon from the goddess, somewhat in the form of an alliance or contract. The king was to establish the worship; the goddess would help and protect him in war and in peace, from threats and calamities. Other legends attest that the contract was further elaborated by the successor kings. The kings were great devotees, otherwise no deity would have had anything to do with them. There is no such devotion nowadays, say the elders of Vishnupur, sadly shaking their heads. The young also recognize the devotion of the early kings of the town; for them, however, what counts is the power (*śakti*) the kings derived from their devotion to the goddess. It is for her power that the goddess is served consistently by many people in the town.

There is a continuing discussion in the town and in Bengal about the kings of Vishnupur, their origin and rule. Some cast doubt upon the Ksatriya origin of the Malla dynasty. The lower castes regard the king at least as someone who is specially related to them, if not quite a member of their caste. A book recently published by a townsman on the history of Vishnupur is of great interest in this regard. Sri Phakirnārāyan Karmakār (1967/68) argues in his book *Bisnupurer Amor Kahini* (*The Immortal Story of Vishnupur*) that had the rājās of Mallabhum not been Ksatriya to begin with, how could they have secured the services of a high-ranking priestly line? The substance of the debate does not concern us. What *is* important is the relation between the priest, king, and deity as well as that between high and low underlying this debate of obviously great antiquity.

The Gājan of Śiva in Myth and Legend

The word gājan probably comes from the Sanskrit *garjana,* meaning cry or shout.[18] During the festival, bhaktas call Śiva, hoping to draw his attention to the acts of devotion they perform. Bhakti and bhakta are general terms, well known in other contexts (see the writings of Edward C. Dimock, especially 1966*a*). In the gājan they denote a special kind of devotion and self denial: bhaktas serve and follow Śiva; their sole purpose is to gain his favor by various ascetic practices. They are separated from everyday life, but they return to the duties of the householder when the festival is over. With the close of the gājan their specific attributes as bhaktas also end. But during the gājan ordinary men become divinelike creatures with special access to Śiva. Among the most striking features of gājan are the processions of bhaktas from one shrine of Śiva to another, and the loud recitation of Śiva's names and attributes by groups of bhaktas, in unison, without rehearsal, just as the spirit of the gājan dictates.

The festival takes place at the end of the Bengali year in the month of Caitra (March-April). The full gājan is performed over sixteen days, of which eight contain rituals of special, cumulative significance. The rituals of the festival as a whole are divided into daily prescribed actions and pūjās specific to the major days. Each of these is designated by a term for the nonrecurrent additional ritual of the day. A month later, at the end of Boiśakh (April-May) the *ābārgājans* are performed (gājan-again). These are on a smaller scale and somewhat different in detail. The following outline gives the framework shared by the two festivals.

Paitāneyoā is the day when the leader of the bhaktas (*pāṭbhakta*) receives the sacred thread (*paitā*) that separates him from everyday life and confers on him certain status, powers, and duties. He has to fast and offer pūjās to and meditate on Śiva and the sun every day. These actions will continue until the end of the gājan sixteen days later. The pāṭbhakta, however, is not joined by other bhaktas till the second major day, Kamilatulā, eleven days later. The ābārgājans of the town are similar in this regard: the gājan of the Boltalā Śiva follows the lunar calendar, and that of Buṛo Śiva the solar calendar (lasting sixteen days). The Caitra gājan is an exception: there the initiation of the pāṭbhakta is followed by the journey of Bhairab on the twenty-second of Caitra, ten days before the end of the festival.

Kamilatulā is the second major day, when more bhaktas receive the sacred thread. In the evening the Goddess Kāmakkā (Durgā) is brought to the gājan (Ṣāṛeśvar, twenty-sixth lunar day of Caitra; Buṛo Śiva, twenty-seventh of Boiśakh; Boltalā, twelfth of Boiśakh).

Rājābheta is the day of paying a visit to the king. Most bhaktas receive the paitā, and the gājan begins in earnest on this day.

Rātgājan, the peak of intensity and excitement, is reached in the gājan of the night.

On Dingājan, gājan of the day, a number of special rites occur in the morning, and at midnight bhaktas eat cooked rice for the first time since assuming the sacred thread.

Paitābisarjan is the final day, when the sacred thread is immersed and bhaktas return to everyday life.

Every year gājan is performed in three different localities of the town. Two of these are ābārgājans. The Caitra gājan takes place in and around the twin towerlike temples of Ṣāṛeśvar and Śālleśvar, on the bank of the Dvarakeśvar River, some four miles out of town. These are perhaps the oldest temples in the district, variously dated to the twelfth or the thirteenth century.[19] Several myths ascribe the origin of the temples to Bisvakarma (the artisan god), who left them unfinished. Even today the towers are incomplete. Townsmen explain that though the British also tried to restore the temples, even they, with all their engineering skill, have failed to put them up and repair them. What they built during the day fell down at night. Śiva himself prefers to live in the unfinished temple. He does not like the weight of the tower: he prefers open, airy places. Another legend ascribes the origin of the temples to the eighteenth-century Marattha invaders whose leader, Bhaskor Paṇḍit, was a devotee of Śiva. Both temples house images of Śiva in the shape of the *liṅga* (a stylized phallic symbol). The temples used to belong to the Vishnupur kings, but now the community as a whole takes care of them. The town is responsible for the organization, expenses, and arrangements of the annual gājan. Indigenous accounts of the gājan emphasize that it commemorates and imitates the pūjās and ascetic practices performed by deities in their worship of Śiva. Men can do no better than follow the example of the gods. Śiva is served by all other divinities (Deb-debīs). All actions that one may observe in a gājan have been taken by men from those performed by the deities themselves. It so happened that a particular āsura (demon) received certain boons from Śiva through the performance of *sādhana, tapassā, yog,* and *upāsanā* (disciplined worship, concentrated ascetic practice, meditation, and adoration). He did these with such intensity and single-mindedness that Śiva had to give him whatever he wanted. So the demon received the power to rule the heavens and the earth. The gods were driven out of the heavens and could find no refuge, since the powers of the demon matched and superseded their own. Neither Viṣṇu nor Brahmā could help. The deities then decided to call on Śiva. But Śiva was immersed in deep meditation. How could he be brought to listen to the distressed gods? The deities decided to break Śiva's meditation (*dhyen bhaṇga*). They called Śiva, performed pūjās, lay on the ground and rolled around Śiva himself, lay on thorny bushes, pierced their tongues, and walked on fire. All the while they repeated Śiva's names and implored him to save them from danger and pain. Śiva rose from his meditation with surprise. All the wounds the gods inflicted upon themselves appeared on his own body. Now he took mercy upon the deities, assumed their sufferings, and defeated the āsura. Men engaged in the same actions with the same purposes.

Alternative accounts state that the first gājan was performed by Śiva's companions—ghosts, *bhuta*s, *raksasa*s, *pisaca*s, and Bhairabas, the riders of the night—the creatures that populate the burning grounds and other inauspicious places. They worshiped Śiva in violent ways (that correspond to the *tamasik* in the tripartite ideology; see pp. 53 ff.). When Śiva joined the gājan and all the deities participated, the form of the gājan as we know it was established. It was a way of acknowledging Śiva's creative and destructive power, and it marked an attempt by all creatures of the heavens to share and participate in the lord's tremendous powers. The deities performed the gājan to secure this divine power for the work of the gods and to prevent it from falling into the hands of the forces of darkness.

When Śiva returned to Parvatī, his consort through the ages (and in different incarnations), he was disheveled and tired, and his body was marked in a frightful way. But he was in high spirits, elated with the worship, intoxicated by the devotion of the gods and his companions. The goddess was surprised and implored him to tell her what happened. Śiva described the gājan with its boundless excitement and joy. Parvatī became moody and jealous since she could not experience all this. So Śiva cried: "*ābār gājan korbo* [I will do gājan again]!" This was the origin of the ābārgājans in the town. For this reason there is an image of Durgā in the Rātgājan procession of the Boltalā festival.

Until the time the gājan was introduced, the gods did not know how to celebrate the greatest of gods, Mahādeb. All the thirty-three crores (crore = ten million) of divinities performed the gājan to express their adoration of Śiva in the most appropriate manner. When men do the same, they too must become deities so that they can worship Śiva as approximate equals. The higher the status of the worshiper, the more meaningful is his self-negation, his unbounded devotion. Different classes (*srenī*) of deities participated in the gājan, and so there are different groups among bhaktas, according to the type of devotional acts they perform.

The above myths are told about the gājan as a whole. Most generally bhaktas use the action of the gods as a precedent for their own performance of the gājan. Many specific myths are told about the actions of the different days of the festival, and I shall mention these as I come to them. A great variety of stories are told about Śiva's own ordeals. There are also many narratives about Śiva in the Purāṇas and other sacred texts. Śiva is a complex divinity with many levels of meaning. But the gājan is not mentioned by name in any of these texts. The dancing, processions, calling of Śiva, and other rites of the gājan are mentioned in the Purāṇas, but they do not explain the significance and meaning of the festival. One myth common to the Purāṇas and the exegesis given by bhaktas is the story of Bana Rājā. This king was a great devotee of Śiva, and the god was pleased with his follower and bestowed many boons on him. Once, however, the king was defeated by rival gods (among them Kṛṣṇa) in a terrible battle, and to recover from his wounds he sought refuge with Śiva. Bleeding and distraught, he danced the dance of the bhaktas in front of the Great Lord. Śiva was pleased and interceded with Kṛṣṇa for his devotee's life. To this day men inflict pain and wounds on themselves to gain Śiva's favor. Bana Rājā is variously regarded by the devotees of Vishnupur as the king of demons or the king of the above purāṇic story.

Purāṇic myths are therefore in some ways, an integral part of the performance and exegesis of the gājan in a particular area of Bengal. Even though gājan is missing from the great purāṇic texts, it is very much alive in the long verse narratives known as Maṅgal Kāviyā. These narratives provide a level of analysis more immediate to our purpose than the Purāṇas. However, just like the Purāṇas that form the most general context for our study, the maṅgals present us with problems of interpretation that cannot be resolved from the discussion of a single festival corresponding to the particular maṅgals of Śiva. Many intriguing problems raised here will be resolved only when all Bengali myths and rituals are analyzed on all levels, in all contexts. The gājan is not an isolated festival; there are other rituals, similar in sequence and detail, in honor of other deities such as Manasā (goddess of snakes) and Dharma

Ṭhākur (Lord Dharma), both in Bankura and in other parts of Bengal. Curiously enough, the most complete description of gājanlike rituals is to be found not in the local myths of Śiva but in those of Dharma Ṭhākur.[20] This deity was popular in the region, but its pūjā is on the wane. The original seat of Dharma worship is only a few miles from Vishnupur. But we also have a few accounts of Dharma and Śiva worship over the last hundred years in other regions of Bengal. In addition to our exegetical data, the Maṅgal narratives and these early accounts enable us to discuss the relation between the rites and myths of Dharma and Śiva. Dharma literature provides almost a book of rules for the performance of Śiva's gājan. The paradox disappears, however, when the performances of Dharma and Śiva gājans are taken in relation to each other in the same locality.

Chapter Two

The Festival of the Goddess

The Organization of Durgāpūjā

The goddess partakes not only of the spatial but also of the temporal dimensions of life. She represents the full cycle of time, within the year and in the cosmos. Annually she visits the town, neighborhoods, households, and temples. At that time all actions revolve around her, and everyone is involved in her celebration. No other festival more fully excites the imagination of the people. There are countless legends about the activities of the goddess, some referring to the timeless past, some going back only a few years. She is worshiped by youth clubs, political parties, associations and institutions, neighborhood groups, families, sects, and individuals. There are exclusive household rituals and there are also large public pūjās performed on behalf of and with the participation of the town. The most striking feature of all this activity is worship in the open: on street corners, in public piazzas, and in any vacant place—in temporary tentlike structures (*paṇḍal*s). The public, community worship of the goddess is a recent phenomenon, about one hundred and fifty years old. Its development has been parallel to the emergence of community involvement in temple worship and pūjā organization. (On the role of voluntary organizations in the festival in Calcutta see Sarma 1969; for a historical account of the worship see Ghosh 1957.)

The Feast of Durgā is characteristically known as "the pūjā of the

Bengalis" or Saradiyapūjā (autumn festival). No other deity's worship is denoted in these terms. This is not the only feast of the goddess, however. She is offered pūjā under a myriad of different aspects and manifestations. Opposed to the autumn is the spring, when the pūjā of Bāsanṭi Debī (the spring goddess) is celebrated. In the early summer the pūjā of Caṇḍī Debī takes place (the fearful goddess who brings disease and pestilence). Caṇḍī is the goddess of power and wrath, just as Durgā is the goddess of peace. Gandheśvarī Debī is worshiped in midsummer: she is the protector of trade and tradesmen. In early winter, Jāgaddhatrīpūjā is performed (the goddess as mother, genetrix of the world) and the goddess Kālī is worshiped, the all-destroying aspect of time, a goddess most dangerous, most powerful (*śaktigoti*). Then there are the feasts of Sankattarinī and Bipadtarinī, the goddesses who deliver from danger (they are protectors of the family, husbands, brothers, and children, and so women are most centrally involved in their worship). Similarly, other aspects of the goddess are worshiped on occasion in relation to specific characteristics or situations. Such are the twenty-four Ṣaṣṭhīs, goddesses of protection and help whose pūjās are assigned to the lunar months of the year, two in each month. Ṣaṣṭhī governs kinship, birth, and death, and so she has a major role in life-cycle rituals.

The societal implications of this elaborate annual cycle are just as obvious as the ideological ones. The annual Durgāpūjā is a general worship, though, as we shall see, the low-caste participation is restrained. The pūjās of Caṇḍī are performed, however, in just about every locality in the town (here the multiple performances give the clue to the societal divisions). Kālīpūjā is the most sectarian of the Debīpūjās, but, owing to its Tantric character, participation cuts across all social boundaries in a special way. Gandheśvarī is worshiped by the Bene caste (*bania,* merchant) and other merchant castes. In the town itself only the Banias have a jāti worship of this goddess. The caste headman's duty is to make all the arrangements for the pūjā. He has to collect subscriptions from the caste brothers, commission the image from the potter or the carpenter (sometimes the blacksmith), buy the objects of worship, invite the priests, bring the offerings, and arrange for the distribution of the deity's *prasad* (food leavings). But in recent years the jāti basis of Gandheśvarīpūjā has been overshadowed by that of occupational trade. Today these are performed all over the town, mostly in the shops and booths of traders big and small, belonging to both merchant and nonmerchant castes. On the other hand, Durgā herself is worshiped by Jele (fishermen) and Śaṅkari (conch-shell workers). These castes claim a special relation to Durgā; the fishermen worship her as the creator of fishermen, the shell-makers regard her as their protectress (fish and shell being important symbols in Durgāpūjā). The worship of Ṣaṣṭhīdebī defines the domestic group and the life cycle, bringing together the private and the public spheres in the rites of the goddess.

Divisions multiply in the worship of the goddess just as they do in the case of her manifestations. Through the goddess alone we get the same spatial division in the town as we do through a consideration of all pūjās. Each of these units is defined through locality, kind of attendance, and type of performance. In the same locality there may be several pūjās: a temple where pūjā can be offered by anyone, a community pūjā in a tent, a line (baṇgśa) temple or a household shrine where Durgā is worshiped as the line deity (kuladebatā) or a chosen deity (*istadebatā*).[1] The pūjā defines the smallest units of locality and society. Under her other aspects she may define situations and experience. She is the one deity most persistently pursued in her diverse aspects, hence the proliferation of her worship through the year. In this way she defines a specifically Bengali ideology (a model for action): the unifying ideology of *debī-upāsanā* (service and pursuit of the goddess). This also follows the discriminations of observed behavior and spatial arrangements. For the Bengalis of Vishnupur, however, the goddess is not at all a means of recognizing social classification. She is engaged in a divine cycle of repetition, returning every year as a destroyer of darkness and the demonic to redress the balance on the side of light and knowledge. She stays with her creatures for a while, confirming them in her grace and protection. Then she goes away, leaving the people with the knowledge that they are not alone, that she will always return. She may come at any time should the need arise. Devotees often take it upon themselves to announce her visit to some favored individual. This is how new rituals arise, should the claim be vindicated.

The question of participation is a difficult one because there is no single criterion of involvement. The vantage point decides the result. Taking the jāti system as the point of reference, we would end up with a confusing picture. On the one hand, the pūjā is open for everyone (depending on the nature of the pūjā: community or line). Does this make a participant out of everyone, especially when pūjās are not congregational in the way Western religious rituals are? To look for concretely definable groups of participants would be a positivist, structural-functional fallacy. Groups in Durgāpūjā do not hold together in *that* way. All we can say at this stage is that Durgāpūjā tends to be segmentary in its organization and participation, with sometimes the larger, sometimes the narrower segments presenting themselves to the viewer. The division into high- and low-caste groups holds in a tenuous way: there are few "low"-jāti, line pūjās (though there may be all-caste pūjās, stressing the larger segments in the social structure of the town). Most of the line pūjās are "high"-caste. Yet the involvement of the low castes in these pūjās is more noticeable than in some of the community pūjās. In the former, the lower jātis still perform tasks for their clients; in the latter, the tasks are performed voluntarily by members of the group (locality-based or goal-oriented). In Calcutta one of the most important public actions during the pūjā is the *puspañjali* (offering of flowers to the goddess while repeating the incantations of the Brāhmaṇ). In Vishnupur this is not the practice, hence a caste-based study of those who do and those who do not perform it would not be very enlightening.

There are no concrete divisions of society in terms of finance, either, for anyone can contribute to the pūjā. There are restrictions in the household and line pūjās, but these do not include outsiders (though caste functionaries are always a part of these pūjās). The restrictions on access to the area of worship are simply in terms of the Brāhmaṇ/non-Brāhmaṇ division (which applies in many other ways too: the performance of pūjā, the recitation of Sam-Vedic *mantra*s, the touching of images, the cooked rice offering, all of which are the privilege of the Brāhmaṇ).

If we look at society through the symbol of pūjā, then Durgāpūjā generally belongs to the high jāti complex, within the high-low opposition of a segmentary social and cultural system. However, the high-low division is only one of many more-or-less inclusive ways of dividing society. In this case the segments and the whole are expressed in different ways (as far as "participation" is concerned) in the course of the festival.

To recapitulate: there are the pūjās of the king relevant to the whole town. Then there are several community pūjās organized by various institutions, designed for general participation. Major *ganja*s (markets) also perform Durgāpūjās for and on behalf of the people in these sections of the town. The same is true of smaller divisions, *pāṛā* (neighborhood) and caste *ṣolaānā*s.[2] Finally there are line, sectarian, and individual Durgāpūjās. Not mentioned in the discussion so far are the pūjās sponsored by voluntary groups. These are also tied to localities and include people with common interests.

Youth and other clubs, political and other groups, may carry out nonsacred social activities during the rest of the year. These groups, or *dal*s, are a basic feature of Bengali social organization, but they are incomprehensible without the pūjā context. They are voluntary, but they have an accepted leadership. They organize pūjās in September but may also work for elections in February. They may be spontaneous, but they link together other forms of organization through locality and shared concerns. Dal is one of the units of social structure invisible to those who require hard and fast boundaries for social groups. The dal organization also characterizes pūjā committees and ṣolaānā groups: the same ways of leadership and following can be found in the functioning of town, ganja, and pāṛā ṣolaānā performances.

The festival as a whole extends through sixteen days, but not all days are observed everywhere. The fullest ritual sequence is observed in the rājā's temple. Even there it has lost much of its luster. Judging from the accounts of older men, from descriptions of the ritual a generation or two ago, and from legendary history, whatever we see today is an abbreviated version of the pūjā as it was in the heyday of the Malla kings. Nevertheless, the myths and rituals reveal a total system. Whatever the role of time and history in ritual continuity and change, a structural view at any one moment tells us more about the meaning and the nature of an ideological system than about the way that system developed and survived. The importance of the rājā's pūjā is not due to its magnificence and magnitude. Rather, it is due to the structural position of the pūjā in the ritual scheme of the town, the position of the royal myths in the indigenous ideology, and the role of the goddess in that ideology. There are several lines in the town that observe the pūjā the same way as does the king. These are hereditary royal officeholding lines, even though they have no duties now, and their pūjās are in no way relevant to the town as a whole. Beyond these there are great nonroyal *baṇgśa*s (lines) that observe the pūjā in their own way (*mat*). But even though these populous, sometimes wealthy, high-caste lines observe the sixteen days of worship, they do not follow the rājā's division of the pūjā into three distinct parts and three goddesses, nor do they have the same position in the annual calendar of townwide rites.

Most household and community pūjās observe only the major days of the festival: the last five. Even in the king's pūjās only the last five days are well attended. The previous days are regarded as preliminaries, as acts of anticipation. In the few cases where the full sequence is performed, the first eleven days consist of rituals of welcome and initial invocations. These are accompanied by the usual daily rituals of the goddess, since in these places there is usually a permanently installed Durgā image.

The first eleven days span the dark and the bright halves of the moon. The first ritual of welcome, the first *saṅkalpa* (or *belbaraṇ* in the case of the rājā's temple), takes place on the first day. From then on the *ghat* of the goddess, installed specially for the festival, is given pūjā every day using special items of food and worship.[3] This is the case even where there is a permanent image and ghat. The new ghat marks the annual, special nature of the pūjā. These offerings and pūjās continue till Mahā-Ṣaṣṭhī, when the goddess is invoked in all pūjās of the town. In between the Amābassā (new moon) phase occurs. Not only is Amābassā an auspicious time for the worship of some aspects of the goddess, as Mahālaya, this Amābassā is the most important new moon of the year. It marks the Debī's fight with the demons, inaugurating a special phase of time: the coming of the goddess. People fast on this day and recite or listen to the myths of the goddess. (Mahālaya is marked at its onset by the recitation of the Caṇḍī myth over the Calcutta station of All-India Radio.) The goddess is invoked in her own form (as seen and described by renouncers, sages, and saints) on Mahā Saptamī, the seventh day. This is the first worship of the Debī herself.

Images of the Goddess

The pūjā revolves around the representation of the goddess. Most of the images that are immersed at the end of the festival represent her as a ten-armed female figure (Dasabhuja, the one with ten arms) in the act of killing the buffalo demon. The image is clothed like a married woman, but the edge of the sāri does not cover the head as modesty ordinarily requires, since here the status of the goddess is accentuated. The goddess wears an elaborate headdress and holds royal insignia in her hands. She is covered with costly jewelry: earrings, wrist and arm bracelets, nose ring, ankle bracelets, necklace, and hair braiding tassles. She has the third eye in the middle of her brow. She is surrounded by her children: Gaṇeś sitting on his carrier, the rat, Kārtik riding on a peacock, Lakṣmī and Sarasvatī both standing on a lotus. The goddess herself is standing on a lion, which is depicted in the act of mauling the half-buffalo, half-man figure of the demon. Above the goddess is Śiva with his followers. These figures are painted on a scroll and mounted in a semicircle behind the goddess. The seven major figures (Durgā, lion, āsura, Lakṣmī, Sarasvatī, Gaṇeś, Kārtik) stand on a pedestal, arranged symmetrically against a semicircular wooden framework. The goddess, her lion, and the āsura form a triangle in the middle with Durgā's headdress the highest point. On her right stand Lakṣmī and Gaṇeś, and on her left are Sarasvatī and Kārtik. More recently the figures have been separated and arranged linearly like a group of actors taking the curtain call (the analogy is apt, since the space behind the figures is taken up by draperies); in Calcutta most of the pūjā paṇḍals boast such "modernized" representations; Vishnupur has few of these, and most images are arranged in the traditional manner.

The images are made by men of the carpenter caste (Suttradhar or Cuttor jāti). The making of images is one of the traditional occupations of this caste; there are, however, image-makers in other castes as well.

In Vishnupur an image-maker of a particular Cuttor line is the rājā's sculptor. He supplies the representations of the goddess for the rājā's pūjā, and he repairs the image of the rājā's Durgā temple. Men of this line have always been associated with the king's worship. They carry the title of phoujdar to signify this. The best images in the town come from this household. The head of the household builds only a few images, for the process is so arduous and time-consuming that he cannot fulfill all orders. In addition to his work for the king, he builds a big image for the Jele (fisher) jāti community worship, another for the worship of the most extensive Brāhmaṇ line in the town, and several smaller images for individual or household worship. He is the guru of two other image-making carpenters; he is not only their teacher but also a relative by marriage.

The clay image is only one of several ways of representing the goddess and her family. Admittedly it is the most popular form and the only one used for public celebrations. But simpler and less expensive paintings (*paṭ*) of the goddess, almost identical to the Mrinmoyī image, are much in use in household celebrations. These are also made by the phoujdar, and the figures are arranged the same way as in the clay images. The goddess is facing the viewer, but her face (like the faces of all the other figures) is shown in profile. Śiva and his attendants are shown anthropomorphically; just above the main group Śiva sits on his bull, Naṇdi, attended by ghosts and demonesses. The paṭ paintings are executed on thin canvas reinforced with glue and plaster to give a firm, smooth surface. The goddess is also fashioned in metal (silver, gold, or a combination of metals), with two, eight, ten, or eighteen arms depending on which of the āsuras this particular form of the goddess has fought and killed. These images are called *bigrahā*; the terms *murti* and *pratima* apply to clay images only. Wooden representations are also found in Vishnupur; these are usually of the ten-armed variety. Images of wood and metal are most commonly seen in line temples. The arrangement of the figures is not constant; the two-armed images show neither the demon nor the family of the goddess. The ten-, eighteen-, and twenty-seven-armed metal images may show only the primary triangle: the goddess, the demon, and the lion. The clay representations are almost always ten-armed, but the most usual variant is a two-armed goddess standing at the side of her consort Śiva: the Śiva-Durgā murti. In this case the divine pair are shown seated on Śiva's bull or sitting on Mount Koilas, no fight with the āsura being shown.

The clay images are often life-size, sometimes even bigger. Their construction takes about a week. The wooden structure that forms the framework for the group of figures is retained year after year. First the figures are fashioned roughly out of bunches of straw and tied onto the wooden poles. Next the artist uses the first of three kinds of clay, rough red clay. The clay is smoothed onto the structure to give the general anatomical shape. It is then allowed to dry, but, since the clay wets the straw below, large cracks appear on the surface. A second and a third layer are added, but this time finer clay is used. The final layer (the fourth or fifth) gives the final shape to the figures; for this a soft, smooth gray clay is used, supplied by the potter. Then the figures are painted and glazed. Durgā has a golden complexion (*gouri barna*). Śiva is white, Lakṣmī golden, Sarasvatī white, Gaṇeś red (but his elephant's head is white), and Kārtik and the lion are golden brown. The demon is blue-black or dark green.

Just before the worship begins, the images are decorated. The heads, hands, and feet are separately prepared and mounted on the bodies with lumps of clay. The image-maker fashions the heads of the figures separately; he may use a mold for the hands and feet. The head is painted separately and placed on the torso, the eyes of the goddess being painted first, before any other painting is done. There is no ceremony at the time of painting the eyes. Nowadays the rājā's Durgā image (in the Mrinmoyī temple) is not touched, the duties of the phoujdar revolving mainly around the painting of the three Ṭhākurānīs. Then the figures are clothed in sāris and dhotis, the usual form of female and male dress. Sometimes the garments are painted on the images. Jewelry is arranged on the female figures, and the ten weapons are placed in Durgā's hands. The semicircular board behind the images is covered with pith and tinsel decorations. In the bigger community pūjās the goldsmith brings out the jewels, a joint property of the ṣolaānā in the safekeeping of the headman. The goldsmith repairs and adjusts the jewels before he puts them on the goddess. The garland maker (*malakar*) mounts pith decorations on the framework. The potter brings earthenware vessels for the worship. Lower-caste men transport the image (if it is not made at the actual place of worship). They also construct the pūjā paṇḍal; the drapes are put on this framework with the help of the pāṛā people. The members of the pūjā committee bring the articles of worship. For family worship, many of these jobs are done by the head and the people of the household. For jāti worship, the work is done by the organizers, the leading men of the locality, or the elders. Everyone can join in: the work is a matter of choice and inclination.

Outside the pūjā context the image is regarded as a doll. It may be called *murti,* a general term for sculpture. When it is the object of pūjā it is called *pratima*. Permanently installed metal images are *bigrahā*s. The various images have different names, the most common being the

Mahiṣamardinī type. All ṣolaānā pūjās are of this type. Line pūjās may honor different images: the two-armed Sarbamaṅgala Debī (*sarba,* all; *maṅgala,* blessing) or the four-armed Caṇḍī and Jāgaddhatrī Debīs. These are not shown with the demon; they refer to different aspects and manifestations of the goddess. The eight-, sixteen-, and eighteen-armed images of the goddess usually appear with the same group as the ten-armed Mahiṣamardinī.

The number of arms, the posture, and the color of the different images distinguish the various identities of the goddess. The image itself corresponds to descriptions of the character (*rūp*) of the goddess given in the different sacred texts. The description of the goddess, *dhyen,* forms part of the recitations in the pūjā, the image itself being a reflection of the word.

Pūjās take place either in permanent temples or in temporary huts. The former contain installed images of the goddess that are worshiped throughout the year and are not replaced until they fall apart or someone steals them. There are few permanent temples of the goddess in Vishnupur. More common are the Durgā *mandal*s (*manca* or *mandap*), permanent but open structures. They are walled in on three sides, the fourth being open with a row of columns and arches. There may be anything from two columns and a single arch to five or six arches and six or seven columns. No permanent image is housed in these buildings. The image is built every year, utilizing the same wooden and straw framework. When the pūjā is over the image is immersed and the clay is allowed to soak off the structure, which is put back into the mandal but is not worshiped. Many families and lines own such a mandal in Vishnupur. The mandal is usually within the residential compound. Paṇḍals are temporary bamboo structures most generally used for community worship. These stay only for the duration of the festival and disappear soon after the immersion of the image. Sometimes the goddess is worshiped in the nāthmandir of a Kṛṣṇa temple. This building is open on all four sides, the roof resting on a series of arches and columns. Usually a place for singing the hymns of Viṣṇu, it becomes the home of the goddess in the autumn.

Temples of the goddess tend to be different from those of Kṛṣṇa and Viṣṇu. It is said that the goddess prefers open places. Most of the permanent Durgā temples in the town are of the mandap type. Those mandaps that house a permanently installed image usually have the open side covered by an iron fence with the bars three or four inches apart. The image is placed on a *bedī,* or altar, a raised platform: no deity can stand on the ground. It is to be mounted on a chariot, a vehicle (lion), or a throne. With the exception of the *liṅga,* no image stands directly on the ground. Line pūjās are performed in the temple of the line (*kula-mandir*). In many cases the line's deity is the goddess Durgā. The only requirement in the construction of a Durgā temple (of the open mandap type) is that the image, when installed, should face south or east, since the Ganges flows to the sea in these directions. Men facing the deity, therefore, face west or north. North is the sacred direction, a most auspicious one, because the Goddess Gaṇgā (Ganges) comes from that direction. Gaṇgā herself is forever striving to turn north, to reach the place where she descended on Śiva's head. The sacred cities (like Benares) are all situated in areas where the river seems to flow to the north, the temporary reversal accentuating sacredness.

The Invocations of the Rājā's Pūjā

The festival in the rājā's temple begins on the ninth lunar day of the moon's dark phase. During the days preceding this rite of welcome, men in some way related to the Malla line collect the necessary items and notify the *rājpurohit* (who still performs the Durgāpūjā but not the daily worship). The king's family receives help from those who want to offer it, but most of the costs are paid from compensation given by the government for lands taken over after 1948. Much of the *debattar* land (endowed to various temples and images) is also gone: without government support the king would not be able to finance a Durgāpūjā. Some of the jātis associated with the temples and pūjās of the king still perform their duties in the autumn festival. Castes previously in the daily service of the king also come at this time, musicians, helpers ("bodyguard"), and a number of individuals who still maintain relations with the palace. The belbaraṇ takes place near the temple, late at night (see fig. 2).

The Nannadi (Nabommadi) Saṅkalpa is performed a short distance away from the Mrinmoyī temple, in a small clearing surrounded by a bamboo grove. This area is sparsely populated; it falls into the palace area, the previously fortified, specifically royal space. There are seven major temples in this area, the temple of the goddess being in the middle. There are few houses here, and the temples are separated by patches of scrub and jungle as well as by the sacred water tanks attached to them. The place of the ritual is called the *beltalā, billastan*: the place of the *bel* (wood apple) tree. From this the rite is also called *belbaraṇ,* the welcome at the bel tree or, more specifically, the welcome of the goddess as manifest in the tree.

The pūjā is performed late at night in the cool silence, when neither man nor animal stirs to disrupt the quiet. The wood apple tree has long since disappeared, but the laterite stone platform is still there, and the

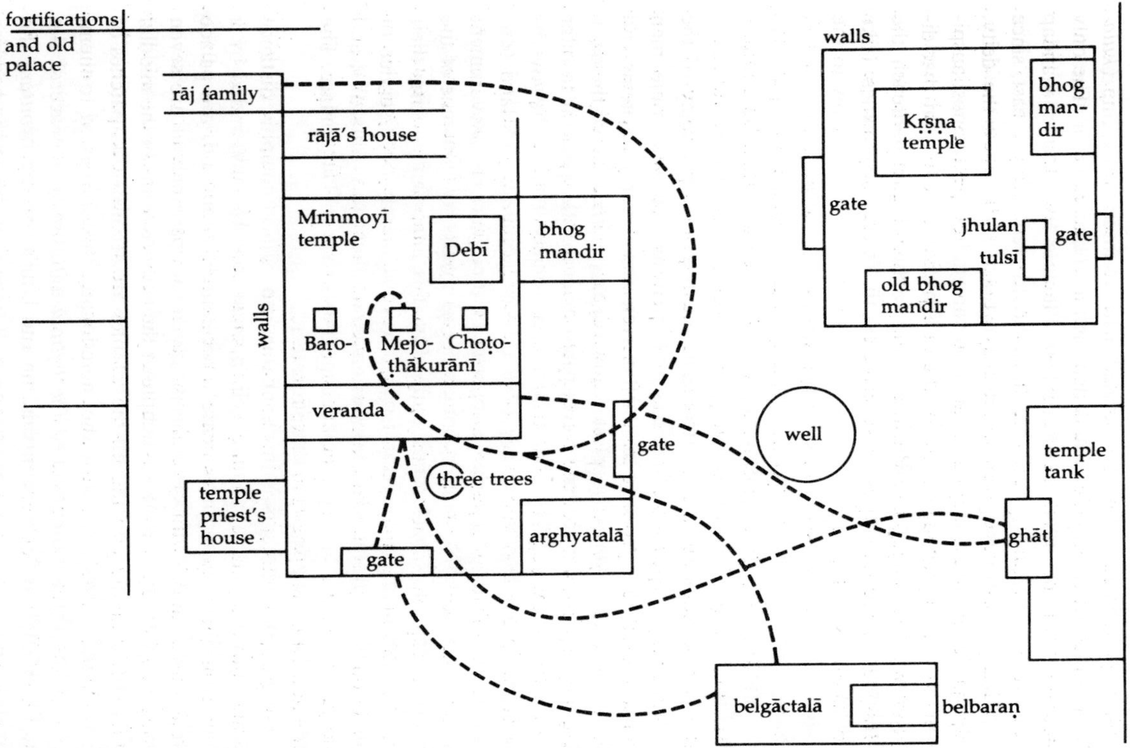

Figure 2. The rājā's temple and the processions of the initial invocations.

pūjā is performed on this flat surface. The bel tree itself is represented by a branch stuck into the ground near the *tulsī* (sacred basil) plant, also necessary for the ritual. Several priests officiate: two from the line of Ādi Malla's original priest, the third the current temple priest. The hereditary priests have given up the daily worship of the goddess since the rājā has fallen on evil days and can devote only a few pennies to the daily worship (hardly enough even for the indispensable items). The outside priest was then engaged, a Rāṛhī Brāhmaṇ ranked higher than the Utkal Brāhmaṇ hereditary priests. Nevertheless, the hereditary line performs the annual worship.

At least two priests have to be present to act as the *tantrik* and the *bhattacharya*. These two terms normally mean a member of a particular sect and the title of a certain class (*srenī*), such as Utkal, Barendra, of Brāhmaṇ. In the context of the pūjā, however, they refer to functions: the tantrik reads out the text from a manuscript or a printed book, the bhattacharya repeats the formulas and performs the acts of offering. Since the correct pronunciation of the formulas is very important, the tantrik is often a *paṇḍit* (a priest knowledgeable in the sacred writings). But all responsibility for the correct performance of the pūjā falls on the often less-knowledgeable bhattacharya. Brāhmaṇs who are priests by occupation are also known as *purohit*s. More accurately, the Brāhmaṇ as the performer of a pūjā is the purohit or the pūjāri (ritualist) or the *jajak* (sacrificer). Not all Brāhmaṇs act as priests, of course, nor are they all capable of performing pūjās. But it is important to remember that all Brāhmaṇs may perform pūjās (even if merely obeying the injunctions of a purohit who knows), since no other jāti is allowed to do so just by virtue of caste membership (this refers to Durgāpūjā; there are non-Brāhmaṇ priests in other festivals).

A group of musicians is in attendance; no pūjā is complete without some music or musical sound (bell, percussion). Usually, men of the low Dom jāti play the instruments at these celebrations. Because of the rājā's association with several low castes, the instrumentalists at the king's pūjās are not Doms as such but a subcaste that has been assigned this particular duty, being known and named for this occupation. The rājā himself rarely attends these welcoming rites; his great moment comes later. But another man of the royal line is always in attendance—the Bābu Sāhib, a descendant of a previous king's younger brother. The agnatic line of descent and succession was broken in the early twentieth century when the present rājā married the last Malla king's daughter. The Bābu Sāhib also contributes to the pūjā, though it is in the name of the rājā and is the latter's responsibility. No one else attends the pūjā this night.

The goddess arrives at the beltalā; a priest brings the painted representation of the Debī (the *Durgāpaṭ*) and props it up on the platform with the two long swords. Next, a small earthenware pot is placed in front of the goddess; this is the *ghat,* in which the goddess will be invoked during the ritual. The ghat is usually shaped like the ordinary vessel for cooking rice, but, unlike other pots, its belly is covered with white geometric designs. The two larger vessels are a pair of ghats, but these are not the vessels of invocation. The small ghat alone is used for the invocation in the bel tree, and it is discarded after the belbaraṇ; but the two big ghats are taken up into the temple and used in the next morning's pūjās. The ghat contains earth and water (gaṅgājal, or Ganges water by definition). A bunch of mango leaves on a single stem is placed in the mouth of the ghat. The purohit marks the ghat with vermilion and, sitting down on a mat (*āsan* or seat), arranges the objects of worship. A small brass jug of water, the *kamandala,* is used in the purifications and in the offering of water. Water is poured from the jug into the *kosakusi,* two leaf-shaped copper containers, the smaller being used to sprinkle water on the offerings. A round stone block is used to rub sandalwood into a paste. Flowers for the pūjā are also placed on the block. The sacred tulsī and bel plants stand at the side of the goddess; a lamp and an incense holder are placed in front of the small trees. These are lit as the pūjā begins, and a plate containing twenty-seven precious and auspicious items (*prasasta patra*) is brought out and placed within the reach of the priest. The tantrik sits with his manuscript a little behind the priest. The darkness is broken only by the flickering oil lamp and the tantrik's hurricane lamp. Incense and smoke (*dhoa,* a more powerful resinous incense) rise in slow folds around the goddess and her priests.

The priest begins to perform the pūjā by reciting Sanskrit words of purification, raising water to his lips. The recitations and offerings fall into separate stages. Words and deeds combine to define these stages. With each unit of recitation (*mantra* and *slaka*) an offering is made (water or flower). In the first stage these concern the objects around the priest, then the priest himself. He places flowers and sprinkles water on all the objects, then recites mantras and performs *mudras* (specific gestures with specific meanings) that prepare the objects and himself for the worship of the goddess.

In the second stage the actions and recitations concern the ghat and the representations of the goddess: painting, *nabapatrika* (a bunch of nine plants placed under the paṭ), and a Dasabhuja image engraved on a small silver plate. These objects form a group in the center of the ritual action. Water and flowers are offered to them while the names appropriate to each are declaimed in a loud voice. The ghat and the bel tree are then "established" or consecrated (*ghatasthapan, billastapan*) by an incantation while the Brāhmaṇ holds his sacred thread to the images. Now all objects are ready to receive offerings on behalf of different deities. More offerings follow: water is poured on the nabapatrika, ghaṭ, and flowers, and a series of mantras are recited. These actions stand for services performed for the deities invoked. Not only Durgā but many other deities are worshiped in this way.

The next group of activities centers on food offerings; first of all, uncooked food is given to all the deities: rice, fruits, and sweets. The main item is rice, *atop cāl* (sun-dried rice), which is sacred (rice eaten every day is *siddha cāl,* or husk-boiled rice, which is less sacred because it is not the "original" rice).[4] Peeled bananas are placed atop the pile of rice (the rice is placed on plates made from the leaves of the *śāl* tree). Sliced and peeled cucumbers, sweets, molasses, the fruit of the bel tree, and other seasonal fruits make up the *noibedda* or *sital,* cold or uncooked fruit and food offerings. These are also the offerings of the daily worship, which is simple in every way.

The next group of offerings consists of cooked food, usually cooked rice. This time no cooked vegetables are given. The food is offered to the deities with gestures (mudras) and words (mantras). A series of pūjās follow, pūjās within the pūjā; as each deity is honored an offering is made. These deities are either represented in the painting or are associated with the objects and words of the pūjā.

The order of pūjās is as follows: after the preliminary purifications Gaṇeś is invoked; all pūjās begin with the worship of the elephant-headed god. Then Pancadebatā, the Five Gods, are invoked: Brahmā, Viṣṇu, Śiva, Durgā, and Surya (the sun). These are followed by a series of other deities (some the manifestations of the Five, others connected with the pūjā in other ways). With each small pūjā the flowers and leaves of sacred trees are placed on the ghat, in the water container, or under the bel (wood apple) and tulsi (basil) trees (both trees are favored by a number of deities). The most commonly offered flowers are *joba* (red in color), *kolke* (yellow) and *cāpā* (white). No pūjā can be performed without the leaves of the bel tree. These are usually offered in sets of three—three leaves on the same stem. When all deities have been served and fed with the cold food offerings, the sacrifice is performed. When the rājās became Vaiṣṇava, they abandoned blood sacrifice (*pasubali*) and changed to a sacrifice (*bali* or *balidān*) of plants, vegetables, and seeds. In the rājā's Durgāpūjā, bali is characteristically different from that in the other pūjās of the town. Here the priest sacrifices grains mixed with pulses. At the moment (*muhurta*) of the sacrifice the musicians begin to play: small drums and wooden wind instruments, the *sanai,* break the silence suddenly. The priest shakes a bell with his left hand and performs the bali, letting the seeds fall from his right hand down onto the stone platform in five or seven small piles. The small piles of sacrificial grain lie on a spot marked by the priest; this mark or diagram is a simple form of *yantra,* an instrument, a geometric design of great importance in pūjā. The diagram is drawn with a finger dipped in oil.

The goddess is approached only after these acts of worship: she is invoked in the tree, bathed, anointed, and dressed through symbolic acts and recitations, and fed with cooked food. The priest anoints the bel tree with vermilion, invokes the goddess into the tree with his sacred thread, and recites verses describing her appearance. At this time the companions of the goddess are also honored, not only Śiva but also his attendants, ghosts and demons, and even deities who stand in some relation to these demons: Rāma, the incarnation of Viṣṇu, and his opponent Rāvan, the demon king of Laṇka. The goddess is offered cooked food (*bhog*), then the sacrifice is performed again with a crescendo of percussions and flutes (this time for the goddess alone). The one rite that is different in this part of the worship is the *adhibas,* or ceremonial welcome: after the goddess is invoked the priest takes the items on the plate, the twenty-seven auspicious items, and one by one touches them to the ghat, naming each item in a mantra. The objects are precious metals, items of beautification, five kinds of grain, milk, honey, and objects with special significance such as conch shell and lamp. Then the mantra or verse of meditation (*dhyen mantra*) of the goddess is recited, the priest standing and offering a handful of flowers (*puspañjali*) to the Debī. Once again the instruments erupt into loud music as the priests take the images and offerings up to the temple in procession. The Durgā-paṭ is then set up in the temple and a final rite of farewell is performed—the evening *ārati,* a ceremonial adoration of the deity with lights and other objects. Then come silence and darkness till the pūjās of the morning.

The offerings are later distributed among the priests and musicians. During the pūjā there is no formality in behavior; the priests carry on a discussion of the proceedings throughout; they decide on the nearest substitute if an item is found missing, the bhattacharya often mispronounces the tantrik's incantations and asks for a repetition, the tantrik asks Bābu Sāhib to pick some more flowers, the latter complies, holding onto his *paitā* (sacred thread) so that the offering should not be polluted, the musicians wander off and miss playing at one of the sacrifices, the priests grumble—but the rhythm of the performance is not disturbed.

The Rituals of Welcome

In the morning the welcome of the goddess is performed at the water's edge (ghāt). This is the *nabapatrika snān* and *ghātpūjā* (the bathing of the goddess in the representation of the nine plants, and the worship at the landing ground of a river or lake). The ghāt plays an important role in everyday life: people wash and bathe there, boats may be tied up there. This rite used to be performed in the town's biggest lake, with a procession of pomp and circumstance through the town. Now the ghāt-pūjā is done in the temple tank not far from the Durgā temple. The Durgāpaṭ is brought down from the temple in a procession of priests, musicians, and children. The paṭ is set up and the nabapatrika is placed under it. On the nabapatrika stands the small silver paṭ of Durgā. These two are bathed with water from small vessels of different sizes, shapes, and materials. A new ghat is used for this ritual alone; it is discarded afterward. The big ghats are now in the temple. Grains of rice and the oil-drawn yantra are under the ghat. The pūjā is just like the one we described except in the rites specific to the day. The preliminaries are the same, and so are the series of pūjās leading up to the encounter with the goddess. This time, however, there is no bel tree, and the nabapatrika stands in the center of the pūjā. The *saṅkalpa* is recited, stating the intention to perform the worship of the nabapatrika. The previous night the saṅkalpa declared the intent to worship Baroṭhākurānī for sixteen days, the number of days to the end of the festival.

After the different deities' pūjās, the ritual bathing begins; first water is poured on the silver paṭ and the nabapatrika from a *dakkhinābarta śaṅkha* (a conch shell with mouth opening to the south). Normally the shell mouth curves in the opposite direction, and so the dakkhinābarta shell is rare, hence especially sacred. Then water is poured from the *aṣṭa kulsi,* eight small ghat-shaped earthenware vessels that are filled with water again and again and emptied over the nabapatrika while the priest recites mantras of offering to the different deities. Raw and cooked food is offered; the moment of the offering and the time of its consumption by the gods are marked by playing the bell. After bali the goddess goes in procession back to the temple. Three cannons at the rājā's house go off with a loud report, marking the arrival of Baroṭhākurānī in the town. The Durgāpaṭ is rested against the temple steps; here the goddess is again invoked in a new ghat, the ghat being discarded after the pūjā. There are further bathing and toilet rituals; this time the actual objects are also used, not just flowers and mantras. Red *āltā,* with which women paint their feet, is touched to the feet of the goddess, black *kājal* that decorates the eyes is applied to the eyes of the goddess, the branch of the *nīm* tree used for brushing teeth is also given to the Debī, and appropriate gestures with a piece of wood represent the cutting of the goddess's nails. All the items on the *maṅgal patra* (auspicious plate) are offered to the Debī. Then cooked food is offered, differing from the morning's bhogpūjā, given specifically to the goddess in her own temple. Blasts from the rājā's cannons mark the moment Debī accepts the bhog. Baroṭhākurānī is then set up in the temple and is worshiped daily till the end of the festival.

The same pūjā is offered every day: purification of priest and objects, celebration of the deities associated with the goddess, daily service symbolized by offerings of water and flowers. A special food offered during this time is *pāyas,* rice cooked with milk and sugar, fulfilling the requirement of *mistanna* (sweet rice) offerings throughout the festival. Every evening the *sandharati* is performed. First the lamp with five flames, then the flame of camphor, a red flower, a red cloth, and the sacred yak tail are waved in small circles around the goddess.

Several households and temples observe the pūjā of the goddess from the Nannadikalpa on. In these cases, however, the Debī is invoked in a ghat alone and then worshiped daily until the major pūjā itself. The series of rites described above can be observed only in the rājā's temple or those of the rājpurohit and rājguru. But where the pūjā is begun from this early date the mistanna offerings must be given every day. From this day onward many people visit the rājā and pay their respects. There are more and more visitors as the five major days of worship draw near. The king receives many people in the yard of what was previously a palace; surrounded by people who perform special duties and still come year after year, the king comes closest to what was a daily practice in days gone by.

Welcome of the Middle and the Youngest Ṭhākurānīs

The next major rite takes place eleven days later when the Mejoṭhākurānī arrives at the Durgā temple. This is the Śukla Pakkha Caturthī (the fourth of the bright phase, the fourth day of Mahālaya). This pūjā is very different from that of Baroṭhākurānī: Mejoṭhākurānī has no image, belbaraṇ, and no consequent ghātpūjā. She comes in the morning and is invoked in a ghat, but she departs in the evening, her ghat immersed at nightfall. But Mejoṭhākurānī does not depart for good; two days later she comes again, in a visible form, together with Choṭoṭhākurānī, amid great rejoicing and special rites. The belbaraṇ of the two sister goddesses takes place on the night of the sixth in the bright phase.

The Ṣaṣṭhīpūjā or Durgāṣaṣṭhīpūjā (the worship of the sixth) is the first major day of the festival. On the evening of the sixth, the paṭs of Mejo- and Choṭoṭhākurānī arrive together at the *belgāctalā* (at the foot of the bel tree). The ritual is much the same as on the night of the Eldest Sister's welcome. The two painted images are accompanied by two small ghats (for the night's invocation alone) and two large ghats (for the pūjā of the seventh lunar day). Each has a nabapatrika placed under it. The Choṭoṭhākurānī is, in addition, represented by a ten-armed engraving on a gold plate; this golden paṭ is placed on the nabapatrika leaning against the larger painting. The two paintings of the goddess are placed one over the other, the ancient swords supporting them. All three paintings (Baṛo, Choṭo, and Mejo) are identical. They are kept in the rājā's house and the phoujdar is called to repaint and repair them every year. Yantras (triangles forming a star) are drawn under the two ghats, and two shells are placed at the side. Every other item needed for the pūjā comes in twos. The number of ritualists is the same as before, yet the pūjā is somewhat different. The saṅkalpa refers to the particular day, the two goddesses, and the number of days during which pūjā will be done (five in this case). The series of preliminary rites (purifications of the object and of the body and soul of the ritualist) are also more elaborate. Correspondingly more flowers and more food items are offered. There is a greater concern among the priests and musicians, since the whole pūjā revolves around Choṭoṭhākurānī from now on. Several members of the rājā's family attend the ritual this night.

The Exegesis of Pūjā: Concepts, Actions, and Objects

The most common account of pūjā given by the people is based on an analogy between the service of a deity and the treatment of a guest. The guest is to be honored above everyone else. The host invites his guest, goes part of the way to meet him, and welcomes him. In the house the guest is received with joy and respect, given refreshments, bathed to be clean from the dust of the road, rubbed with scented oils and perfumes, given new cloth to relax in, fed and entertained, and finally bade goodnight and allowed to rest. When the time comes for him to leave the host bids him farewell and reminds him to come again. The ideal way to treat a guest is the way to treat the gods: guests are like deities, and gods are guests among men.

Deities are part of the world as men know it, but when the special festival of a deity is celebrated the god is regarded as a traveler from a distant land visiting his followers, devotees, and subjects. The gods live in the Himalayas and travel across the land through the sacred rivers.

◀ Picture 1

▼ Picture 2

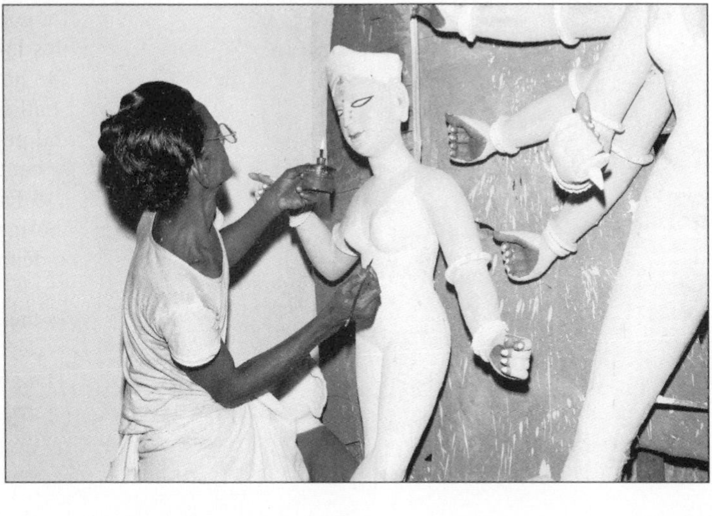

Picture 3

Picture 4

Picture 5

Picture 6

Picture 7

Picture 8

Any geographical landmark may be the abode of a god, just as any lake or river may be a vehicle for deity. Land and water are linked closely to the idea of divinity. Any hill is related to the Himalayas in some way, and the water of *pukur*s (water tanks) and streams is related to the sacred Ganges. A deity can be in two places at the same time. Like men, the gods are tied to localities, but unlike men they have different manifestations in different places and situations. The deities who come and go at the seasonal festivals are the same as the ones whose pūjās go on for the twelve months of the year in permanent temples. The seasonal pūjās are more intense, however, concentrating on particular aspects of the deity in question.

In the devotional and line cults the aspects of a certain deity are deliberately separated and celebrated apart from the general meaning of the same deity. The deity who comes to his devotees in the seasonal worship has just as specific a meaning in the particular festival as do the purely regional, local deities. Men choose these aspects themselves, or the deity forces people to note his presence in a particular locality. The intensity of worship itself separates the manifestations of the same deity; the god that dwells in the Himalayas is also the god of the local temple, the object of seasonal worship, and the inhabitant of the local jungle or hill.

When a deity is invited for a celebration out of time and out of place, one of his many functions and meanings is selected for special contemplation.[5] Then the house of the worshiper becomes the dwelling of the god, the Himalaya itself. The house or the temple is transformed into a festive place where a distinguished guest is honored and entertained. The gates are decorated with mango leaves, a sign of auspiciousness (*maṅgal*) and joy. The gateposts have *maṅgalghat*s leaning against them, with banana leaves stuck inside. These are different from the invocation vessels, being ordinary pots, signs of welcome and happiness, marking the passage of a deity and bringing welfare to the inhabitants. They also mark the place of the worship, the approach to the locality of the pūjā. The banana tree itself is sacred, being one of the Nine Durgās (nabapatrika).

The pūjā itself consists of many parts, each of which is a step in the service of the deity as a guest. Usually this service is performed through the offering of sixteen items, *saladān*. The god is welcomed in the place of the pūjā, invoked into the ghat, offered a seat, water to wash his feet, a towel to dry him, and oil and turmeric to rub on his body. A goddess is offered red lacquer to paint her feet, collyrium to paint her eyes, a mirror and sacred thread to prepare herself for the public. Then the deity is honored with beautiful and precious things, all representative of certain attitudes and thoughts found in the human world: light, incense, camphor, flowers, sandalwood, silk garments (unstiched, complete, and uncut), and food, raw and cooked. These are all honorific items, varying in amount and preparation according to the occasion. These steps are to be found in any pūjā, big or small. The items are offered in deed and in imagination, through mantras and oblations of water.

Just as the deity is prepared for the homage of his subjects, so the worshipers must ready themselves for the encounter with the deities. They bathe and fast, so that both the inner and the outer person may be purified. They wear pure cloth and tie it in the fashion peculiar to rituals. But only a priest can perform the full service of the deity; he is pure by the definition of his office, and the worshiper must use him as an intermediary. But even the priest must go through a series of elaborate purifications in order to perform the pūjā. In these purifications all the constituent elements of life are treated separately, and so we can find in the pūjā the indigenous ideas of creation and the functioning of living things symbolized in clear, explicit ways. The priest knows the rules of the worship, the actions, the incantations, and the proper pronunciation. There must be a specialist, since the rules are complicated and only a Brāhmaṇ can follow them correctly. There is an element of magic (*kriyā*) in the doings of the priest, especially in the way the image of a deity is invested with life.[6] The priest is not necessary for all acts of worship. Non-Brāhmaṇs can perform the pūjās of their *kula* (line) deities and of their personally chosen gods. But images that have been invested with life, the powerful images of major temples, must be worshiped by Brāhmaṇ priests. The annual festivals of all gods, regardless of their investiture with life or their appearance as direct manifestations of a deity, also must be worshiped either by Brāhmaṇs or by particular non-Brāhmaṇ ritual specialists. Only the Brāhmaṇ can offer cooked rice to the gods, and only the specialist can offer cooked food to the deities in the non-Brāhmaṇic rites.

The idea of pūjā is built around service, respect, and honor. People refer to pūjā as *ṭhākur sebā*, the service of the lords, or *sammān deoyā*, the expression of honor. Sebā is an attitude of devotion and, together with sammān, constitutes subservience. Sebā is also the offering of food, an act that symbolizes honor and respect. Sebā in other contexts symbolizes the same range of attitudes: a service given to husband by wife, children to parents, *sissa* to *guru* (disciple to preceptor). But only the offices of priest and king are institutionalized objects of sebā on behalf of society.

The Goddess and the Three Qualities

According to the Caṇḍī legend, there are three forms of the goddess, corresponding to the three guṇas: Mahā Kālī, or *tama guṇ,* Mahā Lakṣmī, or *raja guṇ,* and Mahā Sarasvatī, or *sattva guṇ.*[7] These three forms issued from the goddess as her first creation; they also form the basis of the social order and of the people's participation in the pūjās. This classification differs from *jāti-bicār* (caste divisions) in that it refers to types and ways of worship (mat). There are different approaches to the gods, varying from one guṇ to another. The *sattvik mat* is the way of Vaiṣṇavas; most commonly this means worship without animal sacrifice, a purely devotional attitude in which the worshiper does not demand anything for himself. The *rajasik mat* is worship with pomp and great insistence on power, the ego (*ahaṃkār*), stressing the self, aiming to derive many benefits from the pūjā. *Tamasik mat* is the pūjā of the householder who wants all kinds of things from the deities in carrying out his everyday duties: help to continue some kind of existence in the bondage of *sangsār,* the world of daily living that according to the sattvik mat is but a world of illusion. Though the three goddesses correspond to the three ways of worship, each one of them can be worshiped according to the other ways as well. Thus sattvik Kālīpūjā is the worship of the goddess without animal sacrifice, liquor, or Tantrik symbolism, a way that concentrates on the benign aspects of this terrible goddess, who is represented without the garland of skulls and the blood that is associated with tamasik worship.

Mat refers to the Purāṇa or the Upapurāṇa followed in the ritual sequences: the different sacred books about the worship of deities prescribing different objects, mantras, and offerings as well as different rules of action.

Sattva, raja, and *tama* are qualities (*guṇa*s), types, and styles of life. They correspond to the three major deities Brahmā, Viṣṇu, and Maheśvār. The first is truth, the way of the renouncer; the second is power, the way of the ruler; the third is the way of everyday life, the householder pressed by social burden. *Dharma, artha, kām, mokṣa* are categories of experience, in terms of which one ought to lead one's life. *Dharma* designates duties, *artha* the means of living, *mokṣa* the liberation from contingencies of living, and *kām* the desires of worldly life. Sattva is the way to mokṣa; dharma is primarily rajasik, the responsibility of rule; kām and artha are the units of everyday life—*tama.* These categories are linked together in a hierarchy—there is dharma for the householder: the dharma proper to tama, just as the dharma proper to the action of the king is the rajasik way of life. The links are progressive; there is no mokṣa in the tamasik way of life. Renunciation, or sattva, is the way to liberation. Hence these categories do not define discrete areas of experience: to any action there are several dimensions: rajasik and tamasik, and dharma, kāma, or artha all together or in varying combinations. The complex process is determined by the laws of *karma* (action in terms of these categories) resulting in the ever-recurring cycle of rebirth (*janmantar*) that is ended only by mokṣa.

Dharma, artha, kām and mokṣa mean something and do something. They tell people how to act in a given context with a certain aim in mind. They limit the possibilities within a set, and they provide the ways of exploring these limitations. A significant feature is the shared or overlapping characteristics of categories. Kṛṣṇa, a sattvik debatā, and Kālī, a tamasik debatā, may have rajasik festivals.

The goddess expresses the created world, and the three qualities define the whole of creation. The goddess herself is māyā, or illusion, which again characterizes the created world. She engages in līlā (cosmic play) giving rise to birth and death, the process of creation (*sristhi*). These terms define the nature and origin of life. Dharma, artha, kām and mokṣa, the four principles of experience, the rules proper to living things, include both models for and models of living. *Bhakti* (devotion), *mānsik,* and *brata* (vows and wishes), *sādhana, āradhanā, yogā,* and *kriyā* are aspects of action governed by these principles. These actions are also attitudes proper to the three qualities and their corresponding categories in society. The goddess, the qualities, and the created world (*prakriti*) are different ways of defining the same totality. The goddess is defined in relation to the *puruṣa* (male) principle, expressed through various divinities in different ideologies. The supreme deity Bhagavan is the hierarchically highest expression of this principle.

The ways of knowing this system and the processes within it are also given to us by indigenous accounts. Ultimately everything (goddess, Bhagavan, qualities) issues from brahman, the Immense One, the One without Gender, Quality, or Characteristic. Everything is one in brahman. The many necessarily participate in the one. This knowledge is *brahmajñān*. It tells of unity and diversity, of elements and units in an abstract scheme that ultimately yield the totality, brahman, the truth (*tattva*). The elements constituting the expressions of brahman, in terms of brahman's līlā with the goddess, creation itself and all the things in the world animate or inanimate are defined in a hierarchical, segmentary way. Tattva is fundamental unity, its elements being water, fire, earth, sky, and ether. These are divided into twenty-five tattvas (ether, for example is divisible into the five winds). These elements constitute and work the human body. Brahman is also the *parmātmā*, the universal soul, a unity in which participate a multiplicity of parts (*ātmā*). Ātmā, as a part of brahman, informs everything else in body, mind, and the constitution of the person. Further subdivisions are consciousness (*caitanya*), mind (*mon*), intellect (*buddhī*), ego (*ahaṃkār*). Some ideologies arrange the relations among these terms (and the direction of the processes in which they partake) differently than others do. I am not concerned here with the parallel between these systems and the major schools of Indian philosophy. Rather, I want to draw attention to these relationships and the processes they designate in action.

The work of element, soul, and consciousness is determined by the law of karma. The different series (tattva, consciousness, or other subdivision of ātmā) partake of a process that eventually merges all diversity back into brahman. Hence a most pervasive feature of the ideological field is a belief in the oneness of the world. Time and time again townsmen wind up their discussions of the work of the gods with the observation that All is One. Whatever god or goddess may be at work, they are all parts (*aṅga*), manifestations, or incarnations of a basic unity. These series (spirit, awareness, object, element), the terms of their relationships, and the laws according to which they act are expressed in the symbolism of pūjā.

Pūjās themselves are part of the processes they symbolize. If there are sattvik, rajasik, and tamasik ways of doing pūjā, the act of performance accomplishes and brings about the state to which the category refers. Pūjās for mokṣa bring liberation, pūjās for kāma result in the favorable intercession of a deity. Rajasik pūjās bring power, tamasik pūjās help with the problems of everyday life. The same pūjā of the same deity can be performed with different combinations of these categories. Debī is pursued by people for profit or desire, liberation or devotion, or just for the sake of the act itself, leaving all work in the hands of the goddess. Any cycle, any arrangement of the categories subject to the law of karma can be brought to fruition by pūjā. Each time a deity is changed, or the direction of the act is changed (from kām to mokṣa for example), the other units rearrange themselves accordingly. Viṣṇu, though the god of mokṣa, may be worshiped for profit; the goddess Kālī, though a tamasik deity, may grant liberation. *Śakti* pūjās of desire, power, and pride may be performed in the way of love and pure devotion (bhakti). The referents of symbols overlap, and categories are not mutually exclusive—they define ideal types of action and can be rearranged within the total system.

Sattva, raja, and tama also define sections of society and ways of living. Kings, though rajasik, may lead a sattvik life, non-Brāhmaṇ castes, though tamasik, may perform rajasik pūjās. The significance of these terms is not in the concrete groups they define but in the principles they refer to, which can be applied to the interpretation of concrete reality.

Categories such as consciousness (reality and ātmā) provide not only a system of meanings but also a way of knowing. Concepts such as buddhī, mon, ahaṃkār give the processes of cognition, the separation of the true (tattva) from the illusionary (māyā). Knowing these terms is brahmajñān. This designates the total indigenous schema of concepts, categories, and meanings. According to local ideologies, no man can sustain this knowledge and awareness unless he is outside the social universe: a renouncer, guru, or saint. Men can achieve glimpses of this truth, only to withdraw behind the veil of illusion and grope toward the truth by means of symbols and metaphors. Men in the world are incapable of the consistency required by brahmajñān. They are aware of the concept, but they realize that their actions are often inconsistent with it. The *tamasik* principle of everyday life is more immediate, giving special concession to those deceived by māyā. Men in particular contexts are bound by lesser principles.

Elements of Ritual

Sacrifice. A sacrifice can be animal or vegetable. In the sattvik way of worship no blood sacrifices may be offered. But in Vishnupur both kinds of sacrifice are common. Durgāpūjā used to have human sacrifice, but since the kings were converted to the devotional Vaiṣṇava movement in the sixteenth century, there has been no animal sacrifice. The Mrinmoyī Debī of the town is the rājā's goddess; when the kings stopped the human and animal sacrifices, the whole town followed their custom. According to old people, the custom of animal sacrifices was not easily abandoned; people used to offer blood to the goddess secretly, against the express orders of the king. Later the blood sacrifice came back in a major way in the observance of Kālīpūjās. But even today there is no animal sacrifice to the Goddess Durgā anywhere in Vishnupur. Nor are nonvegetarian and "hot" foods—meat, fish, eggs, onions, garlic, and certain kinds of pulses—offered to the goddess (except for one temple, a sister temple of the goddess in a nearby village, where the distinctive feature of the pūjā is the offering of cooked fish).

Vegetables are a common replacement of the banned animal sacrifice. *Kumra bali,* the sacrifice of pumpkin, is the most common substitute. Here the pumpkin is treated as a sacrificial animal: anointed with vermilion, it is dedicated to the goddess. In the king's pūjā rice and pulses mixed together constitute the sacrificial animal; the seven small piles of grain made by the priest constitute the sacrifice and stand for the seven śaktis of the Goddess. The meaning of sacrifice is the casting away of one's sins and faults. By sacrificing their sins, making them into demonic beings through mantras, men not only please the gods but recognize what is divine in themselves.

Incantations and Gestures. Mantra is śakti; words have power to accomplish what they say in the context of the pūjā. The word, mantra, is itself sacred, but in the pūjā it is also efficacious. The power of mantra is associated with pūjā and kriyā, otherwise words cannot accomplish what they say: word and action together produce an effect in pūjā. Power comes from "vibration"; word is sound, *sabda,* that produces vibration, energy. This energy has results when allowed to unfold in the ritual context. A mantra is efficacious even when the object to which it is directed is unaware of it; mantra has the quality of a spell. Because of its independent energy, it can act independently. There is widespread belief in Vishnupur in the power of certain religious ascetics who can direct a mantra at a man for good or evil. People accept the action of the mantra when uttered by such an ascetic, even when the man at whom the mantra is directed is unaware of it. Hence mantras have to be pronounced correctly, because they have independent power (power inheres within the proper sound). We noted above that the Universal Being, brahman, is itself associated with sound. In pūjās a mantra can replace all objects and offerings. Mantra is also the aim with which men offer gifts to the deities, the aim being stated and brought about by the recitation. The recitation of mantras has to be done *jatāśakti,* "with all the power possible." Mantras often name a deity in the particular object in which it is invoked: The Goddess Who Dwells in the Bel Tree, the Goddesses in the Nabapatrika. In the mantras of the snān the different waters and objects through which the bathing of the Debī is performed are named, together with appellations of the goddess as the Beloved of Śankar (Śiva), the Lover of Śiva: "Let the Lover of Śankar be anointed. . . ." Mantras always name a wider series of objects in which the goddess is manifest than is explicit in the ritual itself. There is a vocative element in mantra: "Let the seven waters of the seven rivers be contained in this vessel. . . ."

Mudras are gestures similar in efficacy and nature to mantras. Mudra is a sacred figure shown by the hands of the priest. A thing shown is a thing achieved: gesture is both meaning, event, and result. Several mudras are particular to Durgāpūjā, but a particular set is basic to all pūjās. The mudra shows something for a deity and represents something on the worshiper's behalf.[8]

Mudras act in conjunction with mantras: action and idea, mudra adding to the meaning of mantra. In itself the mudra also brings about what it represents. First in the sequence is the *abahan* (invocation) mudra, appropriately formed by two hands cupped together palms upward. The *sathapan* (installation) mudra is the reverse of the above, expressing the entry of a deity, the establishment of the ghat. The *Saṅgbodhani* mudra (joining and union) is made by the two fists placed side by side, the fingers curled under the thumbs. The *sammukhi* mudra is formed by the two fists with the thumbs held up. These mudras occur in the initial stages of pūjā, when a deity is invited with gestures and words, placed on a seat, and asked to stay and to grant safety for the devotees. The same mudras recur throughout the pūjā in the context of offerings for the supporting deities. No matter how often a mudra recurs, regardless of the context, it means the same thing. Initially mudras relate to the main deity of the pūjā, but as pūjās within the pūjā are performed, the same mudra is offered to different deities.

Beyond invocations there are sets of more complex mudras. Such are mudras of union and merging, expressing the relation between a male and a female deity. These mudras are linked to the concept of śakti, just as mantras are, expressing the power and energy that issues from the union of the god and the goddess. The mudra shown at the time of the encounter between Durgā and the male element expresses a union that effects all action, including the actions of the pūjā. The *yoni* mudra symbolizes the possibility and power of action.

Some mudras parallel the categories of pūjā: āradhanā is both an attitude and a gesture (palms together). Others are equivalent to the object of offering, as in the shell mudra, and water mudra. Further, there are mudras invoking sacred images: the tortoise mudra, the sacred mother cow mudra.

There are other actions, designated by the term *nyas*. These are not merely yogic exercises of breathing. Nyas may be any manner of enumeration, dissection, quantification, and qualification. In performing these actions the ritualist is directed to meditate on the Goddess Sarasvatī, and the elements of the world are to appear as parts of a system of knowledge, a unity. *Bhutsuddhi,* the purification of the elements, is also a certain kind of nyas; the ritualist is directed to meditate on the parts of a unity. He is told that in imagination the world is dissolved through fire and gives place to its constituent elements. Enumerating these and joining them with the units of energy and life in the Tantrik scheme (different coils, *kul-kundalini,* in the body), the *ātmā* (soul or self) is made to rise to *parmātmā,* the universal soul. The process is to be achieved through concentration and the utterance of sacred syllables that are efficacious in themselves.

Welcome. *Bodhan* and *amantran* are the initial welcoming rituals in

Durgāpūjā. Connected with the primary invocations, welcome, and respectful reception of the goddess are the rites of *belbaraṇ, kalparambha,* and *saṅkalpa.* They share certain general features, and all welcoming rites include a saṅkalpa, the central act of the rite. Bodhan is the awakening of the goddess, an invitation to the annual festivities.

Amantran, an act of greeting performed for deities alone, is related linguistically to the ordinary word for invitation, *nimantran.* These rites together designate *kalparambha,* the beginning of the period of worship (*kalpa,* age, time, sequence; *arambha,* beginning). Belbaraṇ is also an early act of the Durgāpūjā, the welcome under the bel tree (*baraṇ,* welcome). Baraṇ always refers to ceremonial occasions, whether these are directed at divinities or men. This rite is performed only at the time of Durgāpūjā; no other deity has a welcome under the bel tree. Most generally baraṇ is performed on the evening of the sixth day in the bright phase of Āśvin, Ṣaṣṭhīpūjā (pūjā of the sixth). This pūjā is not yet that of the goddess; it approaches the Debī as manifest in the *belgāc,* Śiva's favorite tree.

Bodhan is not only the initial rite of Durgāpūjā, but also the opening act of the pūjās of the seventh, eighth, and ninth lunar days. The tenth day holds the immersion rite; there is no welcome on the last day. In the welcoming rites the goddess is invoked in a series of items: bel tree, ghat, and nabapatrika. But this is not śakti pūjā—up to the seventh day the goddess is worshiped merely through her creation.

The representations of the goddess are regarded as spectators who do not actively participate in the preliminary rites. Offerings are made to bel tree and ghat, both of which symbolize the goddess. The many companions and attendants of the goddess and other major deities are also invoked. Once the ghat is "established," the gods can be invoked in it. Offerings may be placed on the ghat (flowers and water libations) or touched to the ghat or spread around the ghat (raw and cooked food), but in each case they reach the gods through the vessel.

Time. The kalpa, saṅkalpa is a declaration of intent on the part of the worshiper. The goddess is told who will offer pūjā to her and for how many days. Doing kalpa on the Kṛṣṇa Nabamī means doing pūjās for the next sixteen days till the end of the festival. The rājā's pūjā has separate kalpa for each of the three Durgās. A kalpa on any of these prescribed days carries with it the obligation to do pūjā from then on till the day of immersion. Kalpa for the major days of the pūjā is done on the evening of the sixth, but it can be done on the seventh, eighth, or ninth, but not on the tenth day. So the Durgāpūjā may extend from two to sixteen days, not more, not less. For one pūjā one kalpa is enough, but people may offer kalpa (and pūjā) on any of the prescribed days within the same sequence; in a line pūjā the members of different lines may do kalpa on different days, in honor of the same deity. The most popular pūjā sequence, from the seventh day to the tenth, is the period of Rāma's offerings to the goddess for the boon of killing Rāvan.

The longest period of worship, from the dark ninth of Bhādra to the bright tenth of Āśvin, was offered by the first human worshiper of the goddess—a king, appropriately enough, Surat Rājā. His story is told in the Caṇḍīpāṭ itself, the origin myth of the goddess. With the kalpa go the prescribed pūjās, bodhans, and belbaraṇs. In the kalpa the priest recites some slakas and mantras mentioning the name and the *gotra* of the worshiper, the jajmān on whose behalf the priest offers the pūjā. Name and gotra identify the worshiper, his immediate family, and the agnatic line of a much wider group. Gotra refers to descent from a *ṛsi,* any one of the great saints and seers of ancient India; it does not designate a corporate or even a social group. Gotra is an ideal category whose members never get together and do not know each other. It is a way of creating divisions within a particular caste for the purpose of marriage; one has to marry outside the gotra, the wider agnatic label. (For the multivocality of gotra, see Fruzzetti and Östör 1976*b*.) People of different jāti may have the same gotra, but this does not interfere with marriage rules, since marriage across caste boundaries is proscribed. The effect of gotra in the saṅkalpa is to identify the recipients of the goddess's blessings and grace. The pūjā has beneficial effects on men and their affairs; hence the worshiper tells the goddess just who is addressing her. Through the gotra an actual line is associated with the pūjā, a line of which the members themselves keep count. That this is an important consideration is shown by the manner in which lines split and set up pūjās for the smaller, newly created segments. Alternatively, where a large, often segmented line offers pūjā to the goddess in a temple and the goddess is a famous one, the segments will share in the worship, splitting the costs as well as the benefits. In the case of ṣolaānā pūjās, the saṅkalpa is done either in the name of the king (this is invariably the case for the major, public, multicaste Durgāpūjās) or in the name of a respected figure (for jāti pūjās the rite is done in the name of an elder or a headman so that the whole caste may be represented in the pūjā) or in the name of a Brāhmaṇ. In keeping with the principle of hierarchy, the model in each case is derived from the encompassing relation between king and goddess, since other kinglike figures encompass other worshipers in the more restrictive categories of jajmān.

Celebration of the Ghāt. The morning after belbaraṇ, the bathing of the nabapatrika is performed at the ghāt. The pūjā order follows that of the previous night; only after the ghatasthapan and the initial pūjās is the ceremonial bathing of the nabapatrika performed. The eight small jars used in the rite, together with a single larger one with a hole in its bottom, called the "thousand streams," are the nine necessary items. The eight jars stand for the eight holy waters and rivers, the ninth representing the waters of the holy land, Bharat, India. Each aspect of the goddess is honored in these ceremonial oblations: water, the most sacred liquid, encompasses land and earth, all of creation.

In the *Mahāsnān,* the goddess is bathed with Ganges water and the earth of seven localities. The goddess is symbolized in different ways in these rites; the manifestations in the Caṇḍī legend (the nine Durgās of the Debī Māhātmā) are honored in the bath, the seven śaktis in the bali (the seven "powers"), and the *asthanahika* (the Eight Mistresses, the eight subsidiary forms of the goddess) in the sandhipūjā (see pp. 79 ff.) The forms of the goddess are accounted for in their almost infinite variation. In doing these acts the priest must wear a ring made of the sacred *kusa* grass, a sign of Debīpūjā, and a protection from the dangers of śakti, which will be present when the goddess is invoked. The final object to be mentioned in the ghātpūjā is the dakkhinābarta shell. It is used as a vessel, and its rareness is a sign of sacredness. It belongs to that class of things in nature which, like the *sālāgrām* stone, are living deities, "incarnations" of divinity. Both these things had, at one time, living beings in them; according to the indigenous ideology, the cavity in both once housed small organisms. These objects are "living" in the sense that no ritual is needed to invoke a deity in them; divinity is incarnate in them as they are found in riverbeds and the sea. The motion of water contributes to their sacredness and life.

Elements of Ritual

Objects. In these pūjās the goddess may be represented anthropomorphically, but the images are not as yet invested with life; they are just representatives. In the belbaraṇ, the tulsī tree (sacred to Viṣṇu) is worshiped; it is also an image of the goddess, the consort of Viṣṇu. Its leaves are offered in all pūjās (except that of Lakṣmī, who is her rival). Viṣṇu himself is present through the sacred sālāgrām stone. Śiva is there through the trident or the liṅga. Viṣṇu and Śiva stand for the puruṣa principle here.

Tree symbols are dual; the tulsī plant is a symbol of both Viṣṇu and the goddess, the bel tree is a symbol of Śiva and the goddess. In the rite, divinity is invoked in the trees, and the trees are then worshiped with the various objects, the maṅgal patra, vermilion, oblations, and flowers. The deities most important in the annual ritual cycle are then invoked in the ghat. The ghatasthapan serves to bring the deities to the locality of the ritual. The unseen divinities are thus comprehended through their manifestation in the ghat; the ritual and the symbols allow men to concentrate in a direct way on the otherwise abstract idea of divinity. The invocation takes place at night; no one should disturb the arriving deities. Without quiet, the ritual may not work. The goddess is "called" at night, and in the morning she is received at the ghāt. She is thought to arrive in a boat, and then the nabapatrika becomes the center of the ritual. Later the same morning the image of the goddess itself is invested with life, and from then on the goddess in her own form is the center of attention.

In the belbaraṇ pūjā the tree is treated as a goddess. The first action is the recitation of the saṅkalpa, following the general purification of the whole environment by the name of Viṣṇu and the water of the Ganges. More purifications follow later, but after the declaration of intent to perform pūjā the ghat has to be "established" so that it becomes fit to receive the gods. First to be received by the ghāt is the Goddess Caṇḍī; actions and objects accomplishing this involve the items described above. The recitations of mantras ask the spirits of these items and the gods associated with them to receive the offerings and to come down among men. The sacred thread purifies the items destined for the deities. It is touched to different items: ghat, earth, rice, water, branch of mango leaves, fruits, flowers, vermilion, and *svastik* (a sign meaning peace). Everything must be purified: the seat on which the priest sits, the offerings, and the worshipers. Water is sprinkled around, and flowers are offered to accomplish the aim of the recited words.

There are corresponding changes in the state of the priest. The ritualist must perform *aṅganyas* (counting and touching the parts of the body, purifying them), *niyantran* (a breathing exercise that purifies the five "winds," which constitute life and are symbolic of divinity in men—elements shared by all created things, men and gods), *ekagrota* (concentration on the gods that symbolize these elements so that service may be done and the gods appear at the pūjā to the welfare and benefit of everyone). The priest must recite the *gāyatrī* (the divine mantra that confers twice-born status on the Brāhmaṇ and allows him to approach the gods). *Pranayan* is "deep" meditation that unifies, in an ideal whole, the diverse elements thus purified, allowing the priest to invoke and bring down all the deities to be worshiped.

The pūjās (offerings of flower and water with the appropriate mantras) of Pancadebatā are next. Gaṇeś, Śiva Durgā, Viṣṇu, and the sun are worshiped one by one. All other deities and spirits (*bhuta*s) are worshiped then, with short mantras and a few drops of water on a flower. This part of the pūjā is concluded with sacrifice, uncooked rice, and fruit offerings. The bali consists of making seven small piles of rice and mustard seeds and reciting the mantra that dedicates the offering to the gods. Mustard-seed oil and rice are the two essential requirements of daily life. This sacrifice represents blood sacrifice without bloodshed. The form, *rūp,* of the goddess is given in her *dhyen* (a mantra of meditation describing the appearance of the goddess and aiding human imagination). The mark on the bel tree is a sign of the goddess; Caṇḍī is asked to manifest herself in the tree. The *adhibas,* or welcome of the goddess, is addressed to the divinity in the bel tree. The plate of welcome is offered to the tree as if it were the goddess. After this, all the deities represented in the painting—the goddess, her family, and all gods and demons associated with the origin and subsequent history of the goddess—are honored and served. *Bhog,* cooked rice offering, represents the high point of the ritual. Bhog also means "enjoyment" and "acceptance." It is the most sacred offering men can give the goddess, and only a Brāhman can ask her to accept it.

The Nine Sacred Plants. The nabapatrika consists of nine plants or their leaves, also known as the Nine Durgās. The nine plants are tied together with the vines of the *aparajita* flower, a flower associated with Durgā. The goddess herself is aparajita, undefeated. This collection of plants appears only in the Durgāpūjā, entering the festival the evening of Ṣaṣṭhīkalparambha. But in the rājā's pūjā, where the *kalpas* (aims) of the three Ṭhākurānīs are celebrated on a more elaborate scale, the nabapatrika is worshiped on each of the belbaran nights. Each Ṭhākurānī has a separate nabapatrika, and all three are immersed together on the tenth day. The plants are sacred in the totality of the nabapatrika. Even separately they have great significance in ritual and in everyday life. All nine are valued by men and form basic ingredients of Bengali cooking. Rice is essential for human life, and the others are only slightly less important. These plants are fit representations of the goddess; divinity is comprehended through creation.

Men need images, for they cannot fathom the formless Universal Spirit (brahman). If one has the proper bhakti attitude, one can recognize the different aspects of divinity in the variety of creation. In a way the nabapatrika also symbolizes human life. It represents all that is necessary for maintenance, well-being, and happiness. The nine plants stand for nine aspects of the goddess, nine kinds of *śakti* (power). Each plant is associated with one of the goddess's śaktis, and the goddess encompasses these aspects of her creative energy. Each one of them is a separate manifestation of Siva. The Nine Durgās are the nine goddesses in the Caṇḍīpāṭ (the Debi Māhātmā). Durgā is called Caṇḍī in the sacred texts; Caṇḍī is the name of the most powerful, dangerous, and potent aspect of the goddess, the form in which she defeated her enemies, the āsuras. Caṇḍī is depicted as a fierce goddess in the full flush of victory, shouting her joy so loudly that even distant mountains tremble. The nine plants and Nine Durgās are discussed below.

Rambha is banana or kola (the ordinary word is not used in rituals; the Sanskritic name designates the function of this fruit in the ritual). The goddess Brahmānī (Brahmā's śakti) is associated with it. Banana is an important item of all rituals; not only is it a favorite raw fruit, it is also cooked when unripe, and the flowers are used in curries. It is regarded as a necessary item of ordinary diet. Its leaves are used as plates for eating because they are pure and sacred. The plant itself is auspicious, being used for the maṅgalghat in pūjās and life-cycle rituals.

Kacu is the Goddess Kālikā. This is an edible root; when cooked it resembles and tastes like meat. Many use it to supplement the rice diet. It is an important staple but can be eaten only in a cooked form. Kālikā is the consort of Śiva, the Goddess Kālī.

Haridra or *halud* is the ordinary name for turmeric, an edible root, one of the most important spices. Not only does it appear in all rituals, including life-cycle celebrations (especially weddings), but it is the basic seasoning of any cooked food prepared from vegetables and meat. Mixed with other spices, it is *tarkari,* the "curry" of Bengal. It is pure and good for the body; people use it in treating all kinds of stomach upsets. It purifies the body inside and out and is used in the daily bath along with mustard oil—good for the skin, good for health. It is the plant of the Goddess Durgā herself.

Jayantī is the plant of the Goddess Karttiki, the śakti of Kārtik, Durgā's son, the leader of the heavenly armies. It is a tree, but also a name of the Goddess Durgā. Some images in some temples of Bengal are known as Jayanti Debī. It means rejuvenation, celebration, a jubilee. The leaves of the tree are used to prevent and cure fevers.

Bel is one of the most sacred trees in Bengal. It is indispensable for any pūjā. The leaves are usually offered to all deities, especially Śiva and his consorts. They are offered as picked, in clusters of three, symbolizing the *trisur* (trident), Śiva's weapon. The goddess is invoked in this tree, the *sebā* (service) of the pūjā, the many offerings that are not actually on the scene may be symbolized by the bel leaf. The longest series of offerings in the pūjā are done with water and bel leaves, a symbolic service in which the bel expresses the same attitudes of worship as the whole pūjā sequence. The mantra with these offerings states that the jajmān offers the deities scented flowers for their pleasure. The fruit of the bel tree is highly regarded as cooling in the summer, beneficial to health. It is a valuable medicine, used to treat digestive troubles. In a society where dysentery is the most common health problem, bel and halud are predictably valued. The goddess of this tree is Sivā, the consort of Siva.

Darim, the pomegranate fruit, is also a regular item of offering in most pūjās, especially Debīpūjās. It is opened and spread out on a plate, the small red clusters constituting the offering. It is also a summer fruit, cooling and delicious. The tree is worshiped only in the Durgāpūjā; the goddess associated with it is Raktadantika.

The *asoka* is another of the most sacred trees. Together with the bel tree, the asoka is the most often "established" tree in Bengal. Certain trees (of these species) are selected as objects of worship for a variety of reasons. In a ritual that is similar to the invocation of life in an image of a deity, a god is asked to take up residence in the tree, and from then on the tree is treated as a representation of divinity. Pūjās must be offered regularly after that, especially in the month of Boiśakh (April-May), the month devoted to the pūjās of divinities as they are manifest in trees. Asoka is Viṣṇu's tree; it is also medicinal. Barren women may eat the leaves of this tree, in the course of a ritual, in the hope of becoming fertile. The goddess of the asoka is Sokarohita.

Mankacu is the arum plant, a cluster of flowers enclosed by fleshy leaves. The goddess is Cāmuṇḍā, the fearful aspect of the goddess that killed the demons Caṇḍa and Muṇḍa. According to the myth in the Caṇḍipāṭ, the goddess became increasingly wrathful at the intransigence and impertinence of the demons; her anger left her and stalked the battlefield as the fearful goddess, killing the two great āsuras amid terrible cries of joy.

Dhān is paddy; the unhusked, harvested rice is the most sacred member of the plant world. It is the basis of life, the central part of any meal. Rice is eaten in many forms, and it is sacred, especially when cooked. Men bathe and offer a portion to the gods before eating cooked rice. Rice is essential to pūjās and life-cycle rituals. It is the Goddess Lakṣmī, the goddess of wealth (*dhān* is rice, *dhan* is wealth). The most common representation of the Lakṣmī Debī is unhusked rice in a common measuring pot, the *Lakkhipai* (*pai,* half-*śeer*). The Lakkhipai is worshiped during all Debīpūjās, in temples and *ṭhākurghar*s, being placed at the side of the main deity. It is never moved (except in the New Rice festival when the goddess is ceremonially moved into the house), for the Debī is fickle, and wealth may easily leave the house. It is said that no Bengali feels he has eaten anything unless he has had a large portion of rice.

The day after the belbaraṇs of the three Ṭhākuranīs, the kalparambha in the nonroyal Durgāpūjās, the morning ritual is devoted to the bathing of the nabapatrika. The nine plants are regarded as the goddess, and after the bathing they are wrapped in a saffron-colored sāri and worshiped like the goddess herself. On the tenth day the farewell ritual of the nabapatrika is performed. Especially in baṇgśa worship (in which the kinship basis of Durgāpūjā is most clearly emphasized), women offer milk products and sweet things to the goddess in the nabapatrika form. During the pūjā the nabapatrika stands at the right side of the Durgā image (in the rājā's pūjā the nabapatrika and the Durgāpaṭ together are wrapped in a white, red-bordered sāri). It is also known as Kala Bou, the banana-tree wife, and is honored as mother, the Goddess Durgā herself (see p. 23). In the rājā's traditional pūjā the king himself used to wear this sāri on the tenth day, parading through the town, receiving the homage and *praṇām* (prostration) of his subjects. The women of the royal household used to do praṇām to the king, touching the sacred cloth. Later they themselves wore it draped around their head and shoulders.

The Vessel of the Gods. The ghat is the most essential vessel of the pūjā; without it a rite is hardly possible. For the worship of the goddess especially, no image or temple is necessary and no offerings have to be given; the only indispensable items are water, flowers, and the ghat. Yet even the ghat is replaceable: the yantra, or *matriyantra,* can substitute for the ghat. The ghat is made of earth (clay) and contains mud and water. It is marked in a special way; across the middle is a wide band painted white and filled with cross-hatching. The shape is that of the ordinary rice-cooking vessel (in other parts of the Bengal delta the ghat is painted all over with many-colored designs, and the shape is also distinctive). The mud and water inside the ghat are regarded as *gaṅgāmati* and *gaṅgājal* (earth and water from the Ganges). The items placed on top of the ghat (mango leaves, coconut, towel) must be perfect and unmarked. The coconut (*dāb*) must come with the vine that attaches it to the palm tree, for the stem is regarded as a sign of fruition and creation, symbolic of the goddess's function. All these items, including the svastik sign painted on the ghat and the sacred thread placed around it, are regarded as the most honorable things men can offer (being auspicious, they are fit to be put on a vessel that will become the home of the gods). The ghat is a sacred vessel because it symbolizes the body: the body of men is also the house of the goddess. Bhagavan (god) dwells in all men; through the ghat men invite the goddess to reside in themselves. Water and earth are elements of the body; the ghat is therefore like the living body, the house of the divinity. In the worship of the Goddess Manasā (Debī of Snakes), the ghat is called *Manasābāṛi* (the house of Manasā).

Water, whenever it is found in the open, is associated with the sacred Ganges—even a man-made water tank is Gaṅgā herself. Well or tube water is not used, because only open bodies of water have certain qualities beneficial to the health of men. Hence people prefer to bathe in the open; "natural" water preserves the skin and prevents colds, asthma, and related diseases. The water in the ghats comes from the tanks, and the rite of bringing the water is called *ghat-tula* (lifting the ghat). This involves processions through the town, usually accompanied by the playing of musical instruments. The procession expresses respect for the gods; the assemblage of ghat, priest, umbrella, and fan symbolizes the presence of the gods. The objects associated with the worship are also regarded as potent and worthy of respect. The items carried in the procession are all royal objects; gods are also kings and must be treated as such by men. The vermilion used in painting the svastik sign is also auspicious, as are the other items. These "auspicious things" of the ghat are meant to please the goddess; without satisfying her, the worshiper cannot ask for boons. The svastik is a symbol of men's desire for auspicious results: let the goddess enjoy her stay, let her remember her devotees, let her mind be fixed on auspicious things, let her fulfill the desires of men.

In the Durgāpūjā a pair of large ghats (*jaraghat*s) are needed. One is for the goddess herself, the other for Pancadebatā, the Five Gods, who must be worshiped every day. The ghats can also mean the consort pair, Śiva and Durgā, or king and queen. Not every deity needs a ghat for the worship; the sun is always worshiped directly as a living deity (*sākṣāt debatā*), and Viṣṇu and Śiva are worshiped in sacred stones, the *sālāgrām sila* and the *liṅga* respectively.

The Plate of Auspicious Things. The *prasasta* or *maṅgal patra* is a plate used in welcome of the goddess. It contains auspicious items used in and found essential for everyday life and also honorific items, symbols of royalty and power, wealth and fertility. These are the best things in the world, hence they are good signs, fit to be offered to the gods as a witness of the good intentions of men. The plate is large and round, made of brass or copper. In welcoming rituals it is waved around the image of the goddess, and then all items are touched to the ghat and to the image itself. The plate makes its appearance in many other pūjās.

Whenever an image is "established," given sight and life, the plate is there for the deity to use. It is also used in life-cycle rituals: in wedding ceremonies it is waved around the bride and the groom, then touched to their foreheads (the bride and groom being treated like deities). In the plate all pūjā items are collected and offered together to the gods, and in the course of the pūjā these items may be used separately, with mantras and mudras, to symbolize the different aspects of the goddess.

There are twenty-seven items on the plate, the first being earth, a symbol of the Ganges. Then comes turmeric mixed with oil, especially that of the mustard seed. This oil is very important in pūjā; it is mixed with turmeric and, separately, with vermilion before being put on the ghat, image, or other representation of divinity. Oil is also used in the daily bath; in water it is a cleaner. Mustard oil is used in cooking to make many kinds of fries eaten with parched or cooked rice. The other items or the plate are "rock" or parched rice (shaped like small bits of gravel); unhusked rice; scent or perfume, most often sandalwood paste; fruit, a whole banana (unmarked and with its stem intact); and a flower, an indispensable item of worship and a way of expressing joy as well as respect (note the garlanding of elders, guests, and friends). Each deity has a flower particularly suited to his worship, a flower that delights him most. Then there is *durba* grass, sacred because a drop of sacred nectar fell on it. The nectar of immortality was rescued by the gods when the demons threatened to capture it after the churning of the ocean. Garuda, the carrier of Viṣṇu, was dispatched to rescue the vessel of nectar, but, being tired, the bird made several stops on his way to the Himalayas. Whenever he put the jug on the ground a few drops fell on the grass. Durba thus became immortal, and the localities where the nectar fell are still celebrated at the time of the four major *kumbha mela*s (jug fairs) involving millions of pilgrims every twelve years. Durba is used in rites (*brata*s) of women, being tied to the arm with a yellow or red thread (*suta*) as a sign of the goddess's benediction and protective watch over the wearer.

Curds and *ghī* (clarified butter) are the next items, sacred because they are the products of the cow. All these are used in pūjās. The cow is regarded as the mother from whom all nourishment comes; Kṛṣṇa himself was the servant of cows in Brindaban. Curds are highly prized as the correct way to end a meal; ghī is the purest item of food. Rice boiled with ghī is the most sacred food offering; ghī is the most valuable and highly regarded of all things. It is used in the fire sacrifice; butter burned in the fire goes straight to the gods and incurs their beneficial attention. To please men ghī is poured on the rice at mealtime. It is eaten reverently without mixing it with vegetables and pulses.

The next item is the *svastik,* the sign of peace and grace, of welfare and desire for the blessings of the gods. It is to be drawn with rice powder sprinkled on the plate itself. Then comes white starch, the liquid from the first boiling of rice, then vermilion, another important substance. Mixed with oil, vermilion is applied to offerings, ghat, images of the goddess, and to anything that is sacrificed and given to Debī. It is necessary for all Debīpūjās. Married women wear it in the parting of their hair, and its application is the central act in the marriage ritual. Red is the color of the goddess; vermilion is her favorite, symbolizing auspiciousness, victory, joy, and blood in sacrifice. In the same series belong *āltā* and *kājal;* all are accessories of women and therefore indispensable to the goddess. Āltā is the red lacquer women apply to the soles and edges of their feet. It is used to beautify, but it also saves the skin from cracking. Kājal is the black collyrium women put in and around their eyes to beautify and clean them.

Saṅkha, the conch shell, is another sacred object in the series. As a horn it is used to call and honor deities in the pūjās and brides in the marriage ceremony. From this shell, arm bracelets are made that women wear as a sign of marriage. Durgā herself wears these bracelets and holds a conch in her hand. A special artisan caste, the Śaṅkaris, work with this shell. Durgā is held in special respect by the people of this caste. Metals form the next group—gold, silver, and copper—all the pure and precious metals everyone values. These cannot be polluted, hence most pūjā vessels are made of copper. Gold and silver are royal as well as pure, and so they ought to be offered to the gods, even if in very small quantities. Copper is less pure than gold, but it can be washed with water and ashes; no pollution is bad enough to make men throw away a copper vessel. Gold is unmarked; copper is less pure because it acquires a green deposit when exposed to humidity. The last metal is iron, not precious but necessary for cultivation and work. Women also wear an iron bangle as a sign of marriage. Then there is the arrow, a weapon of the goddess, a sign of Śiva (also the representation of the Bhairabas). Ascetics carry the arrow and the trident with them all the time. A yellow thread (*suta*) smeared with turmeric is also included as an auspicious sign. Men and women wear this at the time of the different Debī bratas when the goddess is worshiped as the one who delivers from danger. The thread is a charm, a lucky sign, protecting men from evil. Threads are worn by children, given at various times after birth to ward off evil spirits and ghosts. But the thread is also a sign of faith; the wearer will fear no danger, because the goddess is watching over him. It is worn at difficult and dangerous rituals like the gājan, also as a sign of the goddess's special relation to the devotees.

The final three items are *ārati,* light or flame, and *cāmor* or yak tail. These are all used in the ārati evening ritual, a short service of the goddess.

They symbolize honor and respect; the cāmor is a rare object, for its touch is beneficial and its presence drives away all annoying things of the summer night, such as flying insects and biting vermin. The lamp is a sign of the sun, a witness to worship. A devotee must have a witness, and the sun, light, and flame are the most faithful (Sīta was failed by trees, waters, and animals when she asked for a witness to her devotion to Rāma). The lamp symbolizes knowledge; the goddess who created all things is also the path to knowledge of the world. Through her māyā and līlā (cosmic play) she hides from the eyes of men the true nature of things, which is oneness beyond seeming multiplicity. Ārati is the act of offering these reminders of her nature and power to the goddess, a reminder that serves men as well. It is a final service before the night interrupts the daily cycle of worship.

There are other important pūjā objects. The oblations that constitute a major part of a pūjā are poured from three vessels; the *kamandala* is the brass water jug in which the Brāhmaṇ keeps the Ganges water and into which he dips the flowers for purification before the offering. From this jug, water is poured into the *kosakusi* (leaf-shaped copper vessels). Water is poured in short streams, repeated three times in the purifications and the bathing of the goddess. These vessels are shaped like the bel leaf, the same shape being represented by the two palms cupped in the gesture of offering, *añjali*. The vessels themselves are expressive of offering. The formal flower offerings in the pūjā, in which non-Brāhmaṇs may also participate, are made with this gesture. The red or yellow sandalwood paste is made by rubbing the block of wood on a wet stone slab. The stone slab is also used in the kitchen to prepare the spices that go into curry. The pūjā ground is often covered by drawings made with rice powder and water. These drawings (*alpanas*) trace the seats of the worshiper and the priest, the place of the goddess, and her footprints leading to her seat. The priest's mat is placed over the drawn seat, and the offerings are placed on the Goddess's alpana (flower, house, and other signs associated with her are also drawn: footprints, fish, sun, or just a flowerlike abstract design, reminiscent of the more exact and specific yantra).

Pradip (lamp) and *dhup* (incense) *dhoa* (resin smoke) are also necessary for Durgāpūjā. Dhup is scent, always a welcome item, associated with honor even in ordinary life. But it is used especially in pūjās, and deities cannot do without it; it is an expression of a devotional attitude. Waving a lighted incense stick around a deity is *sebā,* service. Pradip is light, knowledge (*jñān*). Out of the darkness comes light, dissolving the darkness. In deep meditation everything becomes dark around the devotee; then lights appear, the expression of pure consciousness. The light becomes more and more intense, dazzling white *cāitanya* (consciousness), which makes men capable of conceiving of the brahman. Light is a symbol of brahman. In ārati a lamp with five branches and five flames is used. Camphor is lit in the five small cups, and the lamp is then waved around the goddess.

Five is a sacred number, recurring time and time again. Many offerings, items expressive of service for the gods and items of purification, come in fives: five products of the cow, five nectars, five grains, and so on. Śiva has five faces, and there are five main gods. The five lights stand for the five paths to god: through desire (*kām*), duty (*dharma*), calculation (*artha*), knowledge (*mukti*), and devotion (*bhakti*). It is also the first item to be waved in the ārati, and it sums up the whole little pūjā: the goddess is greeted with lights and offered a bath, fresh clothing, and a garland of flowers; finally, she is fanned with the cāmor. Pradip also means the power of burning, energy, the energy that drives the five elements and the five vital airs that are the basis of life. Ārati also means cessation, rest, and peace, the proper state of Śiva when he is one with the goddess, the time of sleep, of no activity at all.

The Pūjās of Mahā Saptamī

The belbaraṇs and the Mahā Ṣaṣṭhī pūjās are not full Debīpūjās. Participants, ritualists, and householders are careful to point out that the pūjās before Saptamī anticipate and prepare for the coming of the goddess. The festival begins in earnest on Saptamī morning. This is the first śakti pūjā of the sequence, a celebration of power and energy, the essence of Debīpūjā. The two Durgāpaṭs are taken to the ghāt of the temple tank, where they are set up at the water's edge. The two nabapatrikas are bathed and worshiped, the priest reaching down into the waters as he refills the shells and the eight jars, pouring out the water with the recitation of each mantra. Each nabapatrika is given the same service as the Baroṭhākurānī's nabapatrika twelve days before. Two lots of raw and cooked food are offered, and the sacrifice is also performed twice. Uncooked rice is scattered around the two deities. When the ceremonial bathing is over, the two goddesses move in procession to the temple accompanied by music and by cannon blasts from the rājā's house. A Brāhmaṇ boy walks before the deities, pouring a continuous trail of water from a brass jar. At the temple steps the two pots are set up side by side for the first time. Here the priests perform a full pūjā, beginning all over again with the purifications and offerings to dozens of different deities.

Two small ghats are used for the pūjā at the temple steps, and the oblations offered to the deities are performed with a set of eight jars. Gaṇeś, Lakṣmī, Pancadebatā, and Durgā are worshiped, among others. Finally, a series of offerings and recitations are addressed to the goddess alone: a special, detailed service. The number of onlookers grows continuously as the main pūjā approaches. Bhog is offered and bali is done, the ghat is immersed (*bisarjan*) by a mantra of dismissal, and the vessel is discarded. After this it cannot be regarded as the material manifestation of Durgā. Sometimes the ghat is actually taken down to a river to be sunk in the water, but often it is just thrown away. The two deities ascend into the temple. Betel leaves and betel nuts are placed on the steps at regular intervals as the Brāhmaṇs carry the two deities into the temple, touching the images to each leaf on the ground. An old Brāhmaṇ woman pours a stream of water from a jar as the images are taken inside.

Inside the temple the images are set up for the major part of the rite still to come. Baṛoṭhākurānī is already under the arch of the inner temple, farthest away from the permanent image of Mrinmoyī Debī. Somewhat nearer is the place of Mejoṭhākurānī. Choṭoṭhākurānī is closest to the clay image, and she is in the center of the temple. For her a small temple is constructed out of *śāl* wood poles, the framework covered with a white cloth. Choṭoṭhākurānī's paṭ, her nabapatrika, and her golden engraving are all placed inside the small white paṇḍal. To her left the ghats are set up, and on her right are the *Lakkhipai,* two brass rice measuring pots filled with unhusked rice (*dhān*), the common representations of Lakṣmī. The ghats are then prepared: grains of rice are placed under them, Ganges water is poured into them, and mango leaves and small colored towels (used also in the daily bath) and a green coconut with its stem uncut are placed on top of them. Then an earthenware lamp and an incense burner are put in front of the goddess. Directly below her is a wide earthenware pot with a mirror inside it so that she can see herself. The nabapatrika is placed between the goddess and the pot. The same range of objects is spread around the other two Durgāpaṭs. The permanent image receives similar attention, but she has a permanent ghat and is never immersed (so no nabapatrika mirror or Lakkhipai are used in her worship). (See fig. 3.)

The pūjā itself begins the same way as the ones described above. Since this is a full Debīpūjā, the priests are wearing rings made of the sacred kusa grass, an essential item for all Tantric rites. The rites of purification are performed once more. The goddess is invoked in the Durgāpaṭs themselves this time; the priest holds a long piece of kusa grass to the main figures in each painting, wrapping his sacred thread around the stem of the grass while reciting the sacred formulas. A long series of oblations and flower offerings follow in the names of many

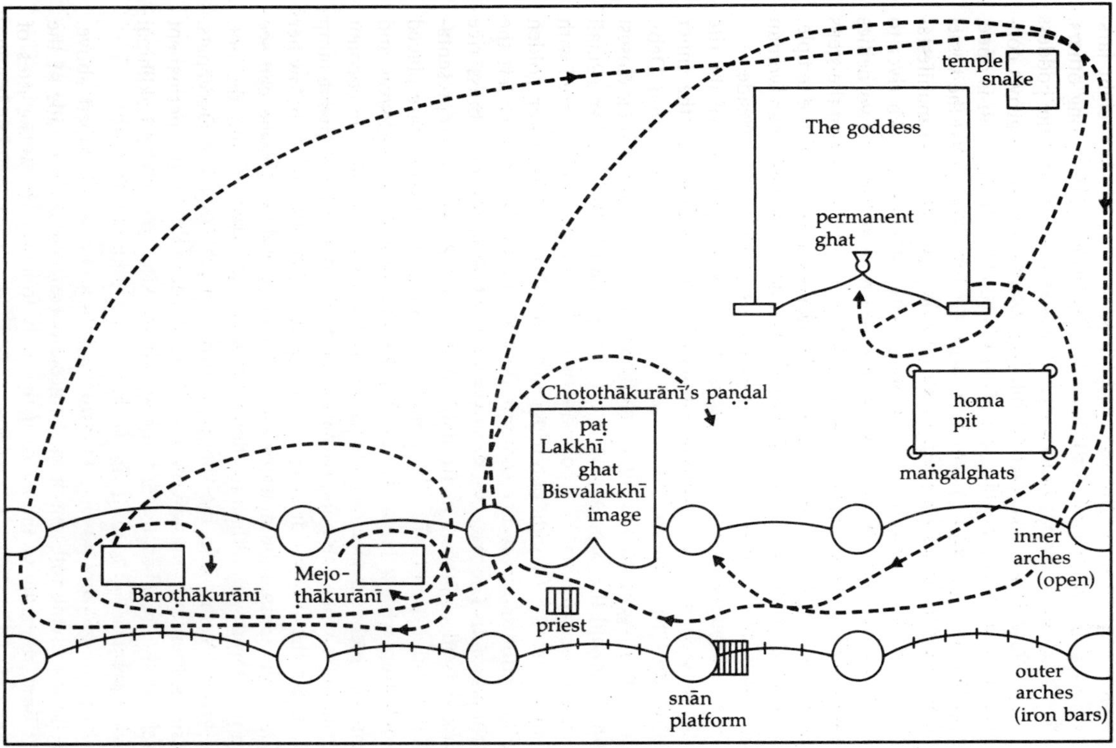

Figure 3. The interior of the Mrinmoyī temple and the circumambulation of the goddess.

different deities. As the deities represented in the paṭ are mentioned, the priest touches them with the kusa. Before being offered, the flowers are smeared with sandalwood paste, and water is sprinkled on them. Rice and flowers are scattered in the four directions, and a silver coin is placed on the ghat. The first lot of offerings over, the ritual reaches its climax in the giving of life, *prānpratiśṭhā,* to the image of Choṭoṭhākurānī. The priest holds a long piece of kusa to the heart of the goddess, then to her eyes. He repeats this with the golden paṭ, and going back to the painting he gives life to the other divine figures. The living deity is then adored by waving incense and camphor flame in front of her. All deities and the demon in the Durgāpaṭ are offered piles of flowers with the recitation of mantras (each group of offerings being made in lots of three, punctuated by oblations). *Noibedda* (uncooked food) and much later bhog are brought out from the temple kitchen (where only Brāhmaṇ males may cook for the gods) and served to the goddess and her companions on śāl-leaf plates.

The priest goes to the altar (*bedī*) of Mejoṭhākurānī, carrying the kusa grass and the copper vessels for the oblations. He gives life to the figures in the painting. The noibedda is spread around the bedī, and the priest invites the Mejoṭhākurānī to partake of the offering (performing the invitation mudra). The same process is repeated at the place of the Baroṭhākurānī. The priest then returns to the Choṭodebī for the bhogpūjā. Cooked food is placed in front of all four Durgā images. The priest offers it three times with the same set of gestures and mantras, then, standing up with a large pile of flowers and sacred tree leaves in his hands, he recites a special verse as the three cannons are fired to signify the moment when the goddess partakes of the food offered to her. The priest lets the flowers drop on the ghat, repeating the act three times. Outside the temple the musicians begin to play, and the goddess herself is now adored with oblations, flower offerings, and recitations. Marking the ground with oil in the shape of a triangle, the priest performs the sacrifice; then, putting flowers into the shell and holding the shell to his forehead, he reaches toward the goddess. After bali everyone bows down, prostrating himself in front of the goddess (*praṇām*). The praṇāms range from bowing, kneeling, and touching the ground with the forehead to lying full length in the ground (*astaṅga praṇām,* the eight-part bow, referring to the parts of the body touching the ground). The same series of actions are repeated in front of the other three images. The priest goes in procession around the temple, circling each goddess clockwise, keeping the deity to his right.

The priest recites a different *dhyen* (meditation verse) in front of each image, offering a flower to each. Another priest performs the *homa* (fire sacrifice) to the left of Mrinmoyī Mother. Fire sacrifice often accompanies major rituals. It consists of burnt offerings: ghī and leaves of the sacred bel tree dipped in ghī are dropped into a fire built in a special enclosure. This sacrifice also follows the order of the pūjā (beginning with the obligatory acts of purification), though the manner of offering is different. The god of fire is the channel through which the sacrifice reaches the gods, and each of the major gods has a special kind of homa. The fire is built in a pit or on a small sand platform, yantra being drawn in the pit or in the sand. While a mantra is recited, a small twig or bunch of leaves is dipped into ghī and put on the fire (śal wood forms the fuel). Twigs of different trees and bushes are used in different types of homa. The final offering consists of milk, a banana wrapped up in a large betel leaf, ghī, and water. Standing, the priest recites a long verse and, with his left hand touching his right elbow (pose of offering), he places the banana in the fire. Still in the same pose, he pours milk, ghī, and water into the fire. From the cinders and the remnants of the ghī he mixes a black paste with which he marks the foreheads of all participants and onlookers.

The pūjā over, the temple is filled by devotees doing their praṇām to the goddess. Water from the oblations of the goddess is taken reverently from the priest, who now sits at the feet of Durgā and dispenses the sacred water. People receive the water in their right hands and, after taking a sip, smooth the rest on their heads, invoking the names of Durgā. The priest receives a few pennies as his fee (*dakkhina*) for this service. These acts continue till evening, when ārati is again performed and cold food is again offered to the gods. A big crowd collects for the evening ritual, and when it disperses the iron gates of the temple are closed.

Text and Exegesis

The pūjā begins by honoring Durgā's female companions, then the goddess herself is offered flowers. After the invocation a kalparambha may be recited (if there has not been one on the night of the sixth). The nabapatrika is worshiped with nine little vessels and the nine mantras of the Nine Durgās. The *Mahāsnān* utilizes different kinds of water: Ganges water, cold water, water in the shell, hot water, scented water, and pure water. The five "nectars" are milk, curd, ghī, sugar, and honey. The five juices are *jam* (rose apple), *simul* (silk cotton plant), *berela* (a shrub), *kul* (jujube), and *bakul* (flowering tree). Other kinds of water are also specified: water mixed with various flowers and juices, water mixed with spices and scents, each offering accompanied by a mantra that mentions one of the aspects of the goddess, corresponding to one of her thousand names. Eight kinds of holy water are offered in the eight small vessels: Ganges, rain, sea, and spring water, the water of the Sarasvatī River, water with sandalwood, and water with lotus.

Bhutapasaran is the separation of the five winds, an act setting the stage for classifying and separating different things in the created world. The pūjās of the five deities honor Gaṇeś, Śiva, Viṣṇu, Durgā, and Surya (the sun). Five "things" are offered: sandalwood, flower, incense, light, and food. These are essential items, but in the major pūjās sixteen things are to be given to the deities. All this must be done before the *mūl* pūjā of the *mūl debatā* is performed (*mul*, root), the pūjā of the deity for whom the entire ritual is intended.

Prānpratiśṭhā and *cakkurdān,* giving life and eyes to the deity, are accomplished by a mantra and certain actions. The images are decorated with flowers, the goddesses in the group are anointed with vermilion, and their eyes are drawn with ghī and collyrium. The *gāyatrī* mantra is recited, the incantation conferring Brāhmaṇ status on a child in the *upanayan* ceremony (the rite of making a Brāhmaṇ, the "second birth" of the Brāhmaṇ jāti). The recitation of this most sacred set of words signifies the divine status of the priest. The Saptamī ghat is "estabḷished" in front of the image: the ghat must stand on the ground, the locality of the pūjā being defined in contact with the earth. The seven kinds of earth are earth from a stable and a cowshed, earth from a termite hill, mud of a river and of a lake, and soil from a cow pasture. The seat of the goddess is purified, and more purifications follow (of the priest, offerings, and so on). In these, five kinds of grain, five "things" of the cow, five nectars, and five leaves are used: cow dung, cow urine, milk, ghī, and curds; leaves of mango, asoka, *asvanth* (a creeper), the fig tree, and the banyan tree; paddy (rice), barley, mustard, pea, and pulse seeds. These actions and offerings belong to the rite of *śuddhācār,* the proper way of purification as laid down in the sacred texts (or as observed in the region).

A triangle, a geometric symbol of the goddess similar to yantra (a magic diagram representing the qualities of *prakriti,* the created world), is painted with oil, and a *bijmantra* (seed mantra) is recited; this way the place of the goddess is defined and pūjā can be offered to the *pīthasthān,* the locality where the goddess stands. This represents the place of the goddess on Mount Koilās, where she stays with Śiva. In the pūjā the locality itself is deified, the original place upon which the goddess manifested herself at her birth. Together with this pūjā, the creation of the goddess (through the place associated with her) is reenacted, and her creative activity is repeated in the recitations and yogic exercises of the *matrikannyas* and *pranayan.* A high point in the pūjā is the worship of the ground on which the goddess stands—itself a deity, *pitha debatā.* This represents the earth and the locality where the goddess first came into being.

When the pūjās of all deities are done, the dhyen of the goddess is recited. The five deities, the nine planets, and Indra (the king of gods) are worshiped, followed by the pūjā of Caṇḍī and the other goddesses. Different offerings are dedicated to these deities (*nibedan kora*) with mantras and libations of water, the sixteen oblations: lotus, *arghya* (oblation), *acaman* (washing teeth and face), *madhuparka* (an oblation of honey, sugar ghī, sugar, milk, and curd mixed together), *punoracaman* (return oblation), bathing, clothing, *ābāran* (ornaments), *śaṅkhabaran* (conch-shell bracelets), vermilion, sandalwood, flower, a garland of flowers, scents, incense, lamp, collyrium, *noibedda* (uncooked food), a house, sherbet, and *tambul* (*pān* and betel nut, the proper way to end meals, offerings, and visits).[10]

In the Saptamīpūjā all three Ṭhākurānīs in the rājā's temple are given large ghats; Mrinmoyī Debī, being a permanent image, needs no seasonal ghat. The double ghats stay till the tenth day; they are the ghats of the śaktipūjā itself. Despite all the purifications of the morning's pūjās, these actions are repeated again in the Saptamīpūjā, because this time the goddess is worshiped in her own form, her own image is given life, and her creative power, śakti, is celebrated—a power that can be harmful to men if not treated with caution (with full observance of the rules for approaching *prakriti rūp,* the form of the female creative principle). The goddess is the Āddā Śakti, the original energy out of which all things were created. This form has many aspects, and all of them have to be honored and served in the remaining days of the Durgāpūjā. The long series of oblations, libations, and flower offerings are devoted to the recognition of and deference to the multiple aspects in the original form of the goddess. This recognition is central to śakti pūjā; *bhed,* division within the one goddess, must be revealed so that the full significance of Durgā may be comprehended and everything may be reintegrated into the idea, form, and appearance of the goddess. These aspects must be adored separately; otherwise the goddess is not satisfied.

According to priests and devotees, the former initiate certain actions, *jogkriyā,* meant to reveal the manifold aspects of the goddess in the human body. *Jog* is yoga, union, putting things together; *kriyā* is action, magic, through which the separated elements of nature and life are brought together and are offered to the goddess. This life is placed into the image. The rites of cakkurdān and *prānpratiṣṭhā* are the most important parts of Saptamīpūjā, giving eyes and life to the image. To accomplish this the priest has to become a deity, for only a god-like being can serve divinity in its own form. The long series of purifications serve to remove the priest from everyday life into the world of the gods, where he can take the life within him and offer it to the image. The life he gives is part of all living things, a part of brahman itself, the Universal Being. There is something of brahman in all things, since ultimately everything comes from brahman. The soul (*ātmā*), which defines the self and separates one being from another is a part of brahman (*aṅga*), a part of Param Brahman, or Param Puruṣ, the original principle. Before all things brahman was, and from that formless principle came sound; sound and brahman are one. From that came *barṇa,* the word or appearance, *mrittikabarṇa,* the appearance of the Mother, who created all living things, hence all deities have to be worshiped before the Mother herself can be served.

First of all the outer organs, *bahirindriya,* are purified, and as these are normally involved in action they have to be "cooled" or rested to help concentration. The external organs are essential to movement; hence they are the primary concern of purification in the pūjā. When the priest is at peace, he can do *bhutsuddhi,* the purification of the five elements: earth, water, heat, air, and sky. These are designated not in terms of everyday language (*calit bhasa*) but in terms of the learned language (*sāddhu bhasa*): *kkiti, ap, tej, marut, bbom.* By making these pure, energy or tej is retained in the body. Tej, vital spirit or energy, is necessary to do pūjā and to give life to the image. Through tej the twenty-five elements of the body are unified to accomplish the purpose of lifting the priest onto the level of the gods. For this, further actions are needed; to unify all the elements of life into teja, jogkriyā, or yogic actions, are resorted to: *niyantran, aṅganyas, matrikannyas.* These refer to certain ways of breathing, gesturing, and touching the parts of the body—mudras and exercises to gather the energy of the body and to purify the elements corresponding to the barṇa of the Mother. Through faith (*astha*), these are joined with the experience of divinity in human life, preparing men to encounter the gods, transforming the priest himself into a deity. Faith, magic actions, incantations, and gestures are necessary to do this; in the pūjā, priests reenact all that pertains to the creation of the gods. The self that experiences divinity becomes a deity through that very experience (anubhab kore). Only by becoming divine can men serve the gods. This is necessary to any pūjā in which the gods are served in the prescribed way and actually brought to the place of worship. Kriyā, spiritual study (*addhatmik,* culture or discipline) are necessary but are not attainable by everyone.

After the jogkriyā and other actions, the life of men is placed into the image of the goddess through a mantra. It is given from the ātmā, the

Isvara (Life; God), that is in all living things. These meanings are expressed by touching kusa grass, sacred thread, and collyrium to the eyes of the goddess and by *pranayan,* the exercise of concentration. The life given to the image is neither the puruṣa nor the prakriti principle, it is the *sayang brahman,* the original principle beyond creation, parts of which are shared by gods and men alike. From brahman issued the goddess as its *icchāśakti,* power of desire. Brahman's desire to see itself in many forms (rūp) resulted in prakriti, the original form of the goddess. The puruṣa (male aspect) of brahman engaged in līlā (divine play) with the goddess, unfolding the story of creation, a continuing event, for līlā is still going on. Prakriti activates puruṣa; from their union issue the *triguṇa,* the three qualities: *sattva, raja, tama* (truth, power or rule, and inertia). From the three qualities come the five vital airs constituting life. Pranayan is the exercise (breathing through the separate nostrils to divide the five winds in the body) through which the internal airs or winds, the stuff of life, are joined together and the ātmā of the self (*sayang ātmā*) merge with the Universal Spirit, Param Brahman Parmātmā. This was the *sādhana* (execution, achievement) of pūjā for those few who attained the merging of their self with the universal soul (*parmātmā lābh kora*). These men gave others the ritual means (sādhana, or necessary action) by which they can achieve the same end. Sādhana is the way to liberate the self, but it is not given to many. In the pūjā this experience is enacted in relation to the gods, and for a fleeting moment men are given a glimpse of the experience of seers, renouncers who are outside society. In the pūjā the achievement is momentary only. The sādhana that finally liberates men is a long process, taking many cycles of rebirth.

Mahā Aśṭamī and Sandhipūjās

Mahā Aśṭamī pūjā begins early in the morning of the eighth day. Many people come early to achieve *darśan* (sight) of the Debī and to give food offerings that the priests place in front of the goddess with the name of the devotee on each plate. These piles of uncooked food are offered to the Debī in the course of the pūjā and returned to the donors on Nabamī day. By that time the food has been touched by the goddess, so it is *prasad,* sacred and auspicious to eat. Reaching home, the householder or his wife distributes the prasad to every member of the household. The devotees also ask the priests to offer small pūjās on their behalf, and much of the morning is spent this way. These individual rites are addressed to Durgā as the deliverer from danger. They are done by the priests for women who want the benefit of the offering for their husbands and children. Such an act is known as nāmgotra pūjā (name-and-descent-label worship), in which the priest takes the food offerings, asks in whose name they are to be offered, and then recites a saṅkalpa while holding the paitā to the image or the ghat. The women receive a few flowers and leaves from the ghat, and a few drops of holy water from the goddess's bath, and in return they give a rupee or four to eight annas to the priest. At the end they prostrate themselves in front of the goddess. Some address the goddess and implore her to help them and listen to them, others just call her their mother, many addressing her aloud in very personal terms. Every jāti can have these pūjās performed on its behalf; the lower castes, however, have their pūjās limited to giving money offerings and receiving flowers and water from the priest.[11] This is not all voluntary; the priests themselves prefer it this way. Nevertheless, some low castes have the full *nāmgotra pūjā* performed: the annual Durgāpūjā is the time for all jātis to participate.

The main pūjā centers around the image of Bisvalakkhī, an ancient eighteen-handed representation of the goddess made wholly of gold. The image was captured by the rājās in one of their raids on a neighboring kingdom. During the year it is kept in the rājā's house, and it is worshiped during the last three days of the Durgāpūjā. Bisvalakkhī is placed on a small seat on which the priest draws an eight-petaled lotus in five different colors. This is a yantra, a diagram symbolizing the goddess herself. The five colors (*raṅ*) correspond to five materials: white, red, black, yellow, and deep sienna. The five colors are used alternately as each line is drawn; a red joba flower is placed in the middle. The image itself stands on the yantra inside the small white temple of the Choṭoṭhākurānī. Behind the Durgāpaṭ a number of *debapaṭ*s are hidden, and the deities represented in them are worshiped today for the first time. No one except the priest can unroll these, but even he should not look at them. They can be opened only in the presence of the king. Only once a year are these images worshiped.

The pūjā is performed in the same way as on the seventh, but there are more offerings and oblations. The already life-endowed images do not have a saṅkalpa recited for them, but a separate kalpa is done for the Bisvalakkhī. The golden image is also endowed with life (*prānpratiśṭhā*). In addition to the goddess, the whole pantheon receives adoration: Śiva and his many forms (especially the powerful Bhairab), consort (*śakti*) figures corresponding to the male gods, Manasā, the sun, Kālī and many other divinities in an unending series of oblations and offerings.

Sandhipūjā is the climactic point of the whole festival, the moment of union when Aśṭamī day becomes Nabamī. In 1968 it came about midnight, and hundreds of devotees gathered to wait far into the night to participate in this ritual. The pūjā begins much earlier with the Mahāsnān, the ceremonial bathing festival of the goddess. At this elaborate ritual only the image of Bisvalakkhī is bathed, but all the Durgāpaṭs are offered the same objects. Four sāris, four towels, scents, and oils are offered for the use of the goddess after the bath. The gifts are placed on a pair of big pots near the image. The priests also receive money and *dhotīs* (men's clothing) from the rājā. The rājā's "bodyguard," members of a particular caste originally created for the service of the king (drawn from among Majhis and Bagdis) bring the items necessary for the bath and prepare the temple for the ritual. Just outside the iron bars of the mandap, facing Mrinmoyī Debī, is a small stone platform, a pedestal for the image in this performance.

The iron gates are opened, and the crowd fills the inner parts of the temple, barely giving the priests room to move about. The stairs and the huge temple courtyard are also filled with people. Traders hawk all kinds of goods. Since any ritual attended by many people becomes a fair, so here the crowd attracts dealers in fried cakes and sweets, bracelets and cheap jewelry and small clay images of different deities. The whole place resounds with laughter, excited conversation, and greetings. The image of the Golden Goddess is placed on the stone platform, and the attendants bring out the pūjā objects: pots and clothes, lamps and incense burners, *maṅgal patra* (auspicious plate), shells, a big earthenware pot in which the oils will be mixed, flowers and cold food offerings, and the eight pots that will be used to pour the scented oils on the golden image. Twenty-one different spices and herbs are necessary for the bath; the waters of different rivers and the oils of different seeds are mixed with various perfumes to make the thick liquid of the bathing water.

Reciting Sanskrit verses, the priest rubs oil on the image. Following the instruction of the tantrik, he performs a series of oblations and flower offerings, pouring water on the image from the shell. Next the scented oil is poured on the Debī, the eight vessels being dipped into the open pot one after another, their contents being emptied over the head of the goddess in sets of eight offerings. The priest shakes his bell and recites a mantra with each act of oblation. The rite over, the image is dried with a red cloth and noibedda is offered. The goddess is honored with light and incense placed on the maṅgal patra and waved around her. Finally she returns to the white house of Choṭoṭhākurānī and the pūjās leading up to the sandhi begin.

All deities are worshiped with flowers, bel leaf, and water, and increasingly larger piles of flowers are offered as the moment of the Goddess's appearance among her worshipers approaches. Brāhmaṇs cook great amounts of food in the temple kitchens and bring out huge vats of rice and curried vegetables. Thirteen śāl-leaf plates of bhog are lined up in front of each pūjā area; in all, fifty-two lots of cooked white rice, pulses, several kinds of curry, and chutney are arranged in rows of six with one plate joining two rows to make thirteen for each of the four goddesses. Meanwhile homa is performed in the sacrificial pit. Offerings brought by townspeople keep piling up around the white paṇḍal. Excitement grows as the moment of sandhi approaches, the crowd pressing right up against the pūjā area. There is so much noise that the voices of the priests cannot be heard. The priests rise and offer increasingly larger piles of flowers (lotus and cāpā) right up to the sandhi. The even bigger crowd outside is not content to wait; some try to push their way in, others jump and strain to catch a glimpse of the events inside. Everyone is talking or shouting about the sandhi, counting the minutes. From far away in the crowd there is a stir, and soon the whole assemblage picks up the cry: the rājā is coming. With his helpers in attendance, the rājā comes quickly through the crowd and into the temple, wearing a white silk dhotī tied in the manner appropriate for worship (the single piece of cloth touching the ground in front and back, with one edge covering the shoulders). The king stands behind the priest (not the tantric, but the performing priest) and holds onto the sacred cloth that covers the Brāhmaṇ's shoulders, his hands folded in the *namaskār* pose (the palms pressed together). Now the attendants wait for the correct time, and everyone stands up as the priest reaches down for a huge pile of flowers to be offered in the final moment. Suddenly a sign is given and everybody shouts *Tob! Tob!* As if in answer, the cannon bursts are felt through the whole temple, a deafening roar, and from all sides the musicians erupt into loud music, people shout the names of the goddess, and the priest relinquishes the load of flowers at the feet of the Debī. All bow down to the ground to honor the goddess who appears this moment. Amid the continuing uproar the priest continues to offer flowers and dhyen recitations. More recitations follow, the priest holding the vessels in the pose of offering (cupped palms). Bali is then performed, then the conch shells are blown as the priest waves the maṅgal patra around the goddess. Then the priest and the king (still holding onto the sacred cloth) go in procession around the temple, ceremoniously circumambulating each altar. Going clockwise, they stop first in front of the Goddess Mrinmoyī, the priest repeating the sacrifice, dhyen recitation, puspañjali (offering of flowers), and the waving of lights. Then they circle the homa pit, Baroṭhākurānī, and Mejoṭhākurānī.

The devotees slowly disperse, and by the time the last mantra is over there is no sign of the hundreds that thronged the temple yard. The rājā waits till everyone is gone; it is only then that he divides the cooked prasad among the priests, musicians, and attendants.

Text and Exegesis

The Aśṭamīpūjā is offered in three parts, the pūjā in the morning (which is the same as Saptamī except that the lunar days in the mantras are changed, and the prānpratiśṭhā is left out), the Mahāsnān (which is performed on the seventh in Vishnupur), and the sandhi, the ritual of "union." Sandhi is the moment of the goddess's appearance. It is said that great devotees may see the goddess taking the form of her image, the image beginning to move, nodding her head, and giving blessings. In neighboring areas the goddess is said to leave footprints in a plate of vermilion dust at this time. But only those who are specially selected by the goddess can witness these things. Besides, townspeople claim, bhakti is no longer in the hearts of men nowadays, so how can they be given such a great honor? Nevertheless, this is the time to approach the goddess with humility and adoration, begging her to fulfill one's wishes and secret desires. The goddess appears among the people and grants their wishes. This is the most crowded ritual of the whole sequence, and the temples and courtyards fill up with hundreds of people.

The Aśṭamīpūjā itself is different from those of the previous days in one very important respect, the drawing of the matriyantra, the diagrammatic representation of the goddess. Together with the yantra appears the golden image of the goddess, Bisvalakkhī. The yantra is an eight-petaled lotus, drawn on a flat surface with five kinds of powder. Red (vermilion) is *rakta,* or blood, yellow (turmeric) is *pit* (also signifying drunkenness), black (collyrium) is Kṛṣṇa (also an incarnation of Viṣṇu), gray (ash) is *dhum* (also meaning smoke), white (rice powder) is *śukla,* which means brightness and dazzling light. A circle and the petals are drawn with these colors alternating one after the other, twice around, so that each petal and circle is drawn with two colors. In the middle a small circle is filled with vermilion, and on top of this a red joba flower is placed. The yantra is the goddess, and all her ābāran deities are worshiped in the pūjā of the lotus. On each petal a different aspect of Durgā is invoked and worshiped; these are the "veils" or covers of the goddess (*ābāran debatā*). Eight flowers are used to worship the eight aspects of the goddess in the lotus. In the Aśṭamīpūjā the Bisvalakkhī image is placed on the yantra, and in the Sandhipūjā they are again worshiped with even more circumstance, the offerings being increased to proportions never seen in other festivals and pūjās.

The rules of yantra pūjā are the following. The five colors stand for the five forms of the goddess. Śiva has five faces, and the five corresponding śaktis are the five Debīs. The five faces of Śiva also stand for the five directions (four cardinal directions and the center), and together these form the ten aspects of the goddess. The Das Mahābiddya or ten objects of transcendental knowledge are the ten main forms of Durgā. All these are worshiped in the petals of the lotus. Color also means form, appearance, and class (*barṇa*). In the seed vessel of the lotus, the original form of the goddess, the Āddā Śakti itself, is worshiped. In the course of giving life to the yantra (the diagram is "activated" just as an image is given life), the different classes of creation as revealed through the goddess are worshiped. The yantra is matriyantra, the diagram of the Mother, the goddess as the cause of creation.

The order of pūjās of these "covering deities" of the goddess is as follows (the series corresponds to the Purohit Darpan): the five śaktis corresponding to the five faces of Śiva; the five main directions (Śiva) and their śaktis, forming ten aspects of the goddess (within Śiva); the ten objects of knowledge: Kālī, Tārā, Sarasī, Bubaneśvarī, Bhairabī, Cinnamastā, Dhumabatī, Bagala, Matangī, Kamalā; the Astanayikā, eight mistresses, eight aspects of Durgā in the lotus (eight qualities of the goddess): Maṅgala, Bijayā, Bhādra, Jayantī, Aparajita, Nandini, Narasinghī, and Koumarī; the eight Bhairavas that correspond to the eight śaktis: Asitanga, Sanhara, Ruru, Kala, Krodha, Tamracuda, Candracuda, Mahā; the fourteen yoginis, the companions of the goddess in her terrible form; the twenty-seven stars, the fourteen lunar days, and the twelve months; the four Ṣaṣṭhīs, the four main aspects of Durgā having to do with the human life cycle.

The duty of the yantra is to join these aspects together with Śiva, the consort of the goddess. *Karja-karma,* the function and destiny of the yantra, is to accomplish creation in and through a symbolic form. The yantra is the goddess, the bijmantra is Śiva. The seed mantra is the male element that activates the yantra and reenacts creation itself. The male and the female aspects of creation thus symbolized are introduced into each other and *saṇgyog,* union, is accomplished. The bijmantra is an utterance, a sacred syllable that is also offered in the form of a flower and is placed on the seed vessel of the lotus. The syllable may also be written in oil on the ground. The purpose is to bring the goddess and the male god together in the symbolism of the pūjā. Only through the meeting of these principles does creation come about, but beyond creation all activity is at the behest of this union. In the yantra the pīthasthān of the goddess is symbolized, the original locality upon which the goddess first appeared and initiated creation. The pith pūjā of the yantra is the *ādisthan,* the original place or seat of the goddess. The jogkriyā have the same purpose: to bring about a union.

The different images of Durgā vary in their construction: the many aspects of the goddess associated with the killing of different demons (*āsurbodh*) have different forms (*rūp*), varying especially in the number of arms. Popularly the arms are associated with the intensity of battle; the goddess needs more arms to kill the greater, more famous āsuras. Different images have a varying number of arms: Jāgaddhatrī Durgā is two- or four-armed, the traditional Durgā image is ten-armed, the Bisvalakkhī image is either ten-, eighteen-, or twenty-six-armed. The rājā's image is made of gold, a sign of wealth and royalty. The image is brought out for public view and worship once a year. Images of clay and of metal cannot be worshiped at the same time in the same locality; deities are mainly identified through their pīthasthān, the locality of their manifestation. Nevertheless, the painting of the goddess is worshiped together with the Bisvalakkhī, and the golden engraving is placed in the little white shrine of the goddess together with the other representations. But these never intrude on each others' locality, since they stand on separate ground.

The Mahāsnān utilizes not only the kinds of water into which texts classify rivers, lakes, and ponds, but also different orders of water within each major class. The waters of sacred rivers and the sea are all represented, and so are the qualities of water; hot, cold, rain, lake, and so on. (This is not an ethnoscientific classification of nature; each division stands for something else and does not merely exhaust a "natural" series.) Earth is also taken from the classes into which soil, mud, and earth are classified not only according to quality but also by locality: earth of meadow and plowland, earth from a prostitute's house, and earth from a Brāhmaṇ's threshold. Different kinds of virtue are symbolized here; the Brāhmaṇ stands for sacredness, the prostitute for the sacredness of all those who visit her and thereby lose their virtue at her doorstep. There is clay from the burning ground and from the sacred rivers. In all, twenty-seven items are mixed into the *snānjal,* the water of the bath or oblation (just as there are twenty-seven items on the maṅgal patra).

The onlookers are a multicaste crowd; all castes, high and low, have access to the king's temples. The temples fall into everyone's sphere of "authority" (*adhikār*). The attitude in Mahāsnān is one of *bhakti* (devotion); people watch in silence, calling Durgā's names from time to time. A sight (*darśan*) of the goddess in this auspicious pūjā is *maṅgalik* (bringing the blessings of the goddess to the participants). Darśan is an attitude of expectation, reverence, and satisfaction—silent and quiet. It is the participation of the whole community in the pūjā, a witness and adoration. Townspeople explain their participation in these terms; to see the goddess, to adore her in a silent way, is a general aim in Durgāpūjā. The fullest meaning of darśan is revealed on the evening of the ninth, when the whole town takes to the streets and crowds flow from image to image, temple to temple, taking sights of and doing praṇām to the goddess.

The Pūjās of Nabamī and Dasamī

The worship on Nabamī morning is shorter and simpler than the previous pūjās. From the early morning devotees are coming to receive their *prasad*. There are more nāmgotra pūjās: this time men and children, as well as women, have pūjās done on their behalf. Some make the flower offering, repeating a series of mantras after the priest and offering flowers to the goddess three times, throwing cupped handfuls of flowers and leaves in the direction of the goddess (*añjali*). Durgāpūjā in Calcutta presents a sharp contrast to that in Vishnupur: festive groups of people go in large groups from one pūjā paṇḍal to another on this day (there are dozens of public pūjās in each major street, rivaling each other in magnificence), performing the añjali in each place. In the public rituals of Vishnupur añjali tends to be done individually rather than in big groups. The exception is Sarasvatīpūjā, when people of all jātis go around the public pūjā paṇḍals offering flowers to the goddess of learning. (This change has been wrought by students, but it can be seen in the occupation-oriented Visvakarma pūjās as well.)

The evening of Nabamī is given to festivities and enjoyment. The whole town takes to the streets, dressed in new clothes, and visits many of the two hundred or more images, admiring the artistry of the carpenters, commenting on the decorations and lights, but primarily adoring the goddess, taking darśan of her, doing praṇām to her, and speaking of her beauty and power. The priests are busy giving drops of the snānjal and petals of pūjā flowers to all comers. People of all jātis participate in this ceremonial circumambulation of the town. However, not all worship is open to everyone; caste and line pūjās may be restricted. Even there, however, taking sight of the goddess is open to all, even in the case of household pūjās.

Greeting the different images is a very meritorious and auspicious activity. People receive their offerings on this day; *prasad* (leavings of the goddess) are sacred (pabittra) because these were touched by the goddess. Prasad is the *ēto* (polluted food) of the goddess, but for men it is the most sacred food. In the same way, at home a wife may eat the ēto of her husband, and children that of their father and of their elders. Sometimes the lowest castes take the ēto of the Brāhmaṇs.

The difference in the Nabamīpūjā comes in the worship of a series of additional deities whose representations are not revealed to the people. A number of paintings are brought from the king's house for just the last two days of worship. These are rolled up and placed behind the painting of the Choṭoṭhākurānī. These paintings represent other forms of the goddess, among them Manasā, the goddess of snakes (daughter of Śiva and rival of Durgā-Parvatī in the mythology). The forms of Śiva, especially Bhairab, are also represented in these paintings. But the worship concentrates on one particular form of the goddess: Kaccarbahini, the Goddess Who Rides on the Mule. This Debī is also a form of Durgā, and she is offered pūjā at midnight on Nabamī day; but no one is allowed to witness the pūjā except the king and the priest. The painting itself cannot be repainted; even the priest offers flowers with his back turned to it.[12] The image is regarded as a very powerful one: there are many legends about foolhardy men who tried to unroll the painting and see the goddess, meeting their death shortly thereafter in strange circumstances.

The tenth and final day, Dasamī, is quite different in character. It is Bijayā day, the Victory of the Goddess, the celebration of her struggle and her defeat of the āsuras. But it is also the celebration of her departure, and so there is an element of nostalgia and sadness in the rituals, especially in the household pūjās. The pūjā is short, since the goddess is already on her way. The offerings are performed with water and flowers only; there is no bhogpūjā; only items that can be carried easily are offered. Instead of cooked rice there is cold *pāyas* (rice cooked with milk and sugar), fried cakes, curds, sweets, and honey. The pūjās of the various deities are perfunctory, and the long series of oblations and acts of service are abbreviated.

The major ritual of the pūjā is the recitation of the *bisarjan* mantra, the sacred formula that takes away the life of the image. The life the priest placed into the image on the seventh morning is reassumed, and the image becomes a mere doll again. The ghat is immersed immediately after the pūjā, and the lifeless image or paṭ is kept in the temple until evening. After the immersion mantra is recited, the ghat must be immersed.[13] The ghat is the abode of the goddess, and after she is asked to leave, the ghat cannot stay. In the mantra the goddess is informed respectfully that the pūjā is over and she can return to her home in the mountains; she need not take offense at the request but should come back again a year later, when she will be called once more to the festival. The immersion is performed at the water's edge. The priests place the Durgāpaṭs on small seats while they recite mantras, gradually dismantling the nabapatrika and immersing the plants one by one. Drops of water are sprinkled on the paintings as a sign of immersion and departure. Oblations are offered to the different deities—milk, honey, curds, ghī, and sugar. Bells and percussion instruments signify the offering, then the ghats are taken out to midstream, the water is slowly poured out, pūjā flowers are immersed, and mango leaves and green coconuts are sunk into the deep. Then the ghats are filled with new water and, together with the Durgāpaṭs, are taken in procession back to the temple. There the priests sprinkle the water of peace, *santijal,* on the worshipers and on the objects around. All bow down, for the water should not touch the feet. Durgāpūjā is over, but the water of peace may be kept in the house during the coming year as a sign of blessing and auspiciousness.

A Provisional Analysis

The goddess is obviously a very complex divinity. The term Debī may designate any one of her myriad manifestations, just as the term for one aspect may designate the whole. "Durgā" is most commonly associated with "Debī," but this does not make the host of other goddesses redundant. As we shall see, the relationship among goddesses is hierarchical: Debī is the most general term, and among her manifestations Durgā is the most encompassing one. There are several levels of meaning in the system of relationships within which the goddess participates: social functions and situations, human dispositions, units of time, divisions of space and locality, rules and guides for living, and so forth.

The pūjās of the goddess divide and unify social and geographical space of the town and beyond. Again we arrive at hierarchy: among other things, the goddess is Bharat Mātā (Mother India), an all-India symbol in Vishnupur. On the most general level of ideology, the goddess designates not merely the town, or the kingdom, or Bengal, but India as a whole. This representation is to be considered quite apart from the quantifiable answer to how many townspeople believe their goddess is also that of India. Next, she is the goddess of Bengalis (no matter where they are), and only then is she Mrinmoyī, the goddess of Mallabhum. More particularly, she may be the goddess of specific jātis, lines, neighborhoods, and sects. These are not exclusive but hierarchical divisions of a whole, and the goddess has meanings on all levels. The individual householder may regard Durgā as his married daughter on a visit home, but he may also worship the same image as Mother India or as the genetrix of his caste.

The divisions of Durgāpūjā designate dimensions of space, society, and ideology (the former two themselves being dialectically related to the latter). Specific pūjās celebrate the timeless, limitless dimensions of the goddess (the community rituals of the Hindu Satkar Samity, for example). In all cases, however, the pūjās relate land, locality, and people to each other in a direct and particular way. Thus we are yielded unity and diversity in one stroke, without contradiction and without either substantive merging or separation.[14]

The levels noted above are immediately recognizable in a different form in the myths and legends of Durgāpūjā. Foremost are the great Purāṇic myths of the goddess as the genetrix of the world and the symbol of the creative principle. These are not just the property of Brāhmaṇic or esoteric knowledge, however, nor are they merely hidden in sacred texts. The great myths are common property and well known throughout the town. On the other hand, the countless stories about the married life of Śiva and Durgā are not emphasized in Durgāpūjā, finding a more ready expression in the bratas of women. The narratives of the Markandiya Purāṇ are selectively present in all Durgāpūjās of the town (including some myths of Śiva and Durgā as a married couple). The most persistent version of the latter is the legend of Durgā's return to her father's house. Here we no longer face a division or discontinuity between oral and written traditions. Nor can we oppose myth to ritual and recitation to performance in narrative. Durgā's return is *śāstra* (as both a verbal and a textual tradition; see p. 17): the performance attests to the reality of the belief, and the belief is enacted in the performance.

The creator goddess is part of an all-India ideology, while other narratives (myths, legends, and stories as well as pūjās) are associated with the smaller segments of society and locality noted above. Thus, starting with purāṇic and other stories, we arrive at the same divisions we found in our account of pūjās and goddesses: hierarchy and segmentation in locality, society, and ideology. We must realize, however, that the same characteristics are true of the Purāṇas themselves: the creator goddess, the mischievous lover, and the chaste wife of Śiva are clearly distinguishable. In each aspect the goddess has a name that applies to a particular context (or contexts) and should not be confused with any others. As genetrix, the goddess is Ādi or Āddā Śakti; as the savior of the gods, she is Caṇḍī, Caṇḍikā, Cāmuṇḍā, or Mahiṣamardinī, depending on the particular situation in which she is involved. As the wife of Śiva she is Gaurī, Parvatī, or Satī, depending on the particular time (*yuga*) and incarnation or appearance of her form. These purāṇic levels are approachable through oral traditions of the goddess in Vishnupur. At the same time, the purely local context of some narratives is equally evident. Yet even the Purāṇas are a territorially and ideologically bounded unit, and the Upapurāṇas are even more localized in their significance. The Maṅgala literature of Bengal is specifically definable in terms of territory and kingship. The Mrinmoyī myths of Vishnupur could well form the basis of an Upapurāṇa or a Maṅgal Kāviyā even if we do not know of such a longer, still extant narrative poem. Several shorter poems and māhīmā katha narratives of Mrinmoyī apparently do exist. This goddess has to be viewed in the same systemic relationships as those we find in the Purāṇas. Surat Rājā, first king to worship Caṇḍī, is in the same relationship to that goddess as the Vishnupur kings are to Mrinmoyī. Thus the hierarchically encompassing deities do not remain constant through space and time: the Caṇḍī of the Markandiya Purāṇ is the Durgā of present-day Bengal, and the Mahiṣamardinī of Surat Rājā is the Mrinmoyī of Vishnupur. The relationships are the same, the identities change.

The narratives of Mrinmoyī designate the town and the region (Mallabhum) as locality or territory in Durgāpūjā. In the same manner, the myths of Durgā as the creator of fisherman and shell-carver jātis define caste, and the stories of the goddess as the returning daughter designate the household group in pūjā. Myths of Durgā as mother and savior have less to do with territory, though even then the locality and society aspects of the performance (and the desired benefits of the pūjā) are unmistakable. At the same time, the goddess does refer us to situations and dispositions. This is evident in the worship of Durgā as mother, as creative principle, and as the protector of the household group (in the brata rituals of women). Myths recited in association with bratas deal with existential situations of danger, fear, protection, and life-cycle transitions.

The festival proceeds through several stages, even in its initial phase: *baran* (welcome), *kalpa* (period), *ghatpūjā* and nabapatrika *snān* (invocations), and the service of the three Ṭhākurānīs. These amount to the sequential aspect of whole pūjā scheme. The performance itself involves several classes of ritualists: priests of the rājā's line and temple priests of Mrinmoyī. The functional divisions of tantrik and bhattacharya cut across this division. The importance of sacred texts is shown clearly in the role of the tantrik: the reciter of the ritual text is separated from the performer. The responsibility for the rites is also divided: the tantrik is the more scholarly (well versed in Sanskirt and proper pronunciation); his presence mitigates the possibility of error. But the bhattacharya does the actual performance, and in repeating the words of the tantrik and executing the actions and gestures, the responsibility is the bhattacharya's. If there is a mistake, if a mantra is mispronounced, all kinds of dire consequences may follow for both the performer and the offerer (on whose behalf the pūjā is performed).

The text used in the rājā's pūjā is an old one. According to the priests and the members of the royal line, the text preserved on palm leaves in a handwritten script is the same one the rājās followed from the inception of the pūjā (and the establishment of the town), dating back to the tenth century A.D. This text is part of a lost Upapurāṇa. Upapurāṇas are usually divided into eighteen parts, and one of these is devoted to the annual worship of the goddess, complete with mantras, meditations (*dhyen*), and rules for the performance of the pūjās. They are limited to particular deities and give a full range of commentary, myths, textual rules, and so forth in relation to that deity as well as a number of other deities (in which case the host of other gods are placed in positions hierarchically inferior to the major deity of the narrative). The rules of performance pertain to annual, seasonal, monthly, and daily worship and include a practical guide for total devotion to a particular deity. Many Upapurāṇas are regional in significance, and many of these are lost, surviving only in fragments. The majority are in manuscript form (whereas the major Purāṇas have been published many times since the mid-nineteenth century).

The rājā's text belongs to a lost Upapurāṇa (the Boli Narayan), and it is significant that the ritual (guide for performance) fragments of the text survive while the stories and legends are lost. Many other line pūjās follow the rājā's texts; still others use different Upapurāṇas (of these some are also fragments of lost narratives). The use of texts shows significant variations. Community pūjās generally utilize the Bengali printed versions of the ritual texts included in the Debīpurāṇa and the Kālikāpurāṇa. These are the most popular Upapurāṇas. The cheap printed editions not only give the rules for the performance of the pūjā, but present them in full, including diagrams for the positions of the hands in various mudras. Jāti pūjās usually follow the same upapurāṇic rules. The texts are printed in large type, with explanatory notes, and even Sanskrit verses are printed in the Bengali script. The rules specify places in the ritual sequence where local, regional, and even household and line variations of performance (*ācār,* tradition, habit, custom) can be accommodated or substituted.

Each major day has its own specific pūjās as well as the daily recurring rituals. A section at the beginning of the Darpan gives these pūjās, mantras, and rules of performance. The Darpan also gives the rites according to the Debīpurāṇa and the Kālikāpurāṇa. The two weeks or so before Ṣaṣṭhīpūjā are divided into several periods in accordance with the various invocations of the three Ṭhākurānīs in the rājā's festival. The new moon falling into this period is a special one and is known as Mahālaya (abode of the great), and the famous Caṇḍī myth of the goddess is recited at dawn.

The daily (*nitya*) pūjās are opposed to the special rites of each "welcoming" day and of the days following Ṣaṣṭhī. Nitya also means eternal, unchanging, and the special rites are in addition to nitya rites. Thus the festival includes continuity and stages of development building up to a climax. The names designating and separating each stage and the nitya pūjās are significant in that they constitute both the continuity and the construction of development in the festival.

Rājā, priest, and deity form the basic relations of Durgāpūjā. But many other functions are performed during the festival, and these are also in the position of a ritualist (or performer) in relation to deity and offerer (king or anyone else on whose behalf the pūjā is offered). The functions I refer to are those of the special jātis surrounding the king (cannon attendants, bodyguards, musicians, flower-gatherers, image-makers, sweepers, and so forth). They are necessary (although not sufficient) for the performance of Durgāpūjā, and, like the priests, they belong to the full complement of groups necessary for the maintenance of large-scale temple worship. They are not equivalent in relation to king and deity: they are inferior to the priest and are hierarchically encompassed by the priest's role vis-à-vis the other two categories. The priest is the performer parexcellence of the Durgāpūjā.

The second phase of the festival lasts from the Debīpūjā of the seventh to the Day of Immersion. Many additional offerings and actions make their appearance in this phase of the festival. It is worth noting the categories of these expanded series of relationships.

The notions of establishment, dedication, consecration, and installation refer to the introduction of life into a representation of divinity. In their different ways, these actions make the material representation of divinity a dwelling fit for the gods. The ghat, the vessel of invocation, is "established" by being placed on a locality and consecrated for the reception of the gods. Locality and divinity are linked in the act of consecration. Images of deities are given life in a complex series of actions that transform the lifeless image into a living god. The priest goes through various yogic actions that amount to the symbolic transference of life from the ritualist to the representation of a deity, thus allowing the service of that divinity as a living being. Not only vessels and images are "established" and consecrated for the purpose of pūjā, but also trees, water tanks, and houses. An "established" object is regarded as auspicious, the dwelling place of divinity. Such objects may then be offered pūjās.

In the prānpratiṣ́ṭhā rites, actions, objects, and recitations have to do with the relation between ritualist and deity. In the course of giving life to the image, a series of classifications and divisions are established only to be unified and reconstituted. The elements of life, force, body, and person (self) are separated and then reunited in order to invest the image of the goddess with life. The classification and recreation of life yields an indigenous system of knowledge and symbolic action: the very act of representing units and elements of an abstract scheme and of bringing them into specific relationships in the ritual brings about the efficacy of what is being expressed or represented. Thus, beyond a classificatory system the rituals set something in motion (in terms of the scheme) to recreate and maintain the way things are supposed to happen in the world, restating the way things (and life itself) were created. However, these actions are brought to bear on the goddess herself, her presence in the town, and her relationship to the people. Therefore the festival is not just a celebration of abstract cosmic forms and classificatory principles: the elements of knowledge are focused on action in the world, among people.

The expanded series of offerings start with purifying water of all possible kinds and progress through different kinds of juices (*ras*), plants, foliage, grains, the sixteen items of pūjā offerings, and the twenty-seven items on the auspicious plate. Then there are seven kinds of earth, emphasizing, in the first instance, the locality of the worship. Footprints of deities and saints are powerful symbols, and dust is gathered from the feet of preceptors, ritualists in festivals, and of elders in everyday life. In all these cases superiority is expressed, but the dust itself is auspicious and, especially in the case of saints and ritualists, is kept by the recipient. The seven kinds of earth also signify different localities and situations or dispositions a locality may refer to.

The yantra of the goddess also makes an appearance: it is another representation of locality, the ground upon which deities stand, the diagram into which the gods are invoked and in which they make their appearance. Yantra is also a symbol of śakti and belongs to the next series of elaboration directly having to do with the goddess. Yantra, ābāran debatās, and so forth reinforce my earlier reflections on hierarchical encompassment. The various aspects of Durgā in the yantra are manifestations of the goddess encompassed in the form centrally celebrated in the Durgāpūjā. As such, the other goddesses are hierarchically inferior to Durgā herself.

The actions performed by the priest concern not only the goddess but the performer and the other participants as well. The meaning of these symbolic actions can be extended to higher levels of abstraction until we reach the theology of worship. But that is not my aim in this discussion, since I want to stay close to the actions and ideologies of the performers. Even then we must distinguish between the esoteric knowledge of sectarian celebration and theological refinement, on the one hand, and the everyday systems of actions, knowledge, ideology, and representation on the other. The former used to be a jealously guarded secret of specialists, initiates, and Brāhmaṇs (the teachers of the Vedas). But this distinction is blurred today by the growth of community worship, the printing of sacred texts, and the growing participation of non-Brāhmaṇs (especially mid- and low-status jātis) in seasonal festivals. Sacred mantras are available to anyone who can read, and devotional movements initiate all who are willing into once esoteric practices. There are several śūdras (men not "twice born") in the town who are celebrated for their knowledge of the Śāstras, superior to that of any Brāhmaṇ. Cheap translations, commentaries, and exegeses of the sacred texts are sold in dozens of places in the town.

Yet these facts themselves should caution us against accepting all pūjā exegeses on the same level. The distinction is not between Brāhmaṇs and non-Brāhmaṇs, or Sanskritic and local, or Great Traditional and folk traditional complexes; rather, it is between the sociological and the theological: I do not propose to elaborate the latter. I discuss levels other than Brāhmaṇic and non-Brāhmaṇic in my account, and I do not skirt the problems posed by the participation of sacred texts in everyday life. Of course the sociological and the theological are linked to some degree, and I make the distinction purely as a heuristic device, to formulate a point for cutting off my exegeses. I follow the ritual specialist and other exegeses to the point where we have grounds for constructing systems in relation to action, since the ideologies assert the systematic nature of the actions we want to understand. But I do not venture beyond, where specific schemes of knowledge are elaborated in great detail. Yet because the two realms are linked the task is simplified: the division of time also forms part of astrology; the classification of the plant world enters into systems of medicine; the gestures of pūjā are part of yogic practices; the principles of worship are related to ancient and ongoing discussions of philosophic systems. Thus we pursue matters that become, at some distance, the legitimate concern of specific disciplines (and form the core of specific systems of indigenous knowledge).

Honoring the gods, bringing them to earth, giving them life, and so forth is based on classification, symbolism, and logic. The task of the anthropologist is not only to construct the system and reveal the elegance of the logic, but to show the relations among the parts and of the parts to the whole. Thus we note pūjā schemes, classificatory series, and indigenous models of the world, but we are also interested in the relationships among different categories; in reciprocity among deity, ritualist, and offerer; and in sharing, replacement, transformation, exchange, and continuity of relationships among groups of people, objects, symbols, and ideologies.

To follow how the gods are given life, how ritualists become gods to serve the gods, how the benefits of the performance reach the people, we must rely on priestly and other specialist exegesis. The rest of the performance (and of the system as I have described it) demands this. Without it the pūjā scheme would not be full, for the priest is an essential factor in the scheme of things. Ideology and action, exegeses of the performers, the performance, and the participants make up the universe of our discourse. From there the anthropologist may reach higher and wider planes in pursuit of understanding, but always in relation to that basic configuration.

The Aśṭamīpūjās introduce further extension and refinement of a logic already noted. The Great Bathing Festival (noted for Saptamī in the texts), Sandhi and yantra pūjās celebrate the goddess in even more ways, manifestations, situations, and localities than any of the previous days' pūjās. But no new classificatory elements are added. Rather, new relationships are established within a wider field to reach the limits of the indigenously known universe. In sociomorphological terms, we note the greater participation of people. The nāmgotra pūjās allow townsmen to have the priest make offerings on their behalf and to receive, in turn, boons and blessings from the goddess. In this sense the people come to stand in the same relationship to the goddess as does the king.

Sandhipūjā reveals the king's relation to goddess and priest most clearly. The moment that renders the structure of pūjā visible also marks the developmental climax of the festival: the arrival of the goddess among the worshipers. Divisions of society, ritual, time, and ideology are thus linked in one moment of the festival.

The sandhi yantra is hierarchically as significant as the sandhi moment itself. The colors, petals, and center of the diagram represent a host of goddesses, with their counterparts in the aspects of Śiva. This yantra encompasses all the hierarchical divisions within the goddess. The exegesis of the yantra confirms our previous account of Durgā in relation to other goddesses. The yantra and its internal divisions is like the court of a king. To reach the rulers one has to pass servants, soldiers, attendants, and advisers. But the different goddesses represent more: the destructive, creative, punishing, and benevolent aspects of the goddess. Each aspect has a separate identity defined in terms of situation, locality, and time. All of them link Durgā to the great purāṇic goddess. Purāṇic events take place in sacred time, the time of the gods; yet even there divisions in the form of ages or yugas separate the manifestations of the goddess. Among men the goddess also represents units of time: the "covering" deities include the phases of the moon and the twenty-seven stars. The moon itself is a female deity, and all the pūjās of the goddess occur in the different phases of the moon. A way of classifying time is symbolic of the goddess. The days of the festival are lunar; thus the lunar cycle from pūjā to pūjā completes the year in the worship of the goddess.

The last two days lend a twofold significance to the festival as a whole. They complete and bring to conclusion many lines of action initiated during the previous days, and they prepare for the return to everyday life. Nabamī is the most active day for most participants: the prasad of the goddess is distributed to the people. This act is also a hierarchical one, since normally the acceptance of food left by somebody else (*ēto*) is polluting. *Prasad* is sacred for men because it is left by the goddess, thus emphasizing the inferiority of men to the gods. Similarly, wives may take the ēto of husbands, children that of adults, low jātis that of high jātis. Prasad is beneficial just because of the separation and the identity of the goddess (and not merely of a general class of deities).

Visiting the images of the goddess is also significant in two ways. Taking sight of the goddess is a reciprocal relationship: Durgā sees the devotee, and the latter receives a beneficial effect. Visitations and processions link the different localities of the town and allow organizations, voluntary groups, neighborhoods, and households to display the magnificence of their pūjās.

The remaining though unique rites of Nabamī are local in every way: the deities served at night and in secret are in a special relationship to the royal line (brought about in ways noted in the legends or through the worship of the service jātis of the kings). These pūjās are not noted in the texts, yet they are important in telling us how new details and additions are created along lines already known. The series of local deities become part of the festival system and confirm our suggestions about the inadvisability of separating the Sanskritic or Brāhmaṇic levels from the local ones. The levels are to be sought within a whole and with more discriminations, on the basis of our data, than simple dichotomies allow.

The final day is a rite of reversal: I have noted the inversion of rules and the unusually free and easy relations between young and old and kin of various classes. The Purāṇas counsel devotees to sing obscene songs and to engage in general revelry—a reversal of normal conduct indeed.

The immersion ceremony is itself symbolic in several ways. Water is the pathway of the gods: the ghat (the dwelling of the gods) is returned to the river or lake, and the clay image of the goddess "travels" through the water (as the vehicle of the departing goddess). The ghat is refilled with water and this water of peace represents the coming year and remains as an a auspicious sign of the Goddess's return. Water is linked to earth: both are placed in the ghat (as, indeed, both are used in making the clay ghat), and both take part in the making and the dissolution—through immersion—of the image.

The whole year is summed up in the mantra of immersion: the festival is brought to an end, and Durgā is asked to return twelve months later. Departure is also expressed by the food offerings: only uncooked, cold foods are given to the goddess. The household pūjās emphasize the role of women: the closing rites of the goddess are performed in exactly the same manner as those of a bride departing after the wedding.

Several rituals follow the end of Durgāpūjā. The image itself (though not the ghat) may stay eight days, when another women's ritual is performed, *aśṭamaṅgala*. In these rites of welcome the goddess is again treated as a married daughter who returns to her father's house after the wedding. The image is then immersed. Three days after Dasamī, several localities of the town perform *Rāvanbodh*—Rāma's killing of Rāvan. Masked dancers proceed through the town dressed as Rāma, Hanumān, and Lakṣman, performing and collecting money as they go. At night the ten heads of Rāvan (represented by a clay or straw image) are cut off by Rāma (amid a display of sword and stick fighting with a statue of Rāma looking on), and the assembled multitude tramples on the headless body of Rāvan. The performance is attended by brief pūjās of Durgā and Kṛṣṇa, thus linking together the Durgā, Śiva, and Viṣṇu cycles of worship.

Chapter Three

The Festival of the Lord

The Organization of Gājan

The Ṣāṛeśvar temple used to belong to the Vishnupur kings, but now the area is the property of a local *zamindar* (a landholder under Mughal and British rule); hence bhaktas call on both the local landowner and the Vishnuper rājā. Daily pūjās throughout the year are performed by a line of Brāhmaṇs. During the gājan several other lines officiate. The pūjā of the Śiva temple originally belonged to the line of the rājā's priest. Today several segmented lines divide up the pūjās of the year among themselves: one line takes care of the temple throughout the year, another looks after the Bhairab temple nearby, two others officiate at the pūjās of the Śiva image, and two more serve at the special rituals of the festival (such as the "burning of incense"). The Brāhmaṇs also cook food offerings (bhog) for Śiva, and they clean the temples and let the organizers know what items are needed for the festival.

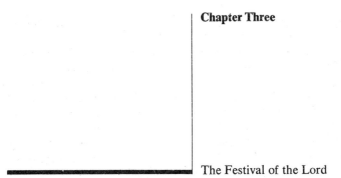

Though the gājan is entirely a voluntary performance, preparations must be made for large crowds. The Ṣāṛeśvar gājan attracts seven to eight hundred full-fledged bhaktas every year (estimates range from six hundred to well over a thousand; my own rough count yielded about seven hundred participants but did not cover the whole area of the gājan). The families of bhaktas, nonbhakta worshipers, spectators, and buyers and sellers at the fairs that accompany every public ritual in Bengal involve fifteen thousand to twenty-five thousand people (in recent years the numbers have been increasing steadily). About one-half to two-thirds of the bhaktas come from the town; the rest are villagers from localities up to twenty or thirty miles away. Other gājans of the region do not attract more than fifteen to twenty-five devotees, the maximum most village performances can cope with. An exception are the ābārgājans of Vishnupur town, where there may be eighty to one hundred bhaktas. The ābārgājans in the town are performed on Boiśakhī Purnimā (full moon) and Boiśakhī Saṇkraṇti (end of the solar month). In 1968 these two rituals coincided because Purnimā fell on the day before Saṇkraṇti. Two of the main Śiva temples are the scene of these gājans.

The ābārgājan of Buṛo Śiva (the Old One) is performed during the days leading up to the Boiśakhī Saṇkraṇti. The Buṛo Śiva temple is in Gopālganj, one of the major *ganja*s (market sections) of the town, and the gājan is that of the Āṭpāṛā division.

The ābārgājan of the Boltalā Śiva temple is the festival of the rival Egāropāṛā (another major division). Some devotees connect the gājan with the traditional rivalry between the two major divisions (clearest in the chariot festival of Kṛṣṇa); others deny it, being faithful to the ideology of Śiva worship. Ceremonial procession take place during each of these gājans, defining and separating the two rituals as well as the two localities. One day of the festival the devotees of Buṛo Śiva call on Boltalā Śiva and offer pūjā as a group. Boltalā bhaktas return the compliment during their gājan. The oldest Śiva temple in the town, Malleśvar Śiva, does not have a gājan in its honor. There were gājans there not so long ago, and old men can recall those times. Nevertheless the Baispāṛā division (the third major spatial unit), within which fall both the Malleśvar Śiva temple and the biggest Kṛṣṇa temple, no longer mounts any of the rituals that define the spatial units of the town.

The Ṣāṛeśvar gājan belongs to the whole town. The organizers, however (by default of the king, who cannot afford to mount this vast festival), come from the Egāropāṛā division. These men are also the leading bazaar merchants, and for this reason the collection of money and food items for the gājan and the preparations for the ṣolaānā celebration are the responsibility of the bazaar.[1] The organizers also become bhaktas and stay at the temple for the duration of the gājan, sleeping and eating there just like the rest of the devotees. The final three days and nights must be spent at the temple itself, and nobody goes home at sunset (as they do on previous days). The gājan is also a ṣolaānā pūjā, a community worship par excellence. There is no line, caste, or individual performance of gājan; it is public by definition. Bhaktas come from different localities, and these ties are visible even in this leveling set of rituals.

Because of the large number of participants, a breakdown into groups is necessary, if only for sleeping and eating accommodations. People from the same locality tend to camp and eat together, especially those from the more distant villages. For the ṣolaānā, the organizers arrange food and accommodations, but not all bhaktas call on these services. Revenue derived from several temple festivals is used for ṣolaānā expenses. The organizers collect money from traders and hawkers at the Ṣāṛeśvar fair held in conjunction with the Pouś parab (January), Baruni pūjā (February), and different Śiva pūjās. Each bhakta contributes a small amount, since the food offerings to the deities also come from the ṣolaānā. The organizers act as the pūjā committee acts during Durgāpūjā. They must let the priests know about the pūjā, choose (in consultation with the priest) a number of leading bhaktas for special duties, confirm the arrangements made for devotees at the temple site, procure all necessary items for the worship, instruct new devotees in the rules (*niyam*) and duties (*dharma*) of the gājan, check that everyone has the required objects for the pūjā, supervise the daily activities at the festival, and be on hand should any trouble or transgression occur. These men are leaders in their own right (especially in their own localities). They tend to be high caste, but this is not a rule. They are, almost to a man, *paricalok* (leading men) or belong to weighty "aristocratic" lines, of dominant position or high in status. These men also take up subscriptions from merchants of the bazaar, townsmen, and anyone who is willing to give. Big men (*baṛolok*) and the wealthy are also asked to contribute. Every new bhakta must contribute a number of items to the gājan, including a small amount of money. The amounts thus collected are spent on offerings, food, and the fees of ritualists.

Everyone has a right (*adhikār*) to take part in the gājan and to worship at the temples. Śiva recognizes no caste differences (*jāti-bicār*). The central feature of the gājan is the obliteration of caste distinctions: Brāhmaṇs and lowest-jāti Mucis (leather workers) worship side by side.[2] Since the king can no longer maintain all temples and priestly lines, the community councils look after most royal temples, but this is not a new feature in this area. The fact that a temple belonged to the king allowed all townsmen to worship there and to take part in the festivals, because people also "belong" to the king. King and subjects (*prajā*) formed a whole, the rājā's authority extending over all lands and people in the kingdom. Conversely, the king had a responsibility to his subjects. One such duty was to maintain worship and rituals. The kings of Vishnupur donated great tracts of land to temples and to lines of ritualists (not just Brāhmaṇs). Hence, even today people say that a festival or a temple is that of the community because it was once the king's.

Men of the bazaar cannot make arrangements for all eight hundred bhaktas, but they look after the needs of about two to three hundred, most of whom are townsmen. This feature of the gājan allows the formation of loose groups, even though there is no conscious separation of people in the performance of the rituals. On the contrary, there is an explicit egalitarian ideology; both high- and low-caste devotees stress the obliteration of caste barriers in the gājan. Such loose groups may not last beyond the period of the festival, nor can they be recognized in the performance of the rituals themselves. The primary division is between townsmen and villagers. Men from the different sections of the town tend to make arrangements for eating and sleeping in the same area. Men of the same village also tend to stay together. Many bhaktas have their wives bring their food every day (both the highest- and the lowest-caste devotees might do this). Many, however, take advantage of the ṣolaānā preparations. Every night after sundown the men of the bazaar distribute food to all who want it. The communal food store is kept in the twin of Ṣāṛeśvar Śiva, the Śālleśvar temple. The lord sanctifies food, keeps it "cool," and everything coming from there is sacred (*pabittra*).

The Ābārgājans

Bhaktas at these gājans average about forty for one and ninety for the other. The locality aspect of participation is also more clearly emphasized. The Śiva temples of the ābārgājans belong to and define larger sections of the town. Participants invariably come from these divisions. The organization is less explicit, mainly because bhaktas can go home to eat and sleep. Nevertheless, the organization of these festivals is in the hands of the temple committees. These committees look after the affairs of the temple and the engagement of a priest (usually a hereditary line for the temple and the main festivals). The members of the committee are agreed upon by the men of the locality; usually those who serve are men who are listened to, who can raise money when needed for ritual purposes. There are neither elections nor disagreement; many can find something to do on these committees.

Committee members live in the named localities surrounding the various temples. They belong to respected families, the lines of the rājā's traditional headmen (there used to be one for each named section of the town, over and above caste headmen), the *pạcjan* (the five, meaning the group of men in an area who used to settle disputes). In addition to these undisputed leaders, there are men on the committee who cannot boast traditional attributes of "respect" and "weight." But they now have influence through new wealth and connections. Many of these are lower-caste men, which does not disturb many. The lowest castes are rarely represented on the committees, however, with the possible exception of the Sunris, liquor distillers(some of whom separated themselves from the jāti as a whole and are now called Saha; they are wealthy and mix freely with the highest castes).

The committees also arrange for the recitation of Rāmāyana or Kṛṣṇa Līlā songs during the gājan. The singers are usually townsmen of the Boiṣṇab jāti.[3] The committee sends out invitations to the gājan and solicits contributions from all over town. On the final day the ṣolaānā gives a feast to all the bhaktas, the community as a whole bearing the expenses. Committees do this for all temple festivals; gājan is only one of many that take place during the year.

Participants

Bhaktas come from all areas of the town and the region, from all walks of life, and from all castes (there are more than a hundred jātis in Vishnupur). Among them are rich merchants and landless laborers, teachers and illiterate men, students, traders, ricksha pullers, artisans, and clerks. They range from the very young to the very old. Some have performed the gājan thirty, forty, or fifty times; many (about one-fourth) are doing it for the first time. In the Ṣāṛeśvar gājan, about five-eighths of the bhaktas come from Vishnupur, and of these about two-thirds belong to the higher castes (especially the Nabasakha, the artisan castes). The remaining one-third belong to the lowest castes and castes like the goldsmiths (Subarnabanik), who are not regarded as "high" but are also separated from the "low." The proportion of these jāti clusters is different among the villagers: about one-half are low caste and one-half are "high" (including the "nonhigh," and "nonlow" castes). The population percentages of town and country are reflected in these divisions. Nevertheless, it is striking that despite the egalitarian strain in the gājan the higher castes are the more numerous participants (this being especially true of the ābārgājans in the town).[4]

In the ābārgājans, Buṛośibtalā corresponds to the divisions observed above among the urban participants of the Ṣāṛeśvar gājan. The lowest castes amount to about one-sixth of the bhaktas (they make up about one-fifth of the town's population). There are only a few participants from the lowest castes in the Boltalā gājan, which is restricted (not without dispute) to a locality where the majority of the "lower" jāti goldsmiths live (this group makes up more than one-half of the Boltalā gājan, whereas they are only one-sixth of the Buṛo Śiva gājan). The highest castes (Brāhmaṇ, Kāyastha) also participate, but in very small numbers (not more than 5 percent).

Once a man becomes a bhakta, all his contacts with the world of everyday life are severed. He is not subject to the normal rules of pollution, and a death in the family does not affect him while he wears the sacred thread. He does not eat with his family, nor does he use the objects of daily life: his way of living, dress, food, and companionship become entirely different. Though there is complete equality among the bhaktas, classes (*srenī*) of devotees are distinguished by the appointed or chosen roles they perform. These are assigned by the organizers.

The pāṭbhakta is the leader of the devotees. He is marked by various insignia that he alone can carry. The gājan and the bhaktas are both his responsibility. His work begins much earlier, since his ascetic practices are meant to secure Śiva's blessings and help for the gājan. He sees to it that all bhaktas obey the rules, and he intervenes and helps when something goes wrong. He sets the tone of the gājan; if the pāṭbhakta is a good one, the bhaktas' spirits are high. He often sits with groups of devotees, reciting stories of past gājans and telling legends about Śiva from the Purāṇas and Upapurāṇas. The *gāmārbhakta* cuts the branch of a *gāmār* tree; the *rājbhakta* is the first to garland the king; the *sannyāsībhakta* is the first to scatter burning coals with his hands in the fire ritual.

These offices of the gājan are often hereditary, and the bearers are agreed upon by the pāṭbhakta, priest, and ṣolaānā in consultation. It is a sign of honor and devotion to perform these acts.

Voluntary roles are the following: *praṇāmsebābhakta*s—devotees who measure the road to the temple with their own bodies, lying down and getting up they advance to the mark made by their outstretched hands, only to lie prostrate again, till they reach the temple; *ghurānbhakta*s—those who roll to the temple through street and field; *śālbhakta*s—those who dance with the *pāṭā* in trance; *agunsannyāsībhakta*s—those who walk on fire; *dhunaporanbhakta*s—those who burn incense in a pot, holding the pot on their heads or limbs.

Bhaktas themselves decide which of these functions they want to perform. The keynote of the gājan is individual (*bektigoti*) devotion within a collective framework. Most of the actions take place in processions, but there are also opportunities for individual worship. One of the prescribed actions of the gājan is the performance of Śiva pūjās every day, in the bhaktas' own time. The second prescription is the performance of collective offerings to the sun every day, *Suryaarghya*. Of course, bhaktas do more than is compulsory: that gives the spirit of the gājan.

Temples and Images

The temple complexes in which the rituals take place vary widely.[5] The Ṣāṛeśvar and Śālleśvar temples form a pair, standing apart from any settlement on a small hill a short distance away from the Dvarakeśvar River. The river, open fields, and a small creek winding its way around the foot of the hill play important roles in the gājan. Strewn around these localities are a series of *ṭhākursthān* (places of the lord) and smaller temples, all of which enter into the mainstream of the gājan. (see fig. 4.)

Most important is the temple of Bhairab, which is deserted during the year but is the scene of many ritual actions in the gājan. Bhairab is the powerful and terrible manifestation of Śiva. He departs from the Ṣāṛeśvar

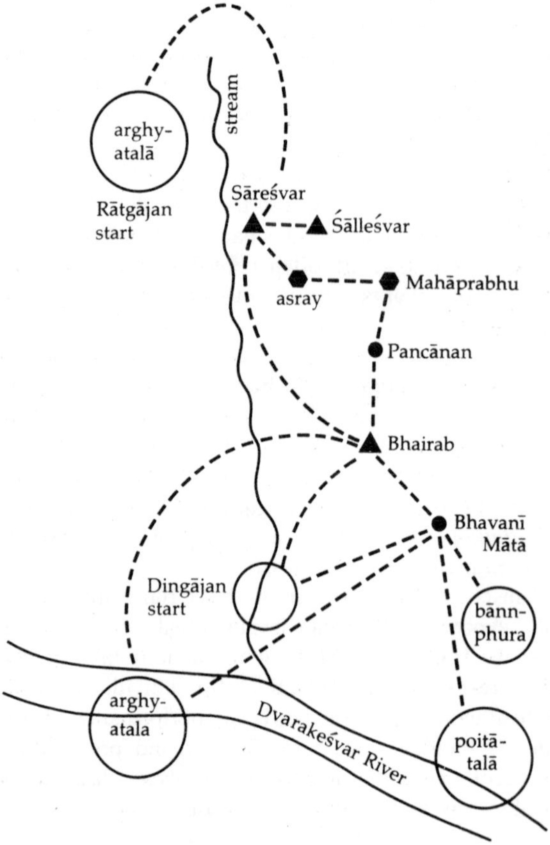

Figure 4. The Ṣāṛeśvar gājan: shrines and processions.

temple on the first major day of the festival and takes up residence in his own temple. Between the Śiva temples and Bhairab's temple is a small shrine of Paçānan (also an aspect of Śiva) and a Baul *asray* (a shelter for mendicants run by an ascetic who belongs to a loosely organized group of Vaiṣṇava initiates famous for their songs in praise of Kṛṣṇa, love of god, and life independent of worldly attachment). Not far from the Bhairab temple is the shrine of Bhavanī Mātā (as aspect of the Goddess Durgā).

The Śiva temples house representations of the deity in the shape of the liṅga and yoni (or *śaktipīth*) that symbolize the unity of Śiva and Durgā as well as the complementary relationship between the male and female principles. This double image usually stands on the floor of the temple or is sunk in a pit below floor level. The Ṣāṛeśvar temple is an example of the latter, Śālleśvar of the former. Guarding the divinity are representations of Bhairab in the shape of earthenware horses and elephants. These have accumulated over the years; having been granted a boon by the deity, grateful devotees often donate such images to the temple. In front of the temple is a stone image of Śiva's bull, Naṇdi, who is also worshiped during the gājan.

The Ṣāṛeśvar temples are of the *rekha* type (towerlike) well known from Orissa. The Boltalā and Buṛo Śiva temples are of the common Bengali type (curved roof in the shape of the straw-roofed mud huts) with a small tower on the top. Another Śiva temple stands near the Boltalā Śiva, an older, terra-cotta structure. Similarly, there are several other Śiva temples around Buṛo Śiva. These may have been established separately by different people; their names perhaps give the clue to the identity of the previous *sebāit* (those responsible for financing temple services). Now all these temples belong to the *ṣolaānā.* The temple of Santīnāth (Lord of Peace) is the most important, the other two, known only as Brāhmaṇ Bābā and Mukkha Bābā (Father Priest and Father Headman), do not enter the gājan in any significant way.

The Buṛo Śiva temple houses some old images in addition to the liṇga. The carved stone images of Suryadeb (the sun) and the goddess (Caṇḍī) are worshiped together with the Śiva liṇga that is situated in small innermost room. The Śiva of the Boltalā temple is sunk in a pit deep in the ground, with small steps leading down to the liṇga. The remarkable feature of the Buṛo Śiva gājan is the participation of a *sāddhu* (ascetic) of the Uddasin Samproday (a sect of renouncers originally from the Punjab). The gājan of this temple was revived by a sāddhu of this order (a preceptor of the present ascetic of the temple) some sixty years ago. This man was a powerful ascetic who was credited with many miracles, his distinguishing characteristic being his silence. Mouni Bābā (the Silent

Father) received a vision from Śiva commanding him to revive the gājan and to participate in it as a deputy of the Great Lord (see fig. 5).

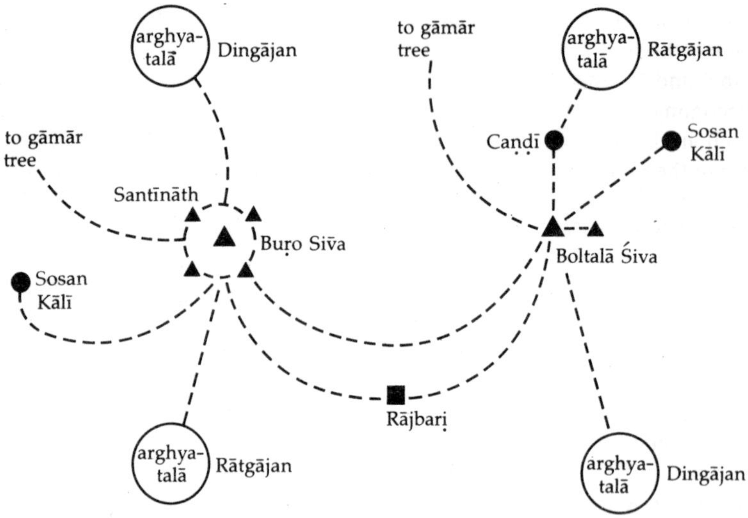

Figure 5. The ābārgājans: shrines and processions.

Receiving the Sacred Thread

Bhaktas receive the *paitā* (sacred thread) in the temple. The pāṭbhakta distributes paitās consisting of many strands that must be separated and rearranged by the Brāhmaṇ before they can be worn. Devotees also wear the sacred kusa rings on both hands. They shave the day before the ceremony but are not allowed to shave again till the paitā is discarded at the end of gājan. *Bhaktakaman* (shaving of the bhaktas) is done individually or in groups, the neighborhood barber, Nāpit, being invited to the house of a bhakta, where several others assemble. That night the devotees eat *habisanna* (ghī and rice) prepared in a special way in their own homes, and then fasting begins. In the morning they bathe in a tank or river and put on a distinctive dhotī of saffron, red, or yellow, the upper part of the body remaining naked. Bhaktas carry long canes (*beṭ*s) of wicker wood. Tying the paitā to the beṭ, they form a half-circle around the *agradhānī*, who recites the sacred verses of the pūjā. The priest's work in a pūjā is now performed by the bhaktas.

The pūjā begins with the agradhānī Brāhmaṇ reciting the mantras of purification, the bhaktas repeating the words and performing the oblations in the name of Viṣṇu. Then they perform other acts of purification: the body, soul, objects, and offerings are all taken care of in a set of mantras at the end of which the bhaktas offer water and flowers to the deities. The paitā is dipped in water and the strands are held apart by all ten fingers. Devotees then recite the most important mantra of the ritual, the formula of reversal whereby they abandon their own descent label and take on the *gotra* of the Great God himself (*Sib gotra*), thus becoming a part (*aṅga*) of the deity. Putting the sacred thread around their necks, they chant the names of Śiva with increasing fervor. They recite the names of the various Śivas in the region: Buṛo Śiva Nāthmuni Mahādeb, Ṣaṛesvar Nāthmuni Mahādeb—Old Śiva, Lord of the Seers Mahādeb. Offering flowers with folded hands, they perform the pūjās of many other deities. They use the objects associated with Brāhmaṇ priests: water jug, incense, food offerings. They mark the body with red sandalwood paste as a sign of purification. Finally, they recite the meditation verse of Śiva and bow down to the ground. Rising, they chant the names of Śiva, loudly imploring the lord to watch over them. This is the time for the priest to impress on the bhaktas their changed status, admonishing them that they are now Śiva's aṅga: you should be devout; perform pūjās; observe the laws (*niyam*), especially the rule of fasting; surrender yourselves entirely to the divinity, calling on him in need and thinking of him in trouble and pain; fix your mind firmly on Śiva, and he will take all your troubles unto himself and grant you the boons you crave. Devotees often discuss the dangers of gājan: there are countless stories of what befell those who inadvertently swallowed a drop of water during the day. Everyone is in high spirits, and the canes are hit together to the chanting of the names of Śiva.

Just after midday the devotees are called to new duties by the drummers of the low Dom jāti, paid from ṣolaānā funds, who assist at the gājan every day, playing the loud, highly resonant *ḍhāk* in unison with varying but distinctive rhythms.[6]

Offerings to the Sun

The sun is worshiped by the pāṭbhakta every afternoon from the first day on. Other bhaktas join the sun worship on the day they enter the gājan. The bhaktas assemble in the temple for the arghya. Usually the rite is done at sunset, but toward the end of the gājan the time varies. These offerings are also in the general pūjā form.[7] Bhaktas line up in the nāthmandir, filling all available space in several lines. They spread towels in front of them, placing the canes on the floor. The offerings of the pūjā fall on colored towels. The items of the worship are spread out over the towel. The pūjā is performed in three parts; bhaktas go through the initial purifications, taking water to their lips three times, reciting the mantras that purify the seat, the offerings, and other objects. At the end of this part they pour water over the flowers and other offerings and begin the worship of the different gods associated with the gājan: the five main deities (Gaṇeś, Viṣṇu, Śiva, Durgā, and the sun). Bhairab, Kālī, the different Śiva images of the region (including the Tarakeśvar Śiva sixty miles away). On reciting each mantra they offer flowers and water. The final set of mantras is accompanied by the offering of fruits, uncooked rice, and sweets. Then, facing the sinking sun, they recite the dhyen (meditation verse) of the sun god, pouring libations in the direction of the sun. After this is repeated three times, all bhaktas prostrate themselves in front of the sun and recite a final verse expressing gratitude.

Burning Incense

Bhaktas, and others also, may perform *dhunaporan* in the temple during the mornings of the gājan. This is an act of devotion in gratitude for a wish fulfilled, or a vow imploring Śiva to bestow a boon on the performer. Such acts are called *mānsik,* a promise or pledge by a devotee to undertake certain acts of worship, thus obligating the deity to act. The incense or resin is burned in an earthenware bowl placed on the devotee's body. Makers of such a mānsik fast for a day, then bathe in a temple tank and go to the deity in their wet clothes, bringing with them a bowl, bits of śāl wood, and resin. They chant the names of Śiva and ring the bell of the inner shrine. Taking their offerings, the priest performs a brief pūjā on their behalf, then kindles the fire and sprinkles resin into the bowl as the flames leap high. The bhaktas start calling Śiva, and the Doms beat the drums in faster and faster rhythms as the priest places the blazing pot on the head of the devotee. Should the devotee be afflicted in any part of the body and his vow concern a cure for disease, pots may be placed on the affected part or parts—stomach, arms, chest, or legs. The devotees rock and sway to the rhythm of the ḍhāk but ordinarily do not fall into trance. Soon the Brāhmaṇ snatches the flaming bowl away and throws it out of the temple, intentionally breaking it. The devotee prostrates himself in front of Śiva and gives the priest a *dakkhina* (small offering in coins). This is also the time for women to have nāmgotra pūjā performed for their families, especially on children's and husbands' behalf (see chap. 2 and Fruzzetti and Östör 1976*b*). Bringing uncooked food, sugar, sweets, fruits, and flowers, people may ask the Brāhmaṇs to perform pūjās for them. The temple is the scene of feverish activity; bhaktas calling the names of Śiva, doing pūjās, keeping the crowd from interfering with the rituals, devotees coming for pūjā, the Doms playing, the temple bells ringing; there is a continuous and general confusion—uproar and complete disorder as far as the unsuspecting outside observer can tell. Beyond the noisy crowd and the colorful confusion, however, there are basic and repeated patterns that everyone knows. Townspeople are used to the mounting of vast rituals without lengthy preparations.

Exegetical Discussion

Bhaktas eat a special preparation of rice, the habisanna, the best possible food. They prepare the rice themselves, in a separate part of the house, using new cooking vessels. Shaving also marks the beginning of the gājan. It may take place in the house of the headman or the house of one of the *poricalok*s (local leaders). It is a rite of purification, signifying the intent and the status of the devotee. One must be pure (*śuddha*) to become Śiva's associate. Fasting, the intent to worship, the making of a vow (*mānsik*), and eating special food define the special state of the bhakta even before he takes the sacred thread. Devotees sleep separately this night, and they wear the mendicant's garb in the morning. To show their respect for Śiva they walk barefoot to the temple. They pick flowers wherever they find them, and no one interferes. It is for the lord, for the pūjā of the father. They chant the names of Śiva and collect fruits and vegetables for the offerings to the sun and to Śiva. These items also are taken from nearby gardens and fields, but no one stops the holy thieves. The offerings cannot be bought in the market; bhaktas must procure them themselves.

The performance of gājan is purely voluntary. People realize that it is not easy to become a bhakta: daily fasting, meals of fruit and milk only after sundown, many devotional acts under the blazing Boiśakh (April) sun, sleepless and exacting nights of procession and dancing around the temples—these are powerful deterrents. Those who take part do so for many reasons. Most commonly they do it to fulfill a vow. One may request a favor or boon from Śiva and when it is received one does gājan out of gratitude. Or one may do the gājan hoping that the deity will look favorably on one's request. The most common explanation of gājan is that people want *maṅgal kāmanā,* blessings and favors that take a tangible form in everyday life. Many promise to do the gājan if the deity does something for them. The initial vow can be made at any time in any Siva temple, even without witnesses, priests, and offerings. The "contract" is between the devotee and Śiva himself. If the deity fulfills the devotee's desires and the latter fails to keep his vow, Śiva or Bhairab can make his wrath felt in many ways. He can bring ill health, wreak havoc among kin and people of the immediate locality, spoil one's livelihood, and ruin one's fortune. Śiva also punishes those who decide to do gājan but fail to observe the laws of the festival. Breaking the rule of fasting is the most common transgression. Specific sins may come to light in trance or possession: bhaktas possessed by Bhairab are questioned about the cause of their distress. The answer will result in a confession or will soon lead the officeholders of the gājan to the culprit. The deity may punish the wrongdoer directly by making him vomit out the offending article. If the transgression is very serious, the unfortunate devotee may die vomiting blood.

The most common reason for making a vow is to recover from some unpleasant and recurring disease. Many suffer from stomach pains and digestive problems that cannot be permanently cured or have not been treated successfully by other means. The last resort is Śiva. Lesser illnesses are also cured by Śiva: skin diseases, rashes, head and chest pains are the common ones. Others approach the god with wishes for male offspring—especially those who have only daughters. In this case women must also go through certain rituals. Young men may do gājan to pass examinations (especially the school-leaving examinations). Others want to secure a job—any job. But there are many gājan regulars who go through the festival year after year, either because they have made such a vow in the past or because they choose to serve the deity in this way. They want to make things a little difficult for themselves, expressing their devotion to Śiva by self-denial. In this way they can step out of the never-ending daily cycle of work, worry, and suffering and can atone for transgressions committed during the year. The life of the householder involves a series of small sins and actions against the rules of proper conduct. Bhaktas are aware that there is a conflict between *dharma* (duties appropriate to one's station vis-à-vis gods and other people) and the exigencies of living. They hope that by serving Śiva in this way, meditating upon him, and spending time with him they will be forgiven and that he may even help them in their troubles. But primarily they do the gājan as an expression of what they deem to be the proper way of adoring Śiva, thus giving the Great God his due. The time of gājan is a time for rendering services to other gods as well, and for reflecting on the role of gods and humans in the scheme of the world.

Bhaktas are also known as *sannyāsīs* (renouncers or ascetics). Siva himself is the greatest ascetic among the gods. Among the devotees the pāṭbhakta or *pradhanbhakta* carries out most of the specialized functions. All bhaktas are associated with Śiva, but the pāṭbhakta is foremost among them. *Pāṭ* may mean a royal sign, but here it refers to the role of the chief bhakta; his association with the temple of Śiva and his relation to the sign of Bhairab (pāṭā) plays a central role. The pāṭbhakta has the primary responsibility for the proper performance of the rituals. A pāṭbhakta may stay with a gājan for twenty or thirty years or more. He cannot eat till sundown, must sleep in the temple, may not touch women, can eat fruit and milk only after sundown, may not drink water during the day, has to do the pūjā and meditation of Śiva, and perform the offerings to the sun every day. He is given a saffron robe, wooden sandals, and beads (*rudramālā*) by the ṣolaānā. He carries an iron trident and a brass water jug for the pūjā oblations. He wears a garland of flowers (which is first offered to the deity). He assists the temple priest in the daily worship, and the priest assists him in the Suryaarghya. Other bhaktas must provide their own equipment, and in addition every bhakta must give a dhotī to the pāṭbhakta and to the priest.

The preferred attitude in the gājan is devotion to Śiva. Once the paitā is received, devotees cannot eat cooked food, rice, fish, meat, or curried vegetables. They may go home to sleep, but they must stay in an empty room, not lie in bed, and generally not take part in the life of the household. They may eat at home also, but their food is to be prepared in separate cooking utensils, preferably by their mothers.

Bhaktas are priests of the gājan. Wearing the sacred thread, they can perform all the pūjās themselves, bathe the deities, and offer food to Śiva and Bhairab. But the Brāhmaṇ priests are also necessary. First the bhaktas must be invested with the paitā. This requires a priest, not only because he knows the Sanskrit mantras but also because it takes a Brāhmaṇ to confer the gotra of Śiva on bhaktas and the sacred thread on non-Brāhmaṇs. The priest is necessary for the recitation of mantras in the Suryapūjā and in the individual pūjās that bhaktas offer to Śiva. The priest always sits in the temple, dispensing the sacred water of Śiva's ceremonial bath to all those who want it.

There are two kinds of Brāhmaṇ priests: "high" and "low." To the former of these major caste clusters belong the highest Brāhmaṇ subcastes, Rāṛhī, Barendra, and the somewhat lower Utkal. The second kind are the agradhānī Brāhmaṇ, a *patit srenī* (lower order). These priests are essential to the gājan, for they officiate at the *arghya* (libations to the sun). This class of Brāhmaṇ can perform all the pūjās, but they are "degraded" (*patit*), their status being lower because of their relation to the mourner in the *śrāddha* (mourning rituals). In the gājan they receive gifts from the bhaktas. High-srenī Brāhmaṇs assist bhaktas in other rituals.

Among the priests there are the permanent temple priests (*mandir purohit*) who perform the worship of temple deities. They are often hereditary priests of the Malla rājās. The priestly lines expanded and segmented so often that the pūjās of the various temples are now divided up among the descendants in such a way that each group receives the worship for a part of the year. The daily pūjās are the responsibility of one or two lines, but the rest claim their part during festival time when the income of the temples increases.

Agradhānī Brāhmaṇs are an endogamous group, performing special rituals at funerary feasts, where they are receivers of the first gift made by the deceased man's son, a gift that is given while there is still death pollution in the house. The Brāhmaṇ receiving this gift ranks lower, for the gift signifies the gradual disappearance of the pollution as the funerary rites go on. This Brāhmaṇ offers the libation of the sun; hence he is called the "giver" of the offering.

The headman of Gopālganj, where the Buṛo Śiva temple is situated, takes a leading role in organizing the gājan. He is not a descendant of the royal headmen but holds office by the consent of the people of the locality, and his duties are almost exclusively ritual organizational ones. The leading men of the locality help him in preparing and mounting major temple rituals. The daily service in the temple, the periodic recitation of sacred texts in the nāthmandir, are also the responsibility of the committee. The Boltalā temple committee functions the same way in that neighborhood except that the leading man there is a lower-jāti Sunri. The locality is inhabited by mid-ranking castes, but the Sunri leader is entrusted with the organization of the temple rituals, mainly because he is regarded as a powerful, wealthy man who is easily antagonized.

Taking the sacred thread is also called paitā pūjā, having the same form as other pūjās. All pūjās begin with the purification of the water. Water itself is purified by the name of Viṣṇu, then the bhaktas themselves are purified by this water: hands, lips, inner and outer self, clothing, objects, and so on. This first set of mantras prepares the bhaktas for the wearing of the sacred thread. The ring of kusa grass signifies their encounter with divinity and is necessary for all Tantric and Debī rituals. The mantra dissolves the self, and when it is stated the transformation of the bhaktas from everyday to divine individuality is accomplished.

Without the context of the pūjā, a mantra is ineffective; without pūjā and mantra the purifications are meaningless. Water in itself is not enough. This is a persistent feature of Bengali explanations of pūjā: action, word, and use of objects go together in a given sequence. After the purification, bhaktas may invoke Viṣṇu or Nārāyan, the names of the supreme being, thus establishing a relation with divinity. The next step is to partake of divinity by taking *debgotra* (the gotra of the gods). Finally they call Śiva for the first time as bhaktas of the gājan, to make him aware of their new status and call his attention to their doings. From then on everything connected with the bhaktas is auspicious. Their beṭs, having been touched by the sacred thread, are not mere canes. Mango leaves may be tied to the beṭs, a sign of auspiciousness. The bhaktas may perform Śiva pūjās as often as they want to. Every day they must perform the worship of Śiva and the oblations of the sun, but no one enforces these rules. Beyond this the devotees follow their own inclination in the performance of devotional acts.

Chanting Śiva's names and the names of famous temples is one of the central acts of the gājan.[8] Individually or together, bhaktas can be heard from afar, day and night, crying out loudly, naming Śiva's characteristics, extolling his powers. The call is meant to break Śiva's meditation. Śiva is the foremost ascetic, sitting on Mount Koilās in absorbed meditation. Devotees must force him to pay attention to the gājan. The chant is also a way of focusing one's attention on divinity. Bhaktas say calling Śiva helps them through the ordeals and creates joy among the people. The louder the better; the spirit and excitement of the gājan is in the joy of devotees in their service of Śiva. In return Śiva himself becomes more involved in the gājan; it is the joy that moves him. He comes, listens, and bestows grace on his worshipers. The more he is worshiped, the more present and visible he becomes in the actions of the gājan. Śiva is not just a silent recipient of adoration; his presence distinguishes one gājan from another, one temple and one image from another. The number of devotees depends directly on the power of Śiva (*mahātmā*) to affect the destiny of his devotees.

The offering to the sun takes place in three major parts; the first has to do with purification, the second with the worship of the different gods and goddesses, and the last is the greeting of the sun itself. Bhaktas purify their bodies, the ground on which they sit, the flowers they offer, the containers they use, and the other items of offering. No one knows whether these items may have been defiled before use; the mantra and the Ganges water make everything pure. Encounter with the goddess comes after the service of all the other deities; so in the Suryaarghya all gods are worshiped before the sun can be honored. The mūl debatā, the god for whom the pūjā is intended, must wait till the very end of the sequence. That all these gods and goddesses make their appearance in the gājan is not fortuitous; bhaktas say that no deity can be neglected even though the special worship is that of Śiva. All deities stand in a particular and unique relation to human life; hence to ignore the other deities would amount to detracting from the totality of living experience in the world.

The pūjās that devotees perform are directed at the major deities, the Five Gods (Durgā, Viṣṇu, Śiva, Brahmā, and the sun), Gaṇeś, the different Debīs (*śakti*), the cardinal directions (in which other deities and other manifestations of Śiva are located). The directions themselves are divine. Each of these pūjās is performed with a mantra and a flower. The name of the flower is included in the mantra. The flower itself is not the offering; it stands for all good things one should offer an honored guest: scent, clothing, and bathing water. In a flower with a few drops of water on the petals, all items of offering are encompassed. By reciting each mantra with the words scent and flower added to the name of a deity, the bhaktas can perform as many pūjās as they want to, throwing flowers after each mantra with the gesture of offering (the two palms held together or the right hand alone in the gesture of añjali). The last set of mantras culminates in the praṇām of the sun. Bhaktas recite the meditation of the sun three times, doing the praṇām (ceremonial prostration) with five parts of the body touching the ground (forehead, two arms, and two knees).

The daily pūjās of Śiva are very different from the pūjā of the sun. Bhaktas worship Śiva individually or with the help of a priest. The simplest acts, placing bel leaves and pouring water on the liṅga, satisfy Siva. The bhaktas, however, also worship Śiva by doing praṇām, calling his name, and asking for help and blessings. The pūjā consists of bathing the image with different liquids: milk, honey, water, the water of a green coconut, curds, and dissolved sugar. Then flowers, water, rice, and sweets are offered without mantras, *bhakti bhābe,* the way of devotion. Central to this pūjā are *bhakti* and *sebā* (devotion and service). The bhakta may address Śiva in his mind, requesting him to accept the offering, to save him, to bestow blessings, to accept the devotion graciously, to listen to his needs and desires. He may call Śiva aloud while performing pūjā. Finally, the devotee places a *mānsik phul* (a votive flower) on the liṅga and addresses a wish or a vow to the god, beseeching Śiva to give back the flower should he look upon the request favorably. Then he remains in a position of prayer (*āradhanā*) with hands folded, waiting for the flower to fall from the liṅga. No matter how long it takes, the bhakta sits meditating on Śiva. When the flower falls he tries to catch it, shouting the names of Śiva in jubilation.

Bhaktas may ask the temple Brāhmaṇ to do pūjā on their behalf with the proper Sanskrit *saṅkalpa* (resolution). The saṅkalpa is also recited when the bhaktas receive the sacred thread, since the gājan is done in the name of Śiva gotra. A nāmgotra pūjā in which the Brāhmaṇ offers flowers and uncooked food items to Śiva on behalf of individuals and their lines may also be performed: the offering then becomes a miniature Brāhmaṇic pūjā. These pūjās are usually performed by relatives of the bhaktas or nonbhakta worshipers, since the gājan is also a time for pūjās by everybody.

Picture 9

Picture 10

Picture 11

Picture 12

Picture 13

Picture 14

Picture 15

Picture 16

The Arrival of the Goddess and the Significance of Power

The Kāmakkātulā (or Kamilatulā) takes place in the dead of the night, in complete darkness and silence. When the goddess comes to join her consort in the celebration of the gājan, she bestows special powers on her devotees. Kāmakkā or Kamila Debī is the Goddess Durgā; her raising or lifting means the filling of a pūjā ghat. Only a few bhaktas assist at the "lifting," and they come to the temple about ten o'clock. They may join for a while the recitation of Rāmāyana songs in the nāthmandir. The *pāṛā* (neighborhood) people often bring parties of singers at gājan time for the nightly recitation of passages from the epic. The singers are Vaiṣṇava either by jāti or by initiation. In the Buṛo Śiva gājan, six bhaktas, the pāṭbhakta, and the sāddhu take part in the ritual. The bhaktas wear the sacred thread, the pāṭbhakta fasting through the day till the pūjā is over. None of the bhaktas may use mustard oil and turmeric when bathing before the *ghat-tula* (lifting of the ghat), but the sāddhu oils his body and then smears himself with ashes after his bath. The sāddhu also carries a trident and a small two-ended drum; his hair is bleached and matted and reaches down to the waist. He too wears wooden sandals and a black loincloth, but as the procession starts the other bhaktas and the drummers remove their sandals. It is a silent procession. They carry the items of the pūjā: the *maṅgal patra* (auspicious plate), the ghat and towel, mango leaves, noibedda (cold food offering), flowers, and incense. Reaching the lake, the men select a lonely spot, leaving the Doms behind, since nobody except the bhaktas should witness the arrival of the goddess. One ghāt is rejected even though it was used the previous year. The reason given is that recently the low-jāti Bauris have begun to use it and have ruined it for this ritual by stirring up the water. The pāṭbhakta wades into the water and bathes the trident, anointing it with vermilion and oil.

The agradhānī arrives and, taking clay from the lake, prepares a small platform, scattering grain as he places the ghat on the *bedī* (altar). The pāṭbhakta and the priest then prepare several *suta*s (*maṅgal suta,* an auspicious bracelet made of thread and the sacred durba grass). The sutas are smeared with turmeric, the Brāhmaṇ tying one on the ghat and the pāṭbhakta putting one on the trident. The priest tells the pāṭbhakta to build a small liṅga of sand next to the ghat, but the two get into a long argument, from which the pāṭbhakta emerges the victor: this night only the goddess is worshiped specifically; the liṅga need not be built. The priest then marks the vessel with vermilion, and by placing the mango branch into the ghat begins the pūjā. After the purification of self and objects is performed, the priest puts all the flowers in the jug of *gaṅgājal*

(Ganges water). With the purified flowers he offers pūjā to the different deities, placing each flower on the ghat. Uncooked rice, sweets, and fruits (noibedda) are offered to the ghat and the towel. With the food offerings, further mantras of the goddess are recited, and flowers and drops of water are placed on the ghat. The pāṭbhakta offers a garland of flowers to the sāddhu, then bathes the red towel that will cover the mouth of the ghat when it is filled with water. The priest does the welcoming rite of the goddess, lifting and touching all the auspicious objects on the brass plate to the ghat.

The most important part of the rite is the installation of the sacred vessel: the priest purifies the parts of the body, the vital airs, the fundamental elements that constitute all matter; invoking the goddess, he "establishes" the ghat, calling upon the Debī to dwell in the house prepared for her. He recites mantras, holding the sacred thread to the ghat. More libations are then poured in the name of the different manifestations of the goddess, and a final puspañjali is offered to all gods and goddesses. The great verse from the Debī Māhātmā linking Śiva and Durgā in their relation to the world ends the pūjā.

The Brāhmaṇ ties a yellow thread on the right arm of the pāṭbhakta, then wreathes him with the mālā (garland) on the ghat. The sāddhu also demands one, and the Brāhmaṇ counters by claiming that the *sāddhu* does not need one till the *gambhari* ritual next day; the ascetic insists. The priest lifts the ghat, and the pāṭbhakta takes it on his head, slowly wading into the water with the six bhaktas following closely. When they reach the deep water the bhaktas form a circle around the pāṭbhakta. As the water covers the pāṭbhakta's head, the ghat slowly fills up. The pāṭbhakta is inert during this process, but when the ghat is full the bhaktas lift him quickly out of the water, the ghat remaining in the same position on his head. The ghat must not be tilted, nor may the pāṭbhakta bend sideways. As the bhaktas see the ghat surfacing, they break the silence by shouting the name of Śiva. Drums roll, and the character of the ritual changes—the somber is replaced by the exuberant. When he reaches the edge of the water the pāṭbhakta places the red towel on the ghat and, turning the vessel upside down, places it back on his head. That the water does not pour out is attributed to the *mahātmā* (power, influence) of the goddess. Should the water pour through the towel it would be a bad omen for the gājan. This time all the signs are auspicious. There is one slight mishap; after a while some water does come through, and on inspection it is found that the ghat was not filled properly. With the addition of some water, the mistake is rectified.

The procession heads back to the temple, the bhaktas calling Śiva all the way, the drummers playing loudly: Everyone must know, even in the middle of the night, that the goddess is being brought to the gājan.

When they arrive at the temple the goddess is placed in the temple of Santīnāth, not in the Buṛo Śiva temple. The pāṭbhakta may eat now and is eager to, but the headman tells him to change his wet clothes, wash his feet, and worship Śiva before breaking his fast. The Brāhmaṇ does pūjā to Santīnāth, annointing the liṅga with vermilion and placing a lotus and leaves of the sacred bel tree on it. Flowers and water are offered together with the recitation of mantras. The bhogpūjā follows, the priest offering the usual items of food, the special dish of this festival being the *cirabhog* (flattened rice mixed with water, milk, and molasses). After the pūjā the Brāhmaṇ performs the evening ārati for the divine couple.

Exegesis of Kamilatulā

The relation between Durgā and Śiva is the key to the gājan, but to understand this relation we must examine more closely the stories, legends, and rites pertaining to these deities.

Kāmakkā is the goddess of Kamarup in Assam. There is a temple of this goddess outside Gauhati, and the locality is venerated as a *pīthasthān*. *Pīth* refers to a locality, usually the place upon which a deity stands, the altar on which a deity is worshiped. *Sthān* means simply a place or locality. The word most commonly refers to particular holy places, however—the fifty-one localities where parts of Satī's body fell when Viṣṇu cut her corpse into pieces.

> Satī was Śiva's wife in the purāṇic legends, an incarnation of Durgā. She gave up her life when her father Dakkha Rājā (the Himalaya mountain) neglected to invite Śiva to his great sacrifice. Dakkha Rājā reasoned that Śiva, an ascetic who roams the burning grounds, would pollute the sacrifice. Satī appeared at the sacrifice and, reproaching her father for the insult, shamed him in front of the assembled gods by giving up her own life through the yogic practices she had learned while wooing Śiva. Śiva became maddened with rage and grief; he took up the body of Satī and wandered all over the world causing destruction and death. The gods were greatly frightened and implored Viṣṇu to stop Śiva's dance of universal dissolution. Viṣṇu followed Śiva and cut the corpse to pieces with his weapon, the *sudangsa cakra* (the discus). Parts of Satī's body fell down to earth, and these localities became manifestations of the goddess; in each place a temple was established and Debī was worshiped as the goddess of that area—a place where Satī's eyebrow, forehead, leg, hand, or foot fell. Satī's genitalia fell on Kamarup, hence the goddess there is known as Kāmakkā Debī.[9]

Kamila is the goddess invoked during the first major ritual of the gājan, the *ugra-śakti,* the most powerful energy of Śiva, the motivating force of the gājan. The identification of Kamilatulā with the invocation of Kāmakkā Debī is not unanimous; some bhaktas regard Kamila Debī as the consort of Śiva or Bhairab, or even as a "part" of Bhairab. Kamila of the Vishnupur gājan is regarded as the expression of a certain power, the female in relation to the male aspect of power.

Kamila Debī comes to the gājan so that she may unite with Śiva (*milan*) and create a certain kind of force that will descend on the bhaktas to allow them to carry out their acts of devotion. This force or power, *śakti,* is effective beyond the gājan; many bhaktas do the gājan year after year to share in this periodic renewal and fulfillment. No action is possible without śakti, and men receive power and vitality through the celebrations of śakti in Durgāpūjā and Śiva's gājan. The ritual itself is considered dangerous, partly because of the śakti the devotees must deal with. The goddess is lifted out of the water amid darkness and silence so that the results of the rite may not be prejudiced by some mistake. The pāṭbhakta's austerities during the previous days lead up to this moment and are put to the test. The goddess is regarded as so powerful and dangerous that great care must be taken in bringing her to the gājan. The pāṭbhakta must concentrate and meditate on the goddess to the extent of losing his own identity; hence the number of bhaktas to assist him. Meditation is important so that the goddess does no mischief on the way, and silence is important in helping the pāṭbhakta avoid her anger. The streets should be empty; no unauthorized person should witness the union of Śiva and Durgā.

The goddess is invoked and worshiped in a vessel (ghat). The pāṭbhakta must prepare the place of the ghat and arrange auspicious items on the ghat: mango leaves, red paitā, āltā for her feet. The locality thus becomes the place on which the goddess herself stands. When the Brāhmaṇ completes the purification of his own body, *ātmā* (self), and vital airs, the elements constituting all matter, then he is ready to worship the goddess who is the creator of all those elements. When all items of the pūjā are purified, they can be used to honor the goddess. Mantras, flowers, and water symbolize acts of service: washing the feet, offering sixteen items to each deity, worshiping the gods with different mantras, attending to the manifold nature of each god.

The actions and recitations of the invocation are meant to establish the ghat as a proper resting place for the goddess. Further, this rite means the bringing of the goddess to a particular place and giving her life there.

In my account the idea of multiplicity in a single deity is clearly demonstrated: the pāṭbhakta objected to building a sand liṅga for the pūjā of Śiva even though the latter was worshiped in the trident and in the pūjā of the ghāt. He insisted, however, that no separate pūjā in the actual image of Śiva was to be done at the ghāt; rather, it should be at the place of the gāmār tree the next day. *Trisur* (trident) pūjā is also Śibpūjā, but the trident is a particular part of Śiva, different from the liṅga, pāṭā, and gāmār tree. Ghat and trident are also worshiped by the pāṭbhakta, who puts yellow *suta*s (bracelets) on them. The priest then gives a similar bracelet to the pāṭbhakta, who in turn gives one to the sāddhu. Garlands are exchanged in the same way, thus defining the relations of these men to each other and to the god and goddess. The suta itself is not only a symbol of the gājan; it is maṅgalik, auspicious, protecting from all danger. All bhaktas receive the suta before they embark on the acts of devotion. It makes a heightened intensity in the development of the gājan, a gradual change in the encounter of deities and men that culminates in the trance during Rātgājan.

The lifting of the ghat is the most dangerous part of the ritual. The pāṭbhakta is inert when he reaches deep water and sinks with the ghat on his head. The pāṭbhakta is said to be in the power of the goddess. The goddess dwells in water, and divinities reach or leave the earth through water. Hence the ghat is brought from a river or a tank, a body of water that is regarded sacred because it is part of the goddess's domain. The Ganges, the sacred river itself, is a manifestation of the goddess. All images of the goddess are immersed in the water after the periodic festivals are over. Water is regarded as the channel through which the gods reach their abode in the Himalayas. Since the goddess will come out of the waters again to visit her devotees, the pāṭbhakta joins her in her own realm. He is not supposed to stir; being in the hands of the goddess, he can be kept there. There is a gājan story in which the pāṭbhakta disappeared during the Kamilatulā; no effort could locate his body. With some difficulty, another pāṭbhakta was chosen (in the bigger gājans several people voluntarily double for the major offices in case a replacement is needed). The next year, however, the vanished pāṭbhakta surfaced with the new man who lifted the ghat. His beard and hair were long, and there were weeds all over his body. As soon as he emerged he died. It is said he had spent that year with the goddess. The meditation, silence, and strict observance of the rules helps to avoid a repetition of this. When the ghat is filled, the pāṭbhakta is pervaded by the mahātmā of the goddess and has to be lifted from the water. People recognize danger in the operation. Also, there is an ambiguity in the role of the goddess; she is the mother of the world, but she is also the creator of all bad things in the world (*khārāp biddhā*—bad knowledge, creature, creation). She must be treated carefully, for many of her manifestations have to do with misfortune. Hence the identities of the multiple aspects of the goddess are not entirely separated, and each manifestation is linked to another till they reach the most encompassing concept, Debī, in whom all others merge.

The mahātmā (power) of the goddess rescues the pāṭbhakta and keeps the water from flowing out of the inverted ghat. The reversal of normal processes is regarded by the bhaktas as a justification for the precautions they have to take during the night. Such acts are interpreted as signs of extraordinary events, comprehensible only in the context of the ritual.

Pomp must surround the goddess when she comes—music and cymbals are part of the festival. The ghat remains in the Śiva temple, then food and *ārati* (the waving of lights) are offered to the divine consorts. The evening ārati is itself a small pūjā, the idea of service being central to ārati also. The waving of lights, incense, shell water-container, and flower symbolize the greeting, bathing, and dressing of an honored guest. Ārati is the last ceremonial act of pūjā, a simple gesture of respect to the deity before everyone bids the divine guest farewell. The objects used in the ārati are used in the pūjā as well.

The goddess is not taken to the main Śiva temple. The combination of the goddess with the main deity of the locality would be too much for mortals to bear; the combined force or power that flows from the union of Śiva and Durgā would destroy the people who want to share in this creative energy. Hence the goddess is placed a little distance from the main deity of the gājan. In the Boltalā gājan the ghat is put into the sanctuary of Śiva, but even there it is placed as far away from the liṅga as possible. The Buṛo Śiva is said to be more powerful than the Boltalā Śiva.

In the Buṛo Śibtalā gājan Kamila Debī is united with Santīnāth, the Lord of Peace. The goddess comes in her ugra-śakti form, and as she nears Śiva he succumbs to a great desire (Śiva's increasing lust can become excessive and end in universal destruction). To avert this disaster the goddess is taken to a lesser temple. Even there she is close enough to Śiva for the desired effect to come about. The fruit of the union is the energy (*tej*) that endows the bhaktas with power (*śakti*) to carry out their duties in the gājan and attain their desired ends in the everyday world. The creative energy that emanates from Durgā and Śiva after their union results in trance (*bhor* or *bhorom*), the effect on the bhaktas being momentary possession. Śiva and Durgā do not possess their devotees, but Bhairab, who is a part of Śiva (*Śiber aṅga*) does. However, trance is a manifestation of the tej of Śiva-Durgā, the divine pair in union. When the bhaktas dance and become possessed, they lose consciousness and cannot remember what they are doing. They are caught by Bhairab, and the deity descends upon them.

Though Durgā and Śiva make the acts of devotion possible, the acts themselves are regarded as dangerous because men are not directly in control. Men must live up to their part in the gājan (fasting, meditating, performing pūjās, worshiping the sun), and especially they must show devotion. Devotion not only averts danger, it also draws the favorable attention of the gods. The calling of Śiva is the most auspicious activity. Śiva cannot but listen when approached in honesty. The other acts the bhaktas perform (fire walking, abstaining from water in the heat, and so on) are in themselves dangerous; hence the importance of bringing them under the influence of Śiva-Durgā's tej. The more difficult the act, the surer is the intervention of the deities.

From the energy of the divine pair is born the power or ability to act, śakti. The personification of Śiva's śakti is Durgā. But even within Śiva, seemingly a single entity, there is the god and the goddess in a state of union. Hence śakti always presupposes two elements: the male and the female. Singly these elements are incomprehensible. The goddess, the female element, is the power of action. The god, Śiva, is the actor. Śiva is in a state of repose and becomes active when the two elements in him become distinct and opposed to each other, hence the separate identities of Śiva and Durgā.

Cutting the Gāmār Tree

The following day (Gāmārkātā) more bhaktas take the sacred thread, and after the Suryaarghya the day's special ritual is performed: *gāmārgāc kata* (cutting the gāmār tree). The bhaktas are called to the temple by the sound of the drums. Before the procession starts, a flagpole is set up, swathed in red cloth and with a red flag fluttering at the top. This is worshiped by the priest: gods and goddesses are invoked in a small ghat, some sacred verses are recited, a little rice is offered, and the ghat is discarded. The flag, a sign of the gājan, remains near the temple throughout the festival.

The sāddhu appears with helpers carrying the photograph of the naked Mouni Bābā. The pāṭbhakta starts off the procession to the place of the gāmār tree, far out of town. The procession is headed by fourteen drummers followed by the main body of bhaktas. Several men carry the objects necessary for the performance of a full pūjā. Last come the pāṭbhakta and the sāddhu. The former carries a trident decorated with garlands and lotuses and is surrounded by the bhaktas who have special duties during the festival. The sāddhu walks under a silk umbrella with two youths carrying silk fans at his side, another bearing the flower-decorated picture of the guru. The procession winds slowly through the localities of Gopālganj and neighboring Rosikganj. At every turn townspeople line the paths; the men do obeisance, the women stop the procession to take the dust off the sāddhu's and pāṭbhakta's feet, asking for their blessings. Women bring small children and place them on the ground in front of the sāddhu; others take dust from the footprints of the devotees.

The gāmār tree stands at the edge of a rice field two miles out of town. All bhaktas do obeisance to the tree. The priest begins the pūjā by sprinkling water on the tree and the offerings. The pāṭbhakta touches a bundle of yellow threads to the sacrificial knife; taking a few pieces of *belpata* and durba grass, he gives the bundle to the bhaktas, who go around the tree three times with the thread, tying the leaves firmly to the tree at about waist height. The priest and the pāṭbhakta mix turmeric with mustard oil, applying the mixture to the trunk of the tree just below the leaves. The Brāhmaṇ paints a trident-like sign in the same place with vermilion and oil. Then ghī is smeared on the tree trunk and grains of rice are stuck into the thick paste. Uncooked rice, fruits, and sweets are spread out on śāl leaves around the tree and the trident.

The Brāhmaṇ performs pūjā, purifying the elements of the universe so that everything involved in the pūjā is ready for approaching the gods. Gods and goddesses are offered oblations and flowers. There is no ghat, so all the flowers are placed at the foot of the tree. Petals of the lotus are offered, and the seed kernel is thrown away. The camphor on the auspicious vessel is lit, and the whole plate is waved around the tree, the priest holding it to the painted trident on the trunk. Invocation of the different deities is followed by more offerings; finally, a formal flower offering is made.

An important moment of the pūjā arrives: the Great God is invoked into the tree; touching the sacred thread to the trunk, the priest recites a long Sanskrit verse. Vermilion and water are sprinkled on the knife, and hashish is offered to Śiva in a *kolke* (a small clay pipe). It appears that one of the bhaktas has already smoked the kolke, so the priest throws it away; everything must be new when given to a deity. Flowers are placed on the knife, and after further recitations, purifications, and mudras the sacred thread is again held to the tree and life is bestowed on this particular manifestation of Śiva (*prānpratiśṭhā*). Finally the priest performs ārati in front of the tree; the bhaktas take the flame and, holding their palms over it, touch their foreheads. The pāṭbhakta blows on the conch three times, then makes a suta from the pile of threads; dipping it into a mixture of turmeric and oil and tying it in a few pieces of durba, he places the suta on the trident. The Brāhmaṇ again scatters drops of water on the knife and the other objects, again holding the paitā to the tree. Then, chanting a verse, he sacrifices the three pieces of *jhinga* (a tuber) cutting them in half with one blow. The pāṭbhakta takes the knife and cuts off a small branch of the tree. Then, as the bhaktas call Śiva, the *gāmārbhakta* climbs the tree and cuts off a large branch. This is taken to the temple in procession.

The sāddhu, the pāṭbhakta, and the gāmārbhakta lead the procession. Reaching the town, the bhaktas rest and wait for complete darkness. When the pressure lamps arrive, borne on the heads of a group of women, the devotees start off again. With lights the procession is more festive, more of a spectacle for the townspeople lining the streets. Back at the temple the tree branch is placed in the Buṛo-Śiva temple. Śiva's pūjā and ārati are performed. The wooden part of the branch is taken to the house of the *kāmār* (blacksmith), who will set three iron nails or spikes in the wood, placing the small pāṭā inside the larger pāṭā (board of nails). This must be done before the rites of the next day.

At night the bhaktas are invited by the kāmār for *jalājog* (drinking water, eating fruit, pulses, and sweets). On several nights of the gājan the bhaktas are invited in this way. The invitations are not random; they are significant and conform to a rule. The kāmār's role is significant in the Gāmārkātā. He belongs to a line of blacksmiths that has been associated with the gājan since Mouni Bābā revived the festival.

Gāmārkātā Exegesis

The tree stands outside the town, but the procession takes such a roundabout way that the actual distance covered is three times longer than the direct route. Part of the gājan's importance is the spectacle it provides. The whole town participates in the gājan by seeing the numerous processions of the bhaktas. To do praṇām to the pāṭbhakta, the sāddhu, and the devotees is an auspicious deed, an act of "minding" the gods, one of the duties of men (*dharma*). Another reason is to show the people of the locality that this is their gājan. Many donate small amounts of money to the ṣolaānā for the mounting of the gājan, and in return the procession passes through the most populous neighborhoods. The spectacle is not only the color and the excitement, it is also the crowd of bhaktas and their actions, their Śivalike appearance, and the whole idea of a festival. The processions in the gājan are just like the circumambulation of a deity in a pūjā, only in the gājan the whole town is circumambulated by a whole crowd of ritualists. The processions establish a connection between temples and deities.

The ritual itself is the worship of a tree. The pūjā is done by the agradhānī Brāhmaṇ and the pāṭbhakta. Śiva's symbols are painted on the tree, the yellow suta is tied around it, and the auspicious plate is offered to it. The tree is Śiva's "part," and the pūjā is also Śiva's. Śiva is invoked into the tree just as the goddess is invoked into the ghat during Kamilatulā. The tree is not marked with the *svastik* (the symbol of peace) as the ghat is; only the trident sign is made with vermilion. But the ghat and the tree are both smeared with the same items in their respective pūjās: ghī, vermilion, and turmeric. All these items are regarded as auspicious, being among the twenty-seven items on the auspicious plate.

The gāmār is a rare tree: its trunk is white, resembling the ash-smeared body of Śiva. It is thorny, and the thorns are significant in one of the rituals: the *jhāpbhanga* (thorn-breaking). In this rite the spikes of the gāmār tree are set within a small piece of gāmār wood. The bhaktas build a liṅga of sand under the *asatva* tree (the sacred pipal) near the pond where the Suryaarghya takes place. They do praṇām to the tree and surround the liṅga calling Śiva's names. The *sannyāsībhakta* then places three thorns from the tree on top of the liṅga and does pūjā. The pūjā mantras are similar to those of Suryaarghya. Offerings of flowers and water are made, and the pāṭbhakta falls chest down on the spikes, invoking Śiva. It is through Śiva's or Bhairab's mahātmā that the thorns do not pierce his stomach. The spikes are set vertically, and the force of the fall is supposed to break the thorns; but without the pūjā and the influence of Śiva, the spikes would impale the pāṭbhakta.

The kāmār (blacksmith) does all the ironwork, even the fashioning of the board. Devotees may commission a new pāṭā as an act of mānsik. Usually people are instructed in a dream to have the kāmār make a pāṭā. In the myths of the gājan, Bisvakarma, the artisan god, prepares the pāṭā, the nails, and the *jhāp* (the thorns). The iron nails in the gāmār tree represent the thorns on which Śiva's followers lay down in order to break his meditation. The kāmār also must worship the gāmār and pāṭā, and must fast before beginning the work. The kāmār is not the only artisan to be associated with the gājan; the *kumār* (potter) also has a role. The kāmār is associated with iron in the gājan, the kumār with the earth. The kumār also invites the bhaktas for jalājog.

The pūjā of the tree is performed in the same way as that of the ghat except that the Brāhmaṇ establishes the tree itself by invoking Śiva into it. All the offerings are made to the tree, and all the other deities are worshiped through the tree (once the deity has been invoked and the tree becomes his manifestation, all other deities can dwell there). Special objects like the tree, the trident, and the sacrificial knife are themselves offered pūjā, since they are associated with the worship in a special way. Just as the weapons of the deities are regarded as symbolic of their owners, so the sacrificial sword (in animal or vegetable sacrifice) is also symbolic of the deity to which the offering is directed. The knife is one of the weapons of Durgā; Kālī herself carries a sword, and the swords used for goat or buffalo sacrifice are shaped the same way.

Paying Respects to the Rājā

The following day is Rājābheta, paying respects to the king; bhaktas spread out in front of the rājā and are feasted by him. The morning is the final opportunity for devotees to take the sacred thread. During the day each bhakta worships Śiva, then together they worship the sun before moving in procession to the rājā's house.

Each bhakta is given a suta by the pāṭbhakta. The kāmār brings the iron nails (*jhāp*) to be set in the gāmār wood. The pāṭā is made of śāl, bel, or nīm wood.[10] It is the length and width of an adult man. Two poles attached across the bottom of the board are used to carry the pāṭā. The middle portion is thickly studded with nails, the top end has an iron neck rest, and the bottom has two iron hoops for the ankles. The kāmār worships the pāṭā before using his hammer to repair and straighten the nails.

The pūjā of the sun is performed at sunset, after which the bhaktas go in procession to the rājā's house, accompanied by the drummers.

The procession is led by the rājbhakta, whose duty is to greet the king first and see to it that everyone else pays respects to the king. This time the silver and silk umbrella is held over the head of the pāṭbhakta. According to the rājā, this visit by the bhaktas of the gājan is symbolic of the king's past power: like good subjects, they come to honor their ruler. But also they come to defend the king; they are like a bodyguard. They respect the king as the servant of all deities, since in the past all major temple images were the king's. Hence the connection of the king with most of the public rituals in the town. In return, says the rājā, the bhaktas must be honored by the king, and so he offers them jalājog.

The procession arrives at the palace gate. The bhaktas enter, lifting their canes high and chanting the names of Śiva. As the king sits on the veranda, the rājbhakta walks up to him and, taking the dust of his feet, garlands him; then, bowing once more, the rājbhakta greets the rājā with his palms folded. The rājā returns the greeting. The paṭbhakta approaches next, then one by one all the bhaktas place garlands around the king's neck. Finally the king presents garlands to the rājbhakta, pāṭbhakta, and the other bhaktas with specialized ritual duties (the sannyāsībhakta, gāmārbhakta). The bhaktas sit in rows in the yard, and the rājā's attendants distribute wetted pulses, fruits, cucumbers, and sweets in śāl-leaf containers. Water and sherbet (of the bel fruit) is then poured for everyone in earthenware cups that are later discarded.

It is dark when the procession starts again, going around the abandoned temples of the rājā's house and setting out for the sāddhus' *āśram* (retreat) across the open fields. At the āśram the bhaktas garland the sāddhu and the old guru (the head of the sect). Pūjā is offered to Śiva, Mouni Bābā, Kṛṣṇa, and Rāmā.

Exegesis of Rājābheta

Most bhaktas take the sacred thread on Rājābheta morning. As the intensity of the worship increases, so the nonbhakta participation grows; *phurti* (excitement and exuberant spirit) attracts more worshipers. There is more śakti and more blessings to come from such a gājan.

Bhetā is a visit, a ceremonial gift to the king. It is complementary: the bhaktas honor the king by presenting him with garlands, the king reciprocates by offering them jalājog. Many festivals include such visits, an expression of the relation between town, people, deity, and king. That bheta is usually part of a major ritual sequence (the three gājans, the Durgāpūjā, and even the Muslim Muharram) highlights the special relation of the king to the people, deities, and ritualists in the pūjā. The Rājābheta is a demonstration of the basic structure of pūjā. The tripartite relations of pūjā are clearly expressed: king and people are related as the encompassing and the encompassed.

The bhaktas honor the king for other reasons also. The three Śiva images are all on land the king once owned. Accordingly, all lands in a kingdom are the rājā's. In the past the king could endow land in the name of a deity or a Brāhmaṇ or even a non-Brāhmaṇ. Hence there is a relation between the king and those who are on the land, since they hold their land by virtue of the king. The king includes within him the land and the people in his relation to the gods, since both the people and the images of the gods are on his lands. Furthermore, the Śiva images are not just placed into a temple. Most of the Śiva liṅgas in Mallabhum are said to have emerged from the earth. The oldest ones, like the Śiva of Ekteśvar in Bankura town are irregularly shaped stones that have erupted from the earth, proving themselves to be extraordinary objects. Many *aloukik* (nonnatural) events surround these images till they are correctly identified by a sāddhu or a tantric as manifestations of Śiva. One such Śiva was a rock in a riverbed, but later a temple was built over it. Śiva usually sends a vision to a devotee about the real nature of such strange natural formations. Alternatively, events and sounds associated with these images are recognized by ascetics as particular aspects of the deity in a particular locality.

The Rājābheta procession is regarded by the bhaktas as the honor due to the king, the owner of the land on which Śiva became manifest. The king, on the other hand, does honor to his subjects (*prajā*) because they take care of the land and worship the deities. The people are the subjects of the king and as such form a part of the king's worship in relation to the gods: this is noted in the gājan in the ceremony of Rājābheta.

Gājan of the Night

Rātgājan is the highest moment of the festival. The Suryaarghya is already a prelude for the special rites of the night. In the middle of the day the bhaktas perform a special Śiva pūjā at the temple, on a ceremonial visit to the other gājan. They carry food offerings which the Boltalā temple priest offers to Śiva on their behalf, and the bhaktas then offer flowers. In return, at their gājan, the Boltalā bhaktas also offer pūjā to Buṛo Śiva.

Just before sunset the bhaktas gather at the temple, waiting for the sāddhu to emerge. The sāddhu wears garlands around his arms, neck, and head. He smokes gāja (hashish) during the night, remaining still at all times. The procession carries several pāṭās, and the biggest of these has the gāmār wood set in it. The procession moves in a different direction, through the center of the town to the lake, in the most populous neighborhood. A short distance away in a fallow rice paddy there is a tumbledown shrine, and as the bhaktas go to bathe in the pond, the sāddhu sits in the shrine, with the picture of Mouni Bābā and the trident next to him. The sāddhu sits in the pose of meditation, and the crowds pay their respects to him, offering small coins to the image of his guru. The sāddhu bestows blessings in return by silently extending his hands palm downward.

The bhaktas place the pāṭās in the middle of the field, the smaller ones flanking the big one. The trident is planted at the head of the middle pāṭā. Then the pāṭbhakta marks the trident and the pāṭā with vermilion and covers the head of the pāṭā with a mixture of vermilion, turmeric, and mustard oil. The rest of the bhaktas follow suit, placing garlands on the trident and the pāṭā. The pāṭbhakta and the priest perform paṭā pūjā with food offerings, rice, sweets, fruits, and flowers. The Brāhmaṇ holds his sacred thread to the pāṭā, then to the offerings, reciting mantras for the worship of Śiva and other deities. The bhaktas then approach, and each one offers fruits; a small mountain of mangoes, bel fruit, and jackfruit quickly accumulates on top of the pāṭā. At the end of the Suryapūjā the Brāhmaṇ takes most of these as his share of the prasad, but those pieces that are firmly spiked on the nails must stay there, as they are essential to the rituals later on. When the offerings are over, the bhaktas sit in concentric squares around the pāṭā and perform the worship of the sun. The final mantra is recited facing the sun, and everyone does praṇām to the sun, prostrating himself on the ground.

Bhaktas garland the sāddhu, touching the dust of his feet to their foreheads. Most bhaktas may break their fast now, though they may not eat cooked food. Many do mānsik to perform additional acts of devotion, and until these are accomplished they must fast. Receiving garlands from the pāṭbhakta, they touch his feet and the ground in front of the trident. Their towels are tied tightly around them by the other bhaktas, and calling Śiva loudly they lie down full length on the ground, slowly rolling around the pāṭās. Still in the same position, they roll toward the road without using hands or feet. They may not get up till they reach the temple; they may not skip stone steps and rocky ground; all the forward motion must be caused by the trunk of the body. Large crowds follow the progress of these bhaktas. They roll, stop for a while, then roll again. The drummers follow, playing only while the bhaktas roll. From time to time they call Śiva to help them move on. Such a mānsik is known as *ghurānbhakta* (the vow of the bhaktas who roll). There are other forms of mānsik, *praṇām sebā* (the service of the deity by doing praṇāms), where the bhakta stands and does *praṇām* to the sun, then lies full length on the ground, rises again, and doing *praṇām,* advances two steps (to where his outstretched hands have made a mark in the dust) and prostrates himself, repeating the same act until he reaches the temple several hours later.

Other ghurānbhaktas have a yet more exacting task; they too roll to the temple, but they wait to start with the main procession—the rising of the gājan itself, the central part of the Rātgājan rituals. This means that they cannot break their fast till the next morning, and should the gājan not finish before sunrise, they cannot eat anything till sunset the following day. These bhaktas keep a vigil near the pāṭā, with the pāṭbhakta. They sit and talk, mainly about past gājans and the dangers that befell men who transgressed the rules, and about the power of Śiva and the power of the gājan. Many smoke gāja and pass the kolke around to the others. The rising of the gājan is at midnight, but many of the bhaktas who go home after the Suryapūjā come back quickly, sitting and talking with the crowds of onlookers. An hour or two later a regular fair has developed around the gājan. Hawkers sell fried cakes, spiced peanuts, parched rice, sweets, and toys.

When the gājan rises at about midnight, a new group of devotees appears who are not initiated bhaktas. They are the *bānnphurabhakta*s, who have their tongues perforated by long iron rods and dance to the temple in the procession. They too may do mānsik, they too fast, but they are not given the sacred thread and the other insignia of the regular bhaktas. Though their performance is essential, no blood can be allowed to flow from the "Sons of Śiva"; hence they are not initiated. *Bānnphura* means piercing of the tongue, an act of devotion that pleases Śiva. No deity can ignore such an emphatic approach. These men are usually from the low castes, but high-jāti people may go through the ordeal for the sake of Śiva, a mānsik that is higher in value than any other form of self-denial in the gājan. The men receive a small amount of money and rice liquor from the ṣolaānā, but the bānnphura is regarded as an act of worship not everyone can perform.

The ritual takes place in the bamboo grove adjoining the field, with two men from the ṣolaānā assisting the devotees. The iron rod is rubbed with hot ghī and the tongue is dabbed with ghī and *snānjal* (ceremonial water) of Śiva. As one man holds the bhakta's tongue, the other pushes the sharp end of the iron through the flesh, while several men support the long rod. Then the rod is turned down and pulled through the tongue till the ends are equidistant from the bhakta's head. It is a painful process, and the men wince but do not utter a sound. They do praṇām and hold on to the iron rod as they join the procession, dancing forward and back in slow steps, always keeping with the falling or rising rhythm of the drums. At the head of the procession are the bānnphurabhaktas, followed by the ghurānbhaktas, and *śālbhaktas* (those who dance with the pāṭā) flanked by the rest of the bhaktas with their canes raised high. The rear is brought up by the pāṭbhakta and the sāddhu.

The streets are lined with people, and the procession is bathed in the light of pressure lamps. The drummers play in several groups; some cluster around the ghurānbhaktas, others walk in front of the śālbhaktas. As the drums begin with a slow beat, the śālbhaktas pick up the rhythm, stepping forward, then back, responding to the faster and faster beat as the steps become jumps and the dance wilder until the bhakta loses consciousness and falls into trance (*bhor*). The movements become more spasmodic and wild, the possessed men jump high with the board of nails. The grasp of the possessed is so strong and convulsive that many other bhaktas have to hold onto the board and control the dancer. A bhakta in trance can carry four or five men with him until the pāṭā is twisted from his hands and he is wrestled to the ground. There he is held while his shoulder muscles are slapped, the holy water of Ganges is sprinkled on him, and pūjā flowers are placed on his neck. Presently the trance passes and the bhakta is helped to his feet. Within a few moments he joins the others. The pāṭā passes immediately to another bhakta, and the dance is repeated time and time again until the procession reaches the temple. The night gājan is a joyous performance: the bhaktas "make joy" by beating their canes together above the pāṭā, shouting the names of Śiva, speeding up the dance and stepping with the śālbhakta in trance, forcing the pace, creating a deeper involvement, bringing possession on faster. Those who do not dance keep the unruly crowd away from the procession, for no one is allowed to touch the bhaktas.

When the procession reaches the temple, all bhaktas circumambulate the temple before entering: the ghurānbhaktas roll around, and up the temple steps, then they lie down at the feet of Śiva. After this they worship the deity and take home a mānsik flower. The iron rods are pulled out of the bānnphurabhaktas' tongues, and the priest puts a sacred tulsī leaf and *pancamrita* on the wounds, which heal within a day or two. The pāṭbhakta performs the final Śiva pūjā by placing flowers and pouring water on the liṅga. The procession ends only at sunrise, but when the sun reaches the horizon the bhaktas have already begun the sixth day's work.

Rātgājan Exegesis

The pāṭā makes its first appearance in the gājan on Rājābheta day when the kāmār repairs it. In the afternoon of Rātgājan the bhaktas take the pāṭā to the *arghyatalā* (the place of the sun worship). There may be more than one pāṭā; the ābārgājans usually have three. The pāṭās are bathed in the temple tank or river and then worshiped. Only one pāṭā in the gājan is meant to support a full-grown man; the rest are much smaller.

Bhaktas explain that in the trance the pāṭā is Bhairab, being both like Bhairab and at one with him. It is Bhairab because the deity "descends" on the bhakta through the pāṭā; otherwise the board is a representative, a sign of the deity. The bhaktas claim that in the trance the deity enters the bhakta through the head, hence the pāṭā is carried on the head. When in trance, the devotee loses consciousness and begins to tremble from within. He is made to leap about in response to the tumult inside him. Finally he thrashes around uncontrollably; the initial rhythm of the dance being lost, the bhakta has to be held down before the trance completely overpowers him and results in damage. The incense, the drums, and the fasting are all regarded as preconditions of the trance. In addition, however, the pāṭā pūjā must be performed, without which the deity does not come down through the pāṭā; nor does he come if the bhakta fails to obey the rules of the gājan.

The pūjā is performed by the pāṭbhakta, and by any bhakta who wishes to become *śālbhakta* (those who dance with the board). In the pūjā the pāṭā is like the ghat, the *gāmār* tree, the trident, and the beṭ in previous days' pūjās. Vermilion, turmeric, and ghī are placed on the pāṭā, flowers are offered, and food (rice and sweets) is given in bhog. The Brāhmaṇ invokes Śiva and the other deities into the pāṭā, and the bhaktas worship by placing different fruits on the pāṭā. The fruits are shared by the Brāhmaṇ, the pāṭbhakta, and the drummers. The fruits left on the nails go through the procession and are regarded as potent: barren women eat them later in the belief that this will bring about conception. When a fruit falls during the dance of the bhaktas women beseech the dancers to give it to them. Bhaktas may also offer pūjās to the pāṭā by placing fruits on it and addressing Śiva in their minds or calling him aloud. They may also offer individual pūjās to the pāṭā, the Brāhmaṇ reciting the mantra of offering, the bhaktas repeating and pouring water and placing flowers on the board. After the Suryaarghya the bhaktas often offer mānsik pūjā to the pāṭā. Mānsik bhaktas then spend the whole night with the pāṭā, first waiting for, then dancing in, the procession and alternating under the pāṭā in the dance.

The pāṭā is complemented by the *cāluni,* a winnowing basket that is also filled with the fruits of the pāṭā pūjā. This is carried by younger bhaktas. Just like the board, the basket has the quality (*guṇ*) of creating joy and bringing on trance. Bhaktas dance with the cāluni also. In the Boltalā gājan there are three women bhaktas who also dance with the pāṭā, but usually they carry the basket. Women do not participate in the other gājans. Women appear in the Boltalā gājan in response to a command of Śiva that women should dance at this particular festival. In the trance and dance the women are treated no differently—the men wrestle them to the ground until Bhairab leaves them.

Gājan of the Day

The following morning the last major rites of the gājan are performed: the rites of gājan of the day (Dingājan). Very early the bhaktas go to the burning ground and pick up charcoal that was used in cremation. Coming back to the temple, they pile the coals on a fire prepared previously in the temple yard. Together they go off again, and after bathing in the lake they cut small branches from a mango tree. Then they return to the temple waving the leaves, chanting the names of Śiva, bringing the sannyāsībhakta in procession. The latter's duty is to scatter the glowing coals with his hands before the bhaktas dance through the fire. Calling Śiva, the bhaktas walk around the fire three times, fanning it with their branches, then stand around it in a closed circle. The sāddhu comes and stands on a stool, a youth holding the umbrella above him, another holding the picture of the guru. The pāṭbhakta and the sannyāsībhakta perform pūjā with red and white flowers, water, milk, and the five nectars. They repeat the mantras chanted by the priest, pouring the libations on the edges of the fire. First they recite the mantras of purification, then they worship the different deities including Āgni (god of fire). The sannyāsībhakta performs the offerings of water and flowers. In the third part of the pūjā he fills the vessel with milk, water, and flowers and offers these to the fire; then the priest puts a banana, rice, and ghī into the milk. These acts are repeated three times. More offerings of milk follow, and finally all the items are offered together three times. The form and the mantras of this pūjā are exactly the same as those of the Suryaarghya except that more items are offered to more deities. By the time the pūjā ends, the yard is overflowing with people. There is great excitement as the pāṭbhakta stands on a bench and the sannyāsībhakta stands under him with his hands folded in the *namaskār* pose (palms pressed together). The bhaktas form a tight circle around them as the huge crowd, pushing and pressing, surges up to the fire. Shouting the names of Śiva, the pāṭbhakta lifts his arms high and leaps into the knee-deep fire. As he jumps, the sannyāsībhakta bends down and lifts up handfuls of burning coals, scattering them three times. The bhaktas take up the chant of Śiva and dance through the fire one by one, holding the canes high above their heads. As the pāṭbhakta lands in the fire, he begins to jump through it in small hops with both feet, his movements becoming uncontrolled as he falls into trance. The bhaktas whirl around the scattered fire, falling into trance one by one. Some move around gently, others thrash about violently, but they are all attended to by the bhaktas who remain unaffected. Bhaktas in wild, uncontrolled trance are quickly carried into the temple before they can inflict damage on themselves or on others. Inside the temple, they gradually regain consciousness, the priest sprinkling snānjal on them, the bhaktas laying them out on the cool temple floor. The crowd then rushes at the fire, doing praṇām as they pick up the darkened coals with śāl leaves. The ashes are auspicious.

The pāṭbhakta remains in the temple and performs the *dhunaporan* (burning incense) for those who make a mānsik; the priest offers pūjās for other worshipers. This day Śiva is worshiped with uncooked rice, flowers, lighted oil lamp, sweets, molasses, and especially a kind of powdered sugar. After nāmgotra pūjā, the Brāhmaṇ gives the worshiper some sweets, flowers, and water, keeping the rice and sugar as offerings to Śiva.

The Dingājan Suryaarghya is performed in the middle of the day. The bhaktas carry the pāṭās down to another pond not very far from the temple, to the ghāt where the Kāmakkātulā was performed five days earlier. They sit around the pāṭā in shallow water and place their offerings on the immersed boards. When the pūjā of the sun is over they hold the pāṭbhakta and gently lower him on the biggest pāṭā. Calling Śiva, the bhaktas lift the pāṭā high, and the pāṭbhakta rests with his back on the bed of nails. Chanting continuously, the bhaktas go in procession to the temple. When they reach the temple, the pāṭbhakta is lifted from the pāṭā; he then does Śiva pūjā, and his back is rubbed with snānjal. Through the mercy of Śiva the ordeals of the gājan do not damage the bhaktas.

In the evening the bhaktas are invited by the Kṛṣṇaganj ṣolaānā for jalājog. They go in procession through Āṭpārā to the Lalju temple. All the way, people line the streets; the men bow in namaskār, the women do praṇām to the sāddhu and the pāṭbhakta. The procession stops in a low-caste neighborhood, a pāṛā of Bagdis. Here the bhaktas sit in the courtyard, chanting the names of Śiva while a Bagdi head of household washes the feet of the pāṭbhakta and the sāddhu. This water is given to the women of the pāṛā, who touch it to their lips and sprinkle it on their heads. They offer milk and sherbet to the sāddhu and pāṭbhakta and water to the bhaktas. As the procession leaves again, the women spread a towel in the dust, and when the bhaktas have stepped on the cloth it is taken into the house. The Kṛṣṇaganj people, the headman, the ṣolaānā leaders, and the Lalju priest are waiting for the bhaktas. The bhaktas witness the temple ārati, then sit in the market square, forming a large rectangle. The temple priests distribute food, śāl leaves, *mukkolai* (wetted pulses), *calukolai* (pulses), jungle fruits such as *talbij* and *licu,* bananas, mangoes, cucumbers, hot peppers, and molasses. Bel sherbet and water are given at the end. All these items are used during the gājan in the offerings to the deities. As the bhaktas finish, the children take the plates and eat whatever food is left; it is prasad.

Exegesis of Dingājan

The fire and the sun are of great significance in the last day of the celebration. Sun and fire are linked together in the bhakti of Śiva: without the heat and the flame to test him, what does a bhakta have to offer to Śiva? Dingājan is the time for putting one's devotion to the test in the *āgunsannyasā* (fire ordeal). Pūjā is offered to the fire the same way the pāṭā was worshiped on the previous days, and the mantras are the same as in the pūjā of the sun. The difference is that the god of fire, Āgni, is invoked, the last acts of the pūjā being the same as those of the *homa* (fire) sacrifice. Again the different Deb-debīs are invoked and libations are poured for them, but the worship centers on the sun, the fire, and Śiva. Śiva is invoked in the fire, but men put their feet into the fire so that honor may be done to the gods. There is an inversion here: Brahmā and the other gods worshiped Āgni by placing fire on their heads; men place their feet into the fire, being unworthy of the act of Brahmā. The offering of milk, banana, and *pān* leaf is the final act in the Āgni pūjā as well as the homa. This is a general offering to all deities; since the fire is the tongue of the gods, all offerings poured into the fire reach heaven. The fire does not burn the bhaktas because they believe that Śiva takes the pain upon himself. Yet the fire hurts, for if it did not it would be no ordeal. The bhaktas claim that it does no damage, especially since trance soon replaces consciousness. Śiva, on the other hand, is said to suffer. Priests and bhaktas inside the temple fan the liṅga and, saying that he is sweating, point to the fine film of water covering the stone. The remnants of the fire are eagerly sought by the onlookers, for they believe that the coals keep insects and other bugs away from the house and the grass cures skin diseases. The coals are brought from the burning ground, a place favored by Śiva. Fire itself is auspicious, and Śiva's attention is drawn to the bhaktas' touching of fire. There is a saying that devotees have to give foot to the fire, *āgune pā dite hobe*. Without such an act the devotion is not true; this is the ultimate test. There has to be fire in the gājan, otherwise Śiva is not satisfied.

The pūjā of the sun is performed early during Dingājan. By then the sun is hot, but the pūjā is done in the cool water. Most ordeals take place when the sun is hottest, this being in itself an act of bhakti. The sun itself is of great importance to the bhaktas. They say that everyone wants the sun in the gājan. All action has to do with the sun, directly or indirectly. The sun is the witness of devotion; trees have failed Sīta as witnesses, but the sun is above deception. The sun is a living deity (*sākṣāt debatā*). He needs no image and no sect devoted to his exclusive worship. The sun gives life and shows men the whole creation; hence in worshiping him bhaktas acknowledge what is central to the functioning of the world. In more abstract terms the core of the gājan is the encounter of Śiva and Durgā. The sun is a witness to creation, and the life of men is regulated (*niyantrita*) by him. In and through the sun the whole universe is revealed. Without the sun there is no life. Through its light the sun allows one to contemplate the creation of the goddess, and worshiping the sun is a direct way of worshiping the creative principle. The sun is greeted every day, and after the daily bath Bengalis do obeisance to the sun, reciting a few words of prayer. Through these qualities the sun leads men to the realization of brahman, the all-encompassing Immense Being, who is without quality and without sex, who is knowledge itself (jñān).

Immersion of the Sacred Thread

Only one ritual of significance takes place during the final day of the gājan: the immersion of the sacred thread. Bhaktas assemble at the temple, bringing special items in addition to the final offerings: turmeric and oil—things they could not use during the gājan.

Standing at the water's edge, bhaktas oil themselves and smear their bodies well with turmeric. They oil their canes and ceremonially rub the feet of the Brāhmaṇ with oil and turmeric. Then they bathe and stand in line in waist-deep water. The final pūjā begins. It is the same as the rite of initiation I described earlier, the difference being that the central concern this time is the giving up of the paitā and Śiva gotra. Holding the sacred threads in their hand, the bhaktas recite mantras of purification and mantras of Śiva's service. Finally they chant the immersion mantra: "I abandon the gotra of Śiva and take back the gotra of my ancestors." Saying this, they shout the names of Śiva, and, rolling the paitā in a lump of clay, they cast it far out into the water. Together all the bhaktas sit down to a meal of items forbidden until now. They eat fried oil cakes with onions, and going back to the temple they partake of cooked rice for the first time. Brāhmaṇ cooks prepare rice, curried vegetables, and sometimes fish. The food is offered to Śiva and then distributed to the bhaktas who sit in the nāthmandir. The expense is borne by the solaānā.

The men are ready to go back to ordinary life. Their first act is to feast the children of the neighborhood: *balakbhajan*. The men are no longer bhaktas, but the power and grace of the gājan remain; this is the meaning of bhakti and bhakta for the participants.

The pāṭbhakta still has his sacred thread, for he has a final rite to perform, the immersion of Kāmakkā Debī. After sundown the goddess departs, as she came, through the waters, in the dark.

Bhakti and the Person of the Bhakta

Bhakti is the way men accomplish the trials set by the gājan. Bhakti is the surrender to the play of the gods in which men are just as necessary as the deities themselves. Bhakti is devotion to and faith in Śiva, an acceptance of his power to deliver men from danger, his ability to intervene in human affairs. Bhakti is absolute reliance on the deity, and calling Śiva itself signifies the bhaktas' acknowledgment that they have no one but Śiva to draw on. To call Śiva when the going is rough, the sun too hot, the thirst unbearable, the rolling painful, and the fire hurting is the only thing that can take a bhakta through the ordeal. When one calls Śiva and trusts him, nothing can go wrong; Śiva is bound to listen and act. Bhaktas often encourage each other to "put the mind" to the lord, calling out loudly—the louder the better. Noise is a sign of great concentration, for the loud cries are bound to distract Śiva from his meditation and bring him to the gājan. The expression *bhaktite bhagavan,* "divinity is in bhakti," points precisely to the dual nature of devotion apparent in the gājan. On the one hand, the devotee tries to become conscious of the identity of Śiva by concentrating on him and repeating his names to a point where he is no longer conscious of himself. On the other hand, the proof of the deity's concern is in this very process of devotion, for without devotion men cannot become aware of the ways of the gods. It is often said in Bengal that men come to have faith through the rites they perform; if one performs the pūjā, then the gods will manifest themselves. Otherwise men can go through life without ever being bothered by the meaning of the sacred. (Edward Dimock's elegant historical and textual studies of bhakti are definitive [1966*a, b*]. As he would expect, the local meanings of bhakti in the gājan add another dimension to an all-India understanding of devotionalism.)

Śiva is the rescuer, the deliverer in the gājan. Bhaktas want to be with Śiva. Whenever someone is in trouble, mostly through exhaustion, he is taken to Bābā (Father). Bābā is Bhairab, Śiva's manifestation who is always present in the gājan. Śiva is immobile in the temple; he cannot be carried around. But Bhairab is where the bhaktas are. The board and basket are regarded as Bhairab, even though they are all *Śiber aṅga* (the parts of Śiva). When the bhaktas go to Śiva, they become "cool." The pūjās they do, on the other hand, cool Śiva. The water of green coconut, milk, and Ganges water are all cooling substances. Bhaktas fan Śiva and hold an umbrella over Bhairab when he moves; both these objects are symbols of royalty. The deities are kings, and the honor they are shown is the due of a king. The bhaktas adore Śiva and are his suppliants; through their calls they beseech him to save them from all hardships. Śiva is *upakāri ṭhākur* (Benevolent Lord). The preferred attitude of the bhaktas is *āradhanā* (prayer) and *prarthana* (begging). The bhaktas offer votive flowers to Śiva. The flower is "given back" to the people when it falls down from the liṅga where it has been placed, signifying Śiva's pleasure with the devotion. Bhairab possesses the devotees; the flowers of Śiva's pūjā and snānjal of Śiva relieve the trance. Śiva gives boons (*bor*) and grace (*upakār*) to his devotees.

Bhakti rescues the mānsik bhaktas from the fire and the bānnphurabhaktas from the pain, the consequences of all actions recoiling upon Śiva himself. Śiva cannot tolerate harm to those who do things out of devotion to him. From bhakti comes a certain ability (*khamata* or *sahas*) to do extraordinary things: *lāphrābhanga* (breaking by jumping), *pāṭā suya* (lying on the pāṭa), *āgunsannyāsā* (fire ordeal), *upās* (fasting). The pāṭbhakta must have this ability to a far greater degree than any other bhakta. It is the bhakti of the pāṭbhakta that keeps the gājan out of trouble. Not everyone has the devotion to make the gods listen. The pāṭbhakta must do acts of bhakti to ensure the safety of all bhaktas. Hence he begins fasting and performing pūjās fifteen days before the major rites of the gājan. In each of the gājan rituals there is the possibility of going wrong. If a mistake is made there is trouble and danger: the worship of Śiva and Durgā is fraught with danger. Not only are the acts themselves dangerous, but the deities are capricious and unreliable. Hence the necessity of performing the rites accurately and trusting everything to absolute bhakti. The pāṭbhakta is responsible for the collectivity, hence his long preparation for the gājan. But the acts of each bhakta are binding on the collectivity; if one bhakta disobeys a rule, all the bhaktas will suffer.

Bhaktas wear a style of dress that symbolizes their relationship to Śiva. The dhotī, the long piece of cloth ordinarily worn by men, is usually tied around the waist like a loincloth reaching the ankles and, being brought up between the legs, is tucked in at the waist in the back, leaving the calves exposed. For ritual purposes this is tied in a different way: the cloth covers both legs entirely, giving the garment a skirtlike, billowing effect. This is the proper attire for rituals; priests wear the dhotī this way, and so do non-Brāhmaṇs in ritual contexts. The ritual wear of a dhotī is distinctive in another way—no stitched garment for the upper body is worn with it.

For the gājan, or any pūjā for that matter, the ritualist must wear an unstitched cloth of certain length. The upper part of the body remains naked or is covered with another piece of cloth, a stole, also unstitched. These garments are also known as *laggā bastra* and *uttariya,* both meaning clothes of modesty. Sāddhus and mendicants wear this kind of clothing, marking their lack of attachment to the world. Not all of them wear the stole, either; Uddasin (Śaiva) sect mendicants wear only a small loincloth, and Vaiṣṇava ascetics usually cover the whole body. The style of wearing clothes signifies an office and status quite separate from those of the everyday world.

The garments are white in the everyday context, but in the gājan they are yellow or saffron. Color also signifies the relation of the bhaktas to Śiva, and most ascetics devoted to Śiva and the goddess wear red clothes. The fact that the bhaktas are a group is brought out by the uniform color of their dhotīs; none wear black, which is the sāddhu's color. Dress thus distinguishes the bhaktas from the Brāhmaṇ priest, the non-Brāhmaṇ ritualist (*pūjāri*), and the renouncer. This kind of classification is central to the symbolism of the gājan: in a way the bhaktas unify within them all three offices, but their dress also signifies very distinctly their participation in one particular ritual, the gājan. The towel itself is an important garment; it acts as a small loincloth, and all bathing rites and acts of devotion are performed with only the towel as a covering. The seminakedness of the bhaktas increases the value of the self-denial in the gājan: men put up with the sun and the heat to win the favor of Śiva.

Each bhakta carries a beṭ (cane) or a sapling of the gāmār, bel, or nīm tree, all of which have an important role in ritual. The cane is often hereditary, fathers handing them down to sons and grandsons. Canes may last a hundred years or more, but their suppleness is maintained by frequent oiling. On the final day of the gājan the cane is rubbed with oil and turmeric, the same items bhaktas rub on the feet of the Brāhmaṇ, and on themselves, before the immersion of the sacred thread. The cane is like the weapon of the deities. Each divinity carries a missile; Śiva carries the trident. The cane is like the trident of Śiva. During the initial ritual of the gājan, bhaktas tie the sacred thread to the cane, then calling on Śiva they hit the canes together, creating a rustling noise. This is the voice of the beṭ, adding joy to the proceedings and reaching Śiva the same way as the calls do. During the *śālpāṭā nāc* (dance with the nail-studded board), the bhaktas hit their canes together above the board, thus helping to induce trance in the dancer who carries the board. This process is also known as "making joy," *ananda korā,* joy being the basis of devotion to and possession by Bhairab, Śiva's "deputy" in the gājan. By hitting the sticks together devotees not only express their emotion and create the environment for trance, they also try to break Śiva's unceasing meditation (*dhyen*) and austerities (*tapassā,* concentration), forcing him to take note of the exuberant devotion to him here on earth and asking him to bestow grace and favor on his followers. Despite the ordeals, the gājan must be full of joy; the attitude of devotion, no matter how hard, is unselfish and joyous, straight from the heart, without regard for the consequences.

From the first day on, the cane stays with the bhakta, an implement of bhakti and a sign of office. Bhaktas take their canes wherever they go, using them to maintain order in the processions. The cane is respected by all those who watch the ceremonies. When the ghurānbhaktas roll through the town, the other bhaktas keep everyone out of the way with the aid of the canes. The cane has a certain power; if a barren tree is hit with a cane during the gājan, it will bear fruit. When the gājan is over, the cane is put away in a high place (usually tied to the rafters) for another year. Canes are regarded as a part of Śiva himself. They are of the lord, a symbol of the gājan. They signify that their masters belong to a different world, the world of the deities, the gotra of Śiva.

Bhaktas wear a *rudramālā,* a garland made of the fruit of the *rudra* tree, a favorite of Śiva. Śiva himself wears this mālā, as do most ascetics. Like the ascetics, the bhaktas wear many kinds of garlands, both as a sign of respect (directed at specific deities) and as a sign of status. Some wear beads of bel wood, tulsī wood, shells, and glass all around their necks, distinguishing them at once from the renouncers of specific sects and from the ritualists in the pūjās of everyday life.

For most of the group rituals in the gājan the bhaktas must wear the kusa grass ring on the fourth finger of the left hand. When they receive the paitā they also receive the ring from the Brāhmaṇ. From then on they use the rings for the Suryaarghya every day. The kusa ring is a feature of śakti pūjās, hence in the gājan it signifies the relation of the bhaktas to the goddess. The ring is sacred (*pabittra*), and its use is purificatory. It means added strength for those who participate in rites that are considered to be dangerous, when a small mistake can result in trouble for all bhaktas. The ring is pure, and it protects from defilement, for any unrecognized pollution can annul the effect of the ritual.

The most important object bhaktas wear is the sacred thread. It is called the *uttarī* or *paitā,* both words denoting the sacred thread worn by the Brāhmaṇs. The threads come from the bazaar, the same threads Brāhmaṇs wear. They must be tied and rearranged by a Brāhmaṇ or by a bhakta who has already received a paitā. Usually the pāṭbhakta ties the threads. But gājan sacred threads are worn around the neck, not across the left shoulder in the Brāhmaṇic fashion. The thread is thicker, being tied many times over and forming a smaller circle than that of the Brāhmaṇs. Nevertheless, it symbolizes a new birth, birth into the gotra of the gods, not birth into the Brāhmaṇ caste. Bhaktas emphasize that they are not like Brāhmaṇs but like deities. The sacred thread is used to purify objects in the pūjā; in the gājan it signifies the ability of the bhaktas to serve, touch, and worship the deities without any restrictions.

Bhaktas carry several items of worship including the *kamandala,* a small brass jug containing *gaṅgājal,* the sacred water of the Ganges. This container is essential to any worship, not only for the oblations of the deities, but for the purification of the ritualist and of the whole environment surrounding the locality of the worship. In the daily rounds of the nearby *ṭhākursthān* ("places," altars of the gods) bhaktas perform pūjās by sprinkling water on the altars (*bedī*) and pouring libations to the divinities, bathing the images of Śiva in the temples. For these acts the kamandala is necessary. The shape of the vessel is the same as that used by the Brāhmaṇ priest in the ordinary pūjā. Other pūjā objects are also used by the bhaktas; the *kosakusi,* a pair of leaf-shaped copper vessels; the grinding stone for making sandalwood paste; the śāl-leaf plates for making food offerings; the flower baskets for honoring different deities. These are used by bhaktas without Brāhmaṇ intermediaries. The bhaktas make the offerings, perform the pūjās; the Brāhmaṇ is often merely a helper.

Bhaktas walk barefoot and cannot even wear sandals. All day they perform their duties with no protection from the sun. They show respect by remaining barefooted. This adds to the ordeal of the gājan, and many walk to the temples when the sun is high as a further sign of self-denial and devotion. At the "lifting" of the goddess, even the pāṭbhakta does not wear his wooden sandals. Bare feet are proper to any pūjā, the Brāhmaṇ priest being barefooted when he prepares for worship. In other ways too the bhaktas must observe a ritualist's preparation for pūjā. They fast before the worship, bathe before touching the object used in the offering, collect flowers for the pūjā, bring water from a river or a tank, rinse the dhotīs worn during the pūjās and hang them out to dry in the open (water must flow down the whole length of the garment before it can be worn for worship).

Only the pāṭbhakta carries a trident. The sāddhu is not a bhakta. He is a representative of Śiva, the guru of the gājan, and of some bhaktas in everyday life as well. Bhaktas garland the sāddhu at certain times, and all do praṇām to him before each of the ceremonial processions through the town. The sāddhu is more like Śiva than the bhaktas are; he is like Śiva even in everyday life. These distinctions are kept in the gājan: only the sāddhu carries the small two-ended drum, and only he wears his hair matted and has his body smeared with ashes, all these being signs of Śiva. The sāddhu is not just like Śiva; as a renouncer he is a deity in his own right. The guru is the incarnate deity of a devotee in the world; as such he is above the gods because he shows men the path to god, and he is incapable of error in his judgment of what is good for his disciples.

Similarities and differences are carefully defined in the gājan through objects expressing status and through actions directed at the holders of different offices. The pāṭbhakta is responsible for whatever happens in the gājan, and so he carries a trident, but this is not just a sign of office.

It is as much a part of Śiva as the liṅga image, the sāddhu, the board, and other objects in which Śiva can manifest himself. Any object associated with Śiva in the myths can become his manifestation. So the trident the pāṭbhakta carries is a symbol of Śiva for the gājan. During the Suryaargya the trident itself is worshiped: it is marked the same way that the ghat is marked at the invocation of the goddess. The trident is offered pūjā and bhog, and all bhaktas who do special acts of devotion also do praṇām to it. At every pūjā it is garlanded and decorated with lotuses just as the sāddhu and the images of the gods are.

A Provisional Analysis

Spatial divisions in the town are faithfully expressed in the organization of the festival. Temples of Śiva define the town as a single unit and as a number of segments in a way similar in effect to other festivals.

Almost all "high" and "low" jātis participate in the gājan. The festival, however, is not dominated by the "low" castes.

The aspect of reversal is not very marked. Bhaktas do pūjā regardless of caste, and there is no separation in eating. Yet people do not use the gājan as a way to carry castelessness into everyday life. The reversal is striking because it is limited. There are no disproportionately large groups of low-caste bhaktas; it cannot be said that the gājan is a way of transcending a social contradiction by ritual means. On the other hand, the egalitarian aspects are also clear. Despite the sacred thread, the bhaktas do not become Brāhmaṇs for the duration of the gājan. Much more, they become a part of Śiva himself (*Śiber aṅga*). The ideology emphasizes a relation to Śiva, and bhaktas are concerned to point out that the status they gain is different from that of the Brāhmaṇs. The latter must go through the initial ritual of separation, just like the rest of the bhaktas. Brāhmaṇ bhaktas recite mantras different from those of non-Brāhmaṇs. The former declaim sam vedic, the latter yayur vedic mantras. The Brāhmaṇs keep on wearing the sacred thread (though they too are given a new one from the ṣolaānā) in the prescribed Brāhmaṇic fashion, across the shoulders. The non-Brāhmaṇ bhaktas wear the paitā around their necks. At the same time, there is a strong element of specific caste reversal in the ceremony of paitā-taking. Bhaktas are like Śiva because without becoming like Śiva they cannot perform the acts of Śiva, cannot attract Śiva's attention, and cannot leave the ordinary sphere of life and participate in the play of the gods. The gājan is the bhaktas' contribution to the acts of the gods in maintaining the cycles of creation and destruction in the world, the proper rhythm that partakes of all things animate or inanimate.

Participants reflect the pattern of jāti settlement in the different localities as well as a marked variation between town and village. About half the bhaktas at the Ṣāṛeśvar gājan come from villages surrounding Vishnupur: among them "low"- and "mid"-ranking castes dominate, with a fraction of "high"-jāti representation. Bhaktas from Vishnupur are overwhelmingly from "high"- and "mid"-ranking jātis. The reverse is the case in the ābārgājans, where the "mid"-ranking castes predominate. At the Boltalā gājan, where "low"-jāti participation is discouraged, the majority come from middle-range castes. The Buṛo Śiva gājan has a preponderance of "upper-middle" and "high" castes. Both gājans have much fewer "low"-jāti participants than the Ṣāṛeśvar gājan.[11]

In the internal dynamics of the gājan, locality is just as important as jāti affiliation in deciding who joins which groups, if not more so. People from the same area (village in the countryside, neighborhood in town) tend to do the prescribed rites of the gājan together.

There is a correspondence between jāti and locality: representations of society and locality are linked in the mythic-ritual field. The categories of the field do not repeat the innumerable jāti subdivisions but group a number of jātis of the same locality into broader divisions. Localities are joined by the processions of the gājan.

Though the gājan honors Śiva before all other gods, we find representations of goddesses such as Manasā, Caṇḍī, Bhavanī, and Kālī in the temples, and bhaktas offer pūjās to these and many other deities.

The professional servants of deities—the priests—are also segmented into several groups. The high-low division is also operative among Brāhmaṇ ritualists: both the "pure" and the "degraded" Brāhmaṇ groups are involved in the gājan. The opposition of high and low is a segmentary one, smaller units being divisible in terms of the same principle. Is then the gājan a "low"-jāti festival, given the free participation of "lower" castes and the significance of the "lower"-status Brāhmaṇ priests in the rituals?

In discussing narratives of the gājan we saw that different deities may share the same myths and rituals. One reason for this is the regional variation in the significance of deities such as Dharma and Manasā. Śiva is worshiped widely even in the areas where scholars have placed the center of the Dharma cult. The myths of Śiva provide several levels of generality. In the most distant sense, Śiva is the Great God of the Hindu triad Brahmā, Viṣṇu, and Maheśvār. This is the level of the ancient sacred texts in Bengali ideologies, and, though bhaktas are aware of the purāṇic Śiva, the gājan itself has only a limited charter in the Purāṇas. Nevertheless, the Śiva of the Purāṇas is one level of gājan exegesis: the Śiva of the gājan is also Maheśvār in addition to being many other things on different levels of Hindu belief. The other levels of *maṅgal, bratakathā, mahātmā* and other forms of narrative (written and oral) are directly related to the festival.

The first day of the ritual defines the person of the bhakta in opposition to the person in everyday life. The objects worn by bhaktas symbolize this transformation. The separation of bhaktas is also expressed in their ability to do things ordinary people cannot. In performing pūjās and wearing the paitā, bhaktas take on the functions of a Brāhmaṇ priest. Bhaktas are Brāhmaṇs in this sense alone.

Not only are the bhaktas Brāhmaṇs, they are also renouncers. The symbolism of dress and the preferred conduct of practicing austerities liken bhaktas to Śiva in the sense that he is sannyāsī, the renouncer, the one who is outside society. Devotees are sannyāsīs, being removed from everyday life. The devotees differ from the sāddhu, who is the guru of the gājan. The sāddhu is also a renouncer; however, he is that during the rest of the year as well. In the gājan his superiority is expressed by his additional role of guru: all bhaktas garland him.

The food eaten by devotees links them to the gods: only the best food is good enough for bhaktas—in other contexts the gods themselves are offered the same items. The essential difference is also expressed: the bhaktas do not eat cooked food, but cooked food offerings are made to Śiva throughout the festival.

Calling Śiva is the most evident corporate activity of the bhaktas, but this feature also stresses the most general meaning of Śiva. In the verses devotees chant, Śiva is Grace-Giver, Deliverer of the Weak, the Ascetic of Koilās, Lord of Sages. All these are attributes of the Great Lord in the all-India context.

Certain jāti functions are to be noted. Barber and Brāhmaṇ are the most important specialists. The barber and the agradhānī Brāhmaṇ share certain duties in other contexts. The barber's presence is necessary for a number of life-cycle rites such as the *upanayan* (the bestowing of the sacred thread), wedding, and *śrāddha* (funerary ceremony). In these rites also, the barber's action of shaving and of paring nails marks the altered status of the person. The same is true of the funeral Brāhmaṇ: he confers the paitā on the bhaktas, and his taking the first offering from the mourner in the gājan signifies the return of the mourner from a polluted state. The offering, however, also signifies the inferior rank of this class (*srenī*) of Brāhmaṇ. Why should *this* Brāhmaṇ officiate at the gājan? Gājan is dominated by middle-order jātis: there are few "twice-born" bhaktas. The rites of the festival are simplified, even though Brāhmaṇic, in the form of abbreviated pūjās, and the lower-ranking Brāhmaṇ ritualist expresses the characterization of the festival in the native scheme of categories. It is important to note that the funeral Brāhmaṇ assists bhaktas in their passage to a higher status and officiates at their offerings to the sun. These are the very acts he performs at śrāddha with the same effect: he ensures the passage of the polluted mourner back to everyday life, but he himself is less pure than other Brāhmaṇ srenīs.

There are clearly defined offices within the gājan: the leading one being that of the pāṭbhakta. He must accumulate bhakti and *tej* (force), the qualities of gurus and sāddhus in other contexts. Clearly, then, the pāṭbhakta is much more than the head of the gājan. His is the hierarchically superior office: his devotion must be greater than that of anybody else. The roles are separated in the requirement that other bhaktas join him in Kamilatulā. The context in which the bhaktas assist him is also significant: the pāṭbhakta is passive at the lifting of the goddess. The goddess herself is the active element. Śakti, the power of the goddess, assumes the center of attention in this rite: but śakti is dangerous (music, in other contexts a symbol of royalty and rejoicing, is played only after Kamila's arrival). As we shall see below, śakti is the active principle, but it also is an aspect of Śiva. In this relationship the pāṭbhakta assumes the role of Śiva. This interpretation is confirmed by the wearing of the "auspicious bracelet," *maṅgal suta.* In other circumstances the bracelet may mean different things depending on the colors used and the way the threads are tied; for example, turmeric-colored threads are used in marriage. In the gājan they symbolize the "initiated" status of bhaktas. But more than that, they signify the role of devotees as they are related to Śiva in Śiva's relation to the goddess. Among men only the pāṭbhakta receives the suta on the occasion of Kamilatulā, but the trident, a symbol of Śiva, also receives it. The day after, when attention shifts to Śiva in the form of the gāmār tree, all bhaktas receive the suta.

Śiva and the goddess unite according to the exegesis, but their union must not be complete: it has danger for the world. Who is this goddess? Durgā, according to all the bhaktas. Why is she called Kamila? One answer is that as the manifestation of Durgā, the hierarchically supreme goddess, the Debī of gājan is Kamila: identity in substance and replacement in structural principle. But it is more complicated than this, and the remaining days of the festival illuminate the puzzle.

The processions of the first three days take in elements of the landscape that are of significance in the latter part of the festival. Categories of space such as land, water, landing and washing platform at the edge of the river, cultivated fields, temples, and streets are defined and brought into relation with each other.

The gāmār tree itself is a complex representation: it is related to cane, trident, sacred thread, and other symbols expressing aspects of Śiva. It is also more: it is an aspect of Śiva. Its trunk is white like the ash-smeared body of an ascetic (the color of Śiva). It is also invested with a bracelet. The only sacrifice of the gājan (a vegetable sacrifice) is performed for the gāmār tree. Hashish, a favorite item of Śiva, is among the offerings.

All these attributes point to the gāmār as representing Śiva himself, not just one of his aspects. There are other reasons for this interpretation. Another name for the gājan in North Bengal is *gāmbhira* (gāmār or gāmbhira is the ornamental tree *Gmelina arborea*). There is evidence that gāmbhira may have meant a place of worship: Śiva's temple gājan is called *ādyer gāmbhira,* the gāmbhira of the goddess.[12] In some texts gāmbhira is an epithet of Kālā, the god of fate, meaning the unfathomable. Kālā is an aspect of Śiva (Scheftelowitz 1929). Most decisive, however, is the evidence gathered by Cintaharan Chakravarti (1935).[13] In discussing a number of texts relating to the cult of Kālārkarudra he quotes the meditation verse (*dhyen*) of a deity called Gāmbhira who is to be worshiped outside the temple. This god is white, a benefactor who must be meditated upon in order to be attained. The texts also give rules for a gājanlike performance. The main deity is a composite Śivalike god who has three aspects: Kālā, Ārka, Rudra. Kālā is the deity of destruction mentioned above, Ārka is the sun (whose eyes are fire), and Rudra is the lord who carries the symbols of a sannyāsī (trident and drum). His body is smeared with ashes. All these deities are related to Śiva. In the context of the gājan, the gāmār tree represents the god, just as the sacred vessel represents the goddess.

The texts of Dharmapūjā follow the actions of the gājan, as so far described, remarkably faithfully. There is a gāmbhāri maṅgal in the *Sunyapurāṇ* of Ramaipaṇḍit.[14] In it the pandit does pūjā to the tree; a small branch is cut off and taken to the house of the kāmār. In accounts of the Dharma rites the cutting of the tree forms a prominent part of the narrative.

It is clear that there are variant performances of the gājan all over eastern India. The rituals differ greatly in action and belief (they are also designated by different terms and addressed to different deities). The festivals are related to each other, however; the hierarchy among deities varies most conspicuously from case to case, the group of deities remaining largely the same.

The blacksmith's role in the gājan is consistent with his duties in other contexts. First of all the blacksmith must fashion the iron nails for the gāmār. Second, he performs the animal sacrifice in all other pūjās. He forges the sacrificial knives (billhook, spike, nail) that are used later in the gājan, appearing also in the Dharma maṅgal, when a queen desiring a son impales herself on a spike to appease Dharma.[15] The role of the kāmār is also stressed in the incantations of the variant gājans.[16]

In a different context I argued that pūjā rests on a tripartite structure of three relational categories: deity, ritualist, and worshiper. In the myths and legends of the royal Malla dynasty in Vishnupur this is expressed through the relations among the king, the king's goddess, and the king's priest. The king is the offerer on whose behalf the priest performs the sacrifice. In the gājan the roles of ritualist and offerer are collapsed in the person of the bhakta. The king is greeted also because he is the owner of the land: in the past people held land as a gift from the king. The deities were also the king's, since they dwelt on his land. The king bestowed pūjās and deities on his subjects and also gave land so that the deities could be served. So the king "owned" the people and the deities on the land. The deities of Vishnupur and the people were linked to the land, since townsmen ideally paid land tax to the deities. These sets of relationships have been changing in a remarkable way during the past hundred years or so, but they are still interpreted and acted out in the above manner. However, the category of rājā is being replaced by that of "community," and this marks a shift in the relation between people and deities of the land.

The processions emphasize the significance of the categories king and sāddhu. The procession to the *āśram* (retreat) separates the renouncer in everyday life from the renouncer in the gājan. Categories may be collapsed temporarily, and different roles may be expressed in one person, but separate identities are maintained, and respective roles and categories are never confused.

The pāṭā is defined through its own pūjās and offerings. It is not by chance that these fruits are efficacious fertility symbols; after all, the pāṭā pūjā follows the coming together of Śiva and Durgā. In establishing the meaning of the board we note a seeming contradiction between the bhaktas' exegesis and that of Brāhmaṇs. The priests hold that the pāṭā is Gaurī, the goddess, the bhaktas insist that it is a part of Śiva, Father Bhairab. We saw that the union of Śiva and Durgā is the cause of all action. The bhaktas are related to Śiva and separately, by virtue of the bracelet, to the goddess. In the trance the effect of the union (*milan*) is revealed to the people. For everyone concerned, this takes place through the joint action of god and goddess. The bhaktas represent Śiva. One aspect of Śiva, Bhairab, "descends" on the devotee in trance. It has to be Bhairab because Śiva is immobile: Bhairab is the active aspect of Śiva. Hence the board is also Bhairab, the representative of Śiva in motion.

The bhaktas relate themselves to Śiva through the pāṭā: for them this represents the same relation to Durgā as that of Śiva. But the symbol is a composite one: since according to the ideology Śiva contains the goddess, the pāṭā can be regarded as Durgā; the dance of bhaktas represents the relation of Śiva and Durgā. There is no contradiction here, just a segmentary hierarchy in relationships. Assigning meanings to individual symbols depends on a subjective orientation to a whole: the point of segmentation one selects for the separation of male and female meanings depends on one's position in the structure of the gājan at a particular moment.

In keeping with the gradual development of intensity in the gājan, the actions of the night culminate in the procession. Here the ordeal of *bānnphura* (piercing the tongue) must be commented upon. The bhaktas involved are not proper bhaktas, but their action comes at a significant point in the festival: it cannot come before this stage. These bhaktas also introduce a "low"-jāti element in that many of them are from scheduled castes. According to them, it takes bravery and power to submit to the ordeal, of which "high"-jāti people are not capable. This is not a jāti role in the same sense as that of the kāmār. Nevertheless, it is a recognition that the bhakti of the "low"-jāti complex, and especially the bhakti directed to the Bhūmidebatā (deity of the earth) cycle of gods is of a specific kind involving blood and pain. In the gājan such devotion is a prerequisite of Bhairab, but in other contexts its distinguishing feature is not caste but different notions of bhakti. In the sects, the devotion to Kālī and other goddesses is of the same type.

Trance is uncontrollable action. It is, however, induced through fasting, incense, dance, and drumming. But it is the action of the gods. It represents the effect of the milan śakti we have already discussed. It is auspicious, beneficial action. There is inauspicious possession also, and this occurs when something goes wrong and a mistake or transgression occurs. Then the deity comes unheralded and enraged and seizes an unsuspecting victim, letting his wrath loose on the wretch. The deity then speaks out and submits his prisoner to all kinds of torture till his wishes are satisfied. Then he departs quickly, leaving the possessed man limp and exhausted.

Siva is the madman of the burning ground, the unpredictable ascetic who abandons his beautiful and languishing wife in favor of an austere power: *tapassā* (a power acquired through meditation and yogic acts). There are other meanings to the bhaktas' procession to the burning ground. In the accounts of other festivals there is a similar ritual at the burning ground that is meant to appease ghosts, Śiva's terrifying companions. Another account conjectures that the ritual enacts rebirth, the passing and reincarnation of souls (see especially Chattopadhyay 1935; Chakravarti 1935; Ghosh 1957).

A new deity appears in Dingājan—Āgni, the god of fire. We saw that fire is an attribute of Kālā in variant accounts of the festival. Here Āgni forms part of the hierarchy of gods in relation to Śiva and the sun. The rituals of the day further emphasize the role of the kāmār (in preparing the thorns for *jhāpbhanga*). The kumār, or potter, appears in several myths. Śiva's body is marked by all the ordeals bhaktas inflict upon themselves. He is further tortured by the summer heat, and so he takes refuge under the potter's wheel. It is dark, cool, and dry there. Potters do not throw the wheel in the month of Boiśakh. When they eventually do resume work, they worship Śiva first. The potter fashions the ghat, the vessel of the goddess. The bhaktas go in procession to the kumār's house during Dingajan just as they go to the kāmār's on Gāmārkātā night. They take fruits and water from the kumār.

Fire walking is an act of self-denial. It is directed at Śiva but involves the pūjā of Āgni. Āgni must be propitiated since bhaktas put their feet into the fire: first they must elevate Āgni to their heads (hence the sannyāsībhakta's gesture before lāphrābhanga). But Śiva is the real sufferer: he takes upon himself the troubles of those who call on him honestly and in faith. After the performance people honor Āgni by taking ashes home from the fire. Śiva is "cooled" by the priests inside the temple all through the ordeal.

The end of the festival is marked by reversal of the rules governing the previous days' activities. Mustard oil and turmeric are again rubbed on the body, and fried food is eaten. Bhaktas express their respect to the agradhānī Brāhmaṇ, but this act also states their lower position in a hierarchical system. The agradhānī, though not the "purest" among priests, is superior to bhaktas, especially because he is *the* ritualist of the gājan. So in this case the office of ritualist is marked, not the jāti category (or, alternatively, the jāti category as it is situated in the structure of the mythic-ritual field).

Immersion is a symbolic act in the context of other rituals: it signifies not an end, but a transition. Deities arrive and depart through water: they are bid farewell as if traveling to some distant land. But they will return. So it is with the sacred thread: a year later devotees will again assume a new identity through the same symbol standing in the same sacred space.

Chapter Four

The Play of the Gods

Structure in the System of Festivals

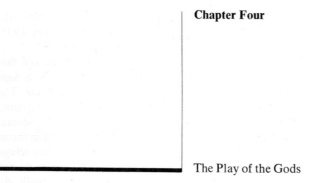

Festivals unify as well as divide the town, according to the deities involved. The three major divinities (Durgā, Śiva, Viṣṇu) are included in each other's festivals; yet the divisions of the town alter according to the cyclical return of pūjās in the annual calendar. The three major deities' annual pūjās define the town as a single unit, a totality of men, objects, and living things in opposition to the divinity. In these pūjās the whole town participates, and all share the benefits of the ritual. Pūjās of other deities define smaller segments of the town. Alternatively, the town is organized both socially and spatially in such a way that major public rituals can be mounted by and for the people as a whole, or by any segment of the town as a whole. The mythology of the festivals elaborates the relationship of these deities to the town. The Goddess Durgā is the divinity of the town; she herself instructed one of the early kings of the Malla line to found a settlement and establish her worship in the place where she manifested herself to him. Townsmen regard the annual pūjā of Durgā as the pūjā of the goddess of Vishnupur, which is performed on behalf the king and the people. The image in the king's Durgā temple is the one the goddess herself commanded the king and his subjects to worship. Similarly, particular manifestations of Śiva and Viṣṇu are also associated with the town in the mythology, both as saviors and as benefactors. The annual festivals of these deities are also pūjās of king and people. Beyond these local manifestations of Durgā, Śiva and Kṛṣṇa (the incarnation of Viṣṇu most widely worshiped in the town) are also honored in others of their manifold aspects, depending on the segment of society and locality that mounts the pūjā in question (see fig. 6).

As I noted above, according to local myths the king entered into an alliance with the goddess when the latter compelled him to worship her. The rājā was to serve her and direct his people to honor her through her pūjās. In return the goddess gave boons, grace, and merit to the royal line and to the people. At a later date the king acknowledged the glory of Kṛṣṇa, and he came to be in the same relation with the town as Durgā. Initially, even before the founding of Vishnupur, the rājās were servants of Śiva. The relation between king and divinity is a significant one; through a king or kinglike figure the people of the locality come into contact with the gods. The king is the enjoyer of the land and the ruler of the subjects; the goddess, also a royal personage (among the gods and in the symbols associated with her earthly representation), appeared to the king on his land. Most deities, their images and their initial appearance in the town, are connected with the king in this way. The king may "give" pūjās to his subjects, and in these pūjās the townsmen stand in the same relation to the gods as does the king himself. In many ways royalty is no longer important in the town; yet it has an enduring signifi-

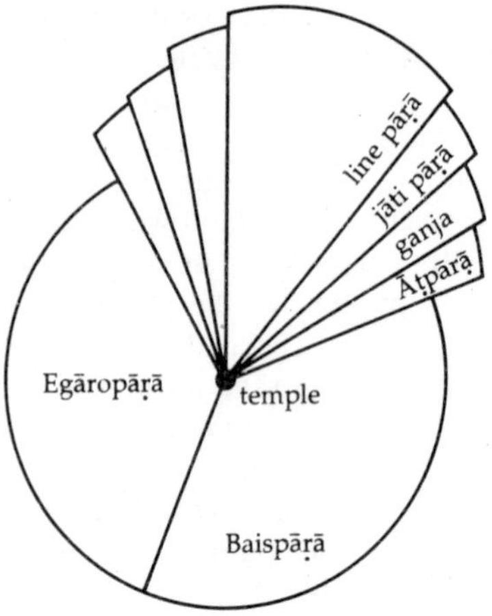

Figure 6. Divisions of the town.

cance that has allowed the emergence of a new category within this system of relationships—the notion of a collectivity, which has come to stand in the same relation to the gods as does the king.

The rituals of Durgā and Śiva express the unity of the town as society and locality. The pūjās of Kṛṣṇa, Viṣṇu, and other deities act the same way. There are three main Kṛṣṇa temples in the town, which divide a single unit into three parts under different manifestations of the same deity. The temples and pūjās of Śiva and the festivals of Durgā accomplish the same subdivision. These major units are made up of pāṛās (neighborhoods) that cluster into *ganja*s (markets). Several ganjas make up the three named main divisions of the town. All these units are significant when viewed through pūjās and festivals. Each of them combines locality and people in opposition to a deity. Each is a whole in the symbolic action of pūjā and in the crucial role of the offerer or *jajmān* (the one on whose behalf the pūjā is offered). The collectivity of men in a particular locality may mount a pūjā in honor of one or another aspect of the goddess. In this case the more recent phenomenon of community pūjās includes all people, just as the king's pūjā includes all subjects. The collectivity is the offerer in ṣolaānā or *sarbajanin* pūjās. The terms are significant: ṣola means sixteen, ānā means a part, one-sixteenth of a rupee, and *ṣolaānā* thus means a totality; *sarba* is all, *jananī* is Mother-Creator, or Durgā, the Creator of All. The community is to the goddess as the king is to the goddess, the king ranking above the community because of his alliance with the goddess. The goddess manifested herself to the kings of Mallabhum, but today she is related to the locality (town, kingdom, district, or region) and to the people in the same manner. It is still the king who performs the Durgāpūjā in the Mrinmoyī temple. There is no reason to doubt, however, that one day this pūjā too will be mounted by the community as a whole, thus letting the process complete a full circle and bring back the Mrinmoyī Durgāpūjā to the most encompassing position on the level of relationships as well as on the levels of action and ideology. The community pūjā of today and the rājā's pūjā of yesterday are parallel in structure, regardless of the passage of time. Thus the community rites also form a totality. Today there is ṣolaānā Durgāpūjā that encompasses the whole town, parallel to the rājā's pūjā. There are pāṛā ṣolaānā pūjās that encompass the people of a locality, jāti ṣolaānā pūjās that are offered by the people of a particular caste living in a locality, and Durgāpūjās offered by the members of a line that is associated with a particular locality. In the latter case the goddess is the deity of a line (see fig. 7).

Pūjā is offered on behalf of a group, and even the ritual performed by an individual affects his line. Pūjā must be a collective act even if the

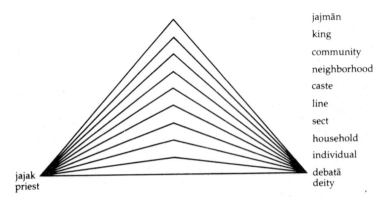

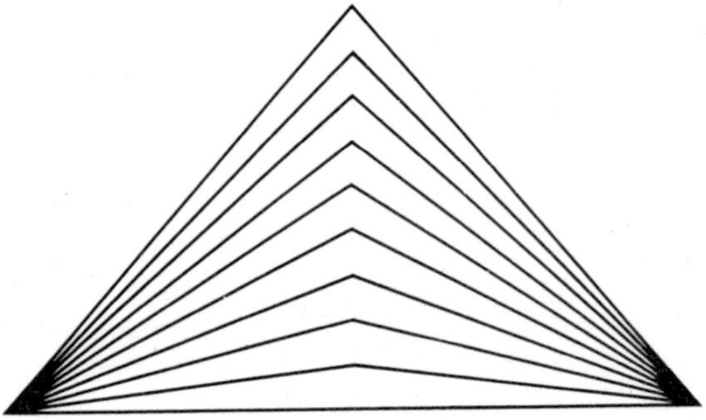

Figure 7. The tripartite structure of pūjā.

collectivity is not present. In the initial rites of a pūjā, the offerer identifies himself through his name and his descent label (gotra). The auspicious motives and results (maṅgal kāmanā) of the pūjā redound on a group of people. Divisions in the festivals have been alluded to above; in the king's pūjā, as in that of the town, all townspeople are merged in the category of worshiper. There is a primary division between king and people, based on a distinction of office and role, but the relationships remain the same. The ṣolaānā is to the goddess as is the king himself, and the same is true of the other units. The model of the king's relation to the gods is followed through the whole society. The unique relation of the goddess to the king remains intact, for we are dealing with relationships and not with the contents of a set of identities. The office of the king distinguishes him from the general worshiper in the ṣolaānā. The people are like kings in their pūjās, but only in the way they relate to the goddess, not in the way they relate to other men. The people are related to the whole (king and goddess) just as they have relationships among themselves.

The third category is the office of sacrificer (*jajak*) or priest (the Brāhmaṇ as purohit), and it completes the structure of the pūjā, which underlies the system of relations within all festivals. Pūjā is offered on someone's behalf, but there is an intermediary between the offerer and the deity. In the myths of the king's accession to the throne the central concern is with the Brāhmaṇ who has to offer the royal sacrifice on the king's behalf. The rājā's priest's line is just as ancient as that of the king. In the case of ṣolaānā pūjā, the Brāhmaṇ is necessary for the approach to the goddess, since only he is equipped (through other rituals) to deal with the dangers involved in Debīpūjā (śakti, the creative energy of the goddess, is destructive when encountered directly). Beyond these dangers, the offices of the priest and the offerer are distinguished not only in the ideology but in the internal order of the pūjā. In the pūjā the basic relations are among the triad of *debatā, jajak, jajmān*. The model for this triad parallels that of king, priest, and goddess as the basic set of relational categories.

Around the king clusters the fullest set of jajmāni relations. In the rājā's traditional Durgāpūjā, each jāti had a certain role. The king is the jajmān to all those jātis, not to the Brāhmaṇs alone. In turn, those jātis are the prajās (subjects) of the rājā. The ritualist and the king are related to each other through their roles in the pūjā (in opposition to the goddess). In this set of jajmāni relations the roles are distinct, even though identities may merge. Those castes that have the king as their jajmān are not identical to the priest, just as the offerers are not identical to the king. The roles of the different jātis are separate from that of the priest, even though they are all "ritualists" in one sense. Only the Brāhmaṇ can approach the goddess directly. Confusion is avoided easily when we realize the full significance of the first ritual in the festival of the goddess, *saṅkalpa* or *kalparambha*. This is a declaration of intent, a vow by the worshiper that he will honor the goddess in a particular way through a certain number of days. The Brāhmaṇ performs this ritual on the offerer's behalf, mentioning the latter's name and gotra.

I argued that the pūjā of the king encompasses the whole town; I also noted that the community pūjās encompass a collectivity. The king's is the fundamental model, however, for only he could bring the high and the low castes together in the festival. Today many ṣolaānā pūjās still have the saṅkalpa performed in the name of the king, since there is no other way of performing a truly ṣolaānā pūjā in which all the people of a locality offer pūjā together. It is the relation of the king to the goddess and to the priest that is replicated in the relations of ṣolaānā, jāti (caste) ṣolaānā, pāṛā (neighborhood) ṣolaānā, baṅgsa (line), and kartā (household head) to the other two categories. In this scheme the roles and offices are distinct and the categories clearly defined, but they are replaceable in a hierarchical segmentary system.

Jātis in pūjās are also grouped in a manner corresponding to the divisions above. The primary separation is between the Brāhmaṇ and the non-Brāhmaṇ. The Brāhmaṇ alone can perform the pūjā. King and Brāhmaṇ together are opposed to the rest of society, for they share a special relation to the goddess (alternatively, another division would oppose the Brāhmaṇs and non-Brāhmaṇs to the king, for the rājā alone concluded an alliance with the goddess). Further, the high castes are separated from the low (Ucca versus Nicu jāti) since the latter are not associated with certain parts of the pūjā as the higher jajmān-jātis are. The Brāhmaṇ does not perform pūjās for the low castes if he has higher-caste jajmān also. The higher castes are subdivided into two groups, called *jal-cal* and *jalacal*. These divisions between high and low castes, and between those whose touch pollutes water and those whose water is regarded as pure, are not a division that can be recognized in the ṣolaānā pūjās or in the internal order of Debīpūjā. I mention them here because the jātiṣolaānā pūjās tend to cluster this way. Further, there are sets of pūjās (of other deities) that are identified with these divisions alone (thus there are particular Nicu jāti pūjās). Even in these pūjās, however, the relations pointed out above hold true.

Every pūjā rests on a structure of tripartite relations—deity-ritualist-worshiper. In this there are two distinct roles for men—the offerer and the one on whose behalf the offering is made—both of which are necessarily linked to the third category, the deity itself. Different hierarchies are established by the replacement of the various categories in this basic structure. The relations entered into by the king are an example of this. We saw how social segments of the town parallel the king in his relation to priest and goddess. However, the king stands in a certain relation to other deities as well, just as the other segments do. The deity of the royal Malla line is Damadār, a manifestation of Śiva (also the name of the sacred river of the Santhals). The chosen deity (the individual or the householder level in the belief system) is Kṛṣṇa, the incarnation of Viṣṇu. This particular Kṛṣṇa is Madan Mahan. The goddess is in a relationship of royalty to the king. Śiva's is a line (*kula*) relation. The same is true of other divisions, categories, and deities. In her relation to the ṣolaānā the goddess denotes the whole town. Śiva effects the same relation in the gājan.

Both the goddess and Śiva are related to the three major divisions of the town, the two festivals, and the smaller ṣolaānā and line segments, the scale being smaller than the region or the town. Viṣṇu is to the town as is the goddess. Since Madan Mahan is the king's chosen deity, the whole town is in the same relation to Madan Mahan as is the rājā. Individual households have independently chosen deities: the structure of the king's relation with categories expressed through symbols is restated through the segmentary social structure. A hierarchy within the town is formed by the kingdom, the town, a collectivity, the threefold division, a locality, a caste, a line, and a household paralleling a hierarchy of deities, manifestations of the goddess, festivals of other deities, which in turn are parallel to elements of space, the major temples of the town, the locality shrines, and household, line, and individual temples and altars. The units occupying the category spaces may vary; alternatively, the same unit may recur in all categories: a goddess may be the deity of a major or lesser social unit, a line, and a chosen deity at the same time.

The three cycles of Durgā, Viṣṇu, and Bhūmidebatā festivals may alternate as units occupying places in the structure of categories. There is a regularity in the transformations: deities not only are discrete in their identity on the level of ideology but are necessarily related within a structure. Hence on one level of analysis we see a parallel structure in the relations of deities and the societal significance of the pūjā system. On another level the social structure is also revealed in certain relationships between cultic deities, the consort pair being the basic unit of a ritual cycle, a self-sufficient microcosm in the domain. The hierarchies are apparent within these cults, and they are repeated from the cults of one god-goddess pair to another. The relation between Śiva and Durgā is a particular realization of the puruṣa/prakriti principle.

From the sequential scheme of the festivals it appears that rituals of male and female deities alternate within the year; in the least they are recognizable as a basic relationship. There are links among the pūjās of the year, not just among worshipers and localities of worship; deities themselves form a system of relationships.

If there is any significance to these divisions and relations, then we may assume that the rites of any divine pair, male and female, share the principles of other festivals. Though structurally each pair is necessarily of equal value, the transformation we referred to would not otherwise be possible. But ideologically the question of values assumes a different significance: on this level we can and must distinguish rituals not only according to their importance to the participants, but in terms of the place the rites occupy in the total scheme. In this way the division of male-female deities is less significant than the recurrence of related pairs within a segment of time.

It should follow that different units may occupy categorical roles. It is not surprising, therefore, that Śiva should be supplemented by Viṣṇu in the rites of Durgā. The puruṣa element may be expressed by different male deities. Śiva is present in Durgāpūjā: the initial rites are performed in his temple or under a bel tree, which is primarily his symbol. The mantras invoking the goddess in the bel tree define the tree as Śiva's dwelling, asking it to receive Śankar's (Śiva's) beloved. Bhairab is also present in the Durgāpūjā (as he is in the gājan) in an active capacity, while Śiva remains at rest. In Vaiṣṇava ideology Śiva is replaced by Viṣṇu, and myths establish the relation of Kṛṣṇa to Durgā.

These structural parallels allow us to reconsider some problems of symbolism and "blocked" exegesis in the two festivals. Bhairab is the male element in "motion," the chief of the gājan. Therefore he is a particular aspect of Śiva in a particular situation. He is also in attendance at the Durgāpūjā, in much the same capacity. But whereas his role in the line and locality pūjās is explicit (moving from the Śiva temple to the Durgā *mela*), in the rājā's pūjā he seems to be conspicuously absent. I say "seems" for good reason, because the role Bhairab performs is not absent—rather, a particular symbol is missing or, more accurately, is replaced by a different unit of the same category. We noted that two swords accompany Durgā's movements in the pūjās. The exegesis recognizes these as signs of royalty. We can extend the reasoning further in terms of the logic of performance. The rājā makes an appearance at the climactic point of the festival, the Sandhipūjā. According to older informants he used to be attired in full battle regalia, sword at his side. The symbol of Bhairab in the line pūjās is a long metal object, a sword or an iron rod. In Durgāpūjā swords symbolize royalty, and the king appears carrying a sword. Though Bhairab is not explicitly named in all this, the relationships are clear. The rājā holds on to the priest's robe in the pūjā (an otherwise forbidden, polluting act). The offices of king and priest are brought together in each of two persons; or, more accurately, the king is associated with the role of the priest in the act of offering.

This must be understood in terms of the relationships among the units in the jajmān category within the underlying structure of pūjā. Only the king is marked out for a special relationship with the goddess in the Durgāpūjā. In the community, caste, and line pūjās, Bhairab takes on the roles of both king and Śiva in the way these appear at the rājā's special pūjā. In the gājan the bhaktas themselves stand in the same relation to the other categories of the structure as does the king in the Durgāpūjā. Therefore the king is to Durgā and the priest as the bhaktas are to Śiva and the priest. The special role of the king is defined by his relation to Śiva (and, by extension, to Bhairab) just as the bhaktas are defined in their special role by their relation to Śiva. The pūjā of the gāmār tree is parallel to the pūjā of the Durgā image once we recognize the relations among deity, offerer, and ritualist. The king and Bhairab represent the male element in the Durgāpūjā in terms of the relationships, just as Śiva, Bhairab, the gāmār tree and the śālpāṭā (board) do in the gājan. The same structure is to be found in the social system as in the world of the gods. The role of Śiva can be performed by Viṣṇu in the Durgāpūjā. In some ṣolaānā pūjās the *sālāgrām sila* (a sacred stone that is a symbol of Viṣṇu) replaces Bhairab.

The significance of the rājā is to be understood in his relation to the goddess and the people. We saw that many myths have to do with the king's relation to the goddess. Mrinmoyī Debī is both the rājā's and the people's (conversely, people and king are hers). Always a relationship is being emphasized—king to goddess, people to king, land to people, land

and people to goddess. These relationships give the unity to the rituals of Durgā and the transformation of categories from king to line, community, and caste in the threefold structure. The system revolves around the goddess, with one or another category brought into relation to her through the office of the priest.

The four-part pūjā of the king, the three Ṭhākurānī, and the worship of the permanent image of Mrinmoyī have an additional significance. Traditionally the kings have four duties (*dharma*) in relation to their subjects: giving protection and peace, ensuring well-being and prosperity, conducting wars, and ensuring the productivity of the land. These functions are enumerated in various myths. In the case of the Vishnupur kings, the four-part pūjās symbolize the fourfold relation of the Mrinmoyī Debī to the rājās: she gives fertility (to women and land), wealth, protection and peace, war and victory. Each of the four goddesses governs one of these fields of experience. The way some accounts have it, the kings divided their worship of the goddess into four aspects; they celebrate the four functions (or the four blessings) in four forms of the goddess. Hence we can see why the role of Bhairab is enacted by the king himself in the pūjā, why the symbolism of Śiva is conspicuously taken over by the rājā. As we shall see below, we are far from dealing with equivalence: king, Śiva, and people are all separate in their identities; but in sets of relationships the roles may be reversed and collapsed into a single category. The significance of reversals can be seen only against an ideology of discrete units and identities. The king's relationships also tell us something about deities in general; divinity is shared by men and gods.

The notion of purity is reversed in the Sandhipūjā to accommodate the relation of the king to Debī and priest. In this triad one of the categories is always primary and the others are secondary: the relations can be reversed in different situations. In the mythology the rājā often appears to be superior to the goddess; the reversal accentuates the ties, a temporary reversal underlies the enduring inferiority of king to goddess and priest. This, however, admits of periodic reversals in the relationships. There are reversals even in the relations among the worshipers: on the last day youths (inferior to elders) smear their elders with turmeric amid general merriment. The same happens with a *sādhak* (adept) who "abuses" a deity and with a king who "defeats" the goddess.

Symbols, Structure, and Sequence

Synchrony and Diachrony in Durgāpūjā

Durgāpūjā refers to the whole festival, but each complete, self-sufficient performance within the sequence is also a pūjā. This allows us to speak of a development within the festival, since pūjās become increasingly complex and intense till the actual manifestation of the goddess between Aśṭamī and Nabamī. From that moment on the pūjās become less complex, graually preparing for the departure of the goddess. Each day there are specific additions to the actions and offerings that are constant throughout the festival. These "additions" should be thought of not in terms of substance, but in terms of relations. Compared with the pūjās of the initial invocations, Saptamīpūjā reveals another aspect of the goddess, her power (śakti), which was realized only through refractions during the previous days. Whereas the invocations are concerned with the goddess as manifested in and through different series of items, the Saptamīpūjā confronts the goddess herself. Aśṭamīpūjā introduces the *yantra,* a diagram of śakti that, as it were, both is something and does something, action itself being symbolized in synchronic form. Here again different things are combined in action, yantra and *bija*: a diagram, an utterance, and an object (point and flower). In *Mahāsnān* the symbolic series are expanded to include more items. This time rivers, earth, segments of society, social groups, objects necessary for everyday life, and items of luxury and high-status living are represented. *Sandhi* itself stands for the joining of two lunar days, but it means more both in the context of the festival and in the position and combination of the symbols introduced specifically for the pūjās of the day. The goddess becomes visible in that moment: locality, society, and divinity are joined.

The sequence in the festival can be diagramed (see fig. 8). It develops through certain distinguishing features that are performed in addition to daily, recurrent rites. Together they yield a distinct form that must be considered separately. From the initial invocations the rites gather complexity to include more and more aspects and properties of the phenomenal and ideational worlds. These aspects are classified and linked together in the ritual sequence.

On the mythical level the development of the pūjā corresponds to the Debī Mahātmā myth: the different days commemorate different exploits and victories of the goddess over the demons. In days past, the killing of the demons was celebrated on the third day following Dasamī. On the ritual level the different days stand for the gradual unfolding of the meaning of the goddess. Śakti is symbolized in the celebration of the specific pūjās of the day. Only in the festival as a whole do we realize the magnitude of the fields encompassed by the goddess.

The scheme of development in the festival is homologous to the sequence of symbols and actions within each pūjā. Here we must discuss the sequence of pūjās with an eye to both the cycle within individual pūjās and the way these units in turn are assigned positions within the

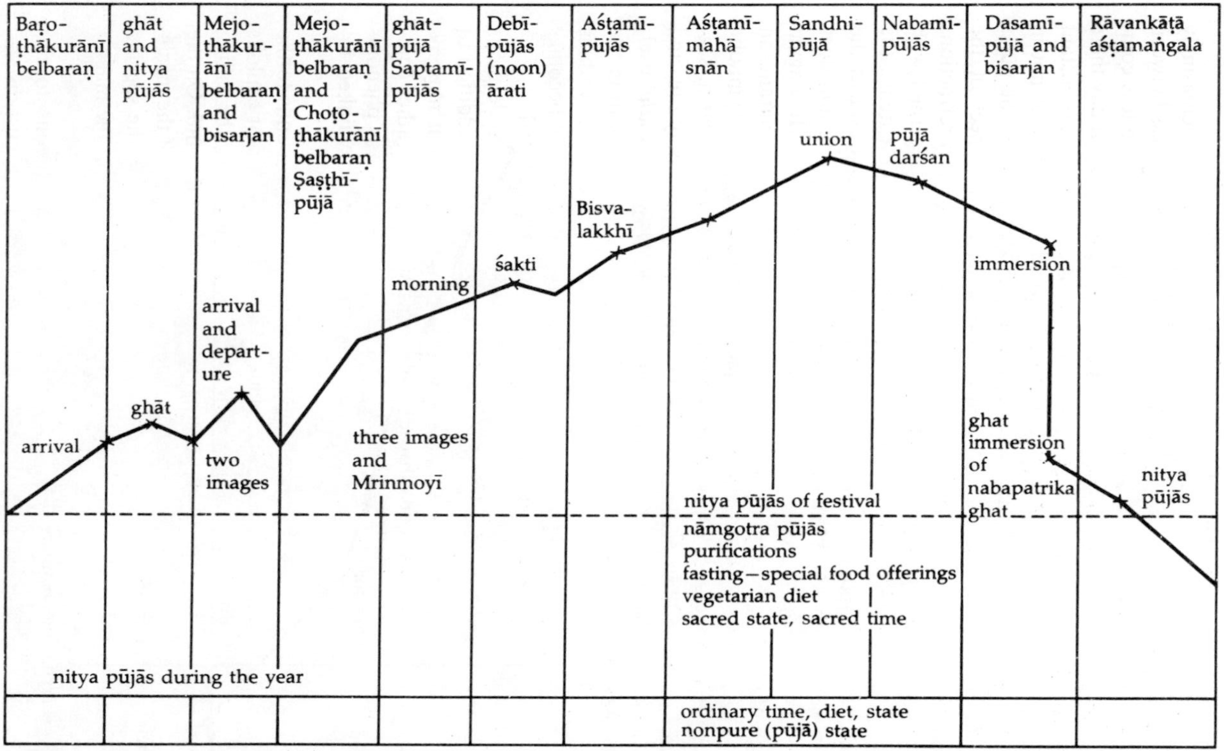

Figure 8. Sequential scheme of Durgāpūjā.

festival as a whole. The developmental scheme of pūjās joins and integrates the series of synchronic relationships (see fig. 9).

In the initial invocations the goddess is seen through the results of her own actions in nature (*prakriti*), in culture (*saṃskṛiti*), and in society (*samāj*). In Bengali ideologies these form aspects of the goddess's creative activity; they add up to creation (not nature in opposition to culture but the created world, including the social world). The sacred bel tree is the dwelling of the Debī, the tulsī tree being the witness to the invocation offering. She is invoked in the bel tree, with tulsī as the witness, and in the ghat, in which some of her aspects and characteristics are represented: earth, water, grains, and fruit-bearing trees as well as the five precious metals. The ghat itself may be made of one of these metals, but if that is impossible then an earthenware vessel (of clay and water) can be substituted. Whatever is basic to life is symbolized in the ghat. Finally, the *putulika* symbol drawn on the outer wall of the vessel is the sign of divinity, the sign of peace.

The goddess is invoked as she is seen and understood in the everyday world: as someone in whom all things are one. The *badhan,* or "awakening," of the goddess marks a beginning, a new departure. In *abahan* she is invited to the locality, a specific place, in the form accepted by the people of the locality.

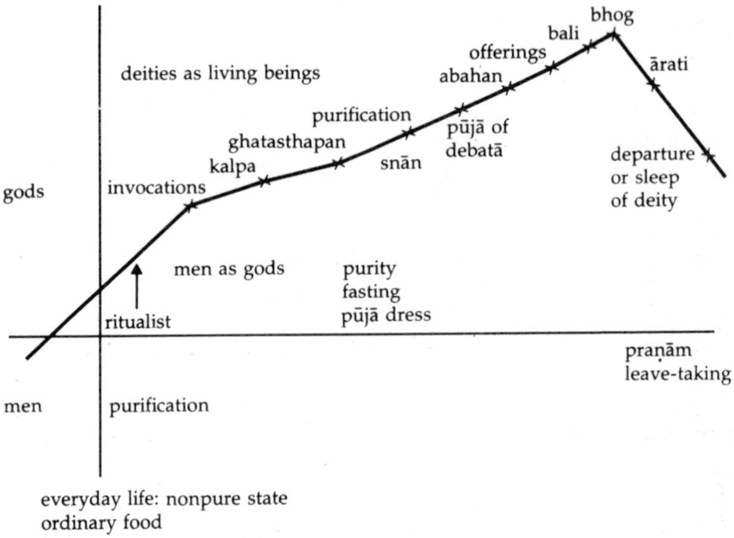

Figure 9. Sequences within a pūjā.

Kalpa (time) is a link between groups of performers: human, divine, and *avatar* (a category that shares in both humanity and divinity). The goddess is worshiped in the world of the gods just as she is served by men. In either case the tripartite structure of the act is clear: the deity, worshiper, and ritualist are separate. The latter two indicate different offices even when merged in a single person. This in fact happens in the case of Rāma, who engages Rāvan to perform the Debīpūjā. The latter agrees but performs only the pūjās of the seventh and eighth; the ninth and tenth he leaves to Rāma. The kalpa not only creates roles or offices, it links the categories of performers (whether men or gods) in the worship of the goddess; humanity, divinity, and other levels are not far apart.

Invocation of the Debī in the bel tree has the effect of realizing the goddess within a tree sacred to Śiva and treating the tree as the goddess herself. The same is true of ghat and nabapatrika. In the course of offerings, many gods and goddesses are recognized in their relation to the Debī. Here development is linked to synchrony: the goddess is defined by her position in the system of relations linking all deities. In this synchronic scheme the goddess is hierarchically the highest because all other deities must be served before the goddess herself can be honored. The series is expandable to thirty-three crores of gods (330 million), but primarily they comprise the Five Deities. These pūjās provide the smallest, least inclusive aspects of the term: a recital of words accompanied by a gesture.

Purifications are a step in the development of the pūjā. The worshiper and the ritualist purify their bodies before going to the performance. They attire themselves in pūjā clothing (pure, *sūddha,* meaning that it was washed and dried in the proper manner). Purifications are effected through the five things of the cow, five nectars, five grains, and so on. Each item is held, placed on the ghat, and mentioned in a mantra, thus relating the name, object, and self to each other.

The discrimination and combination of items in the purification recur in other contexts. Five nectars, grains, trees, metals, and so on may form part of the offerings, the core of a particular pūjā, or only a part of a pūjā. The classificatory principle and the classes into which the units are arranged is common to all contexts in which these items occur. In the bathing of the goddess these items return to symbolize the form and character of the goddess; mantras of the recitation giving the *guṇ* (quality) of the goddess, and meditations (*dhyen*) describing her appearance (*barṇa*) and nature (*caritra*).

Mantras, especially the bijmantra of the pūjā (particular to the deity and to the ritualist involved), are used for concentration and purification. For the pūjā to be performed properly, the purifications should order the series of units in the pūjā universe (designating things in the world) into a synchronic structure. So the *bahirindriya* (outer organs) are purified (with mantras and water) touching the different joints (*aṅga*) of the body. Concentration, *ekagrota,* brings about peace, and contemplation of the One and its elements serves to purify all things. The five vital airs are purified: earth, water, sky, air, and heat, the constituting elements of all things. Through various breathing exercises and meditations (*nyas*), the ritualist dissolves these elements into their constituent parts, five *tattvas* into twenty-five subsidiary elements, and reunifies them into vital cosmic energy (*tej*). In *aṅganyas* and *matrikannyas* (the separation of units that have come to be through the goddess), the ritualist meditates on all that issues from the Debī: different classes of matter and concept, various forms and appearance (barṇa) of men, all of which are activated by *tej,* divine heat or energy.

Elements and units in synchronic relations form ordered successions that enter into certain relationships with each other in the sequence of the rites. These series reveal the true image of the world as it appears to men. The system is self-sufficient, one part being consistent with another, all units being linked through the logic of relationships. Symbols (object, word, and gesture) form a unified whole, representing the elements and units of the created universe. The unfolding of these relationships is of significance in the developmental scheme of the festival. Thus do men become gods so that they may perform the pūjā of a deity; the process through which men cross the dividing line between divinity and humanity is that through which the world and the gods themselves came to be: the action of the goddess.

Most people can realize divinity only through the play of the gods, and so the goddess is experienced through the signs of creation. By displaying the variety of creation and reenacting the process of creation in accordance with basic principles, through the power of word, gesture, and object, men can become deities in experience. Having experienced and understood the work of the gods, they become fit to serve the gods.

All creation (*sristhi*) originates in the goddess. Meditating on this, the priest recreates the order of the world in the symbolism of the rites. Through the symbols and categories of the ritual this system not only is defined and experienced (a divinity shared by all things in the world), but is also brought about in the action of the ritual. Action proceeds on the basis of assumptions that are consistent with the logic of the system: words into deeds. What is *said* is also *done.*

Pūjā is action: the goddess, a totality, is approached through the multiplicity she encompasses. First of all, this multiplicity is separated into symbolic series: objects, words, gestures. Then each of these series is divided into constituent units: concepts and ideas, the vehicles of symbols. At the end of the process we are left with classificatory units dividing "nature" (plants, trees, fruits, and flowers); objects in everyday life (vessels, lights, seats, clothing, and food items, cooked and uncooked); divisions in society; and divisions in space or locality. At a higher order of abstraction these units are grouped together in the twenty-five elements, the internal and external senses, the winds and elements of life. At a yet higher level of abstraction there are the principles of energy and power, and finally there is creation itself, the goddess. The pūjā begins with the postulated unity of the goddess, dissolving that unity into myriad parts. In this process the pūjā reveals the principles of life activated by the goddess. These principles are put into motion by the ritualist in relation to the gods. The relationship is mediated through the sacred power of words. This is the meaning of *kriyā,* the power to transform elements of one series, everyday life, into another, the sacred.

The services of Durgā as the "root" deity, bhog and bali, treat the goddess as a person. Synchronically this completes the universe of objects in the pūjā. All items included have a role and a meaning in everyday life. The offering and sacrifice refer to concepts, which in turn designate items of and attitudes toward life. A goat or buffalo sacrifice equates the killing of a demon with the renunciation of sin (*pāp*) and evil (*khārāp biddhā*). Kinds of experience are consecrated to the goddess and transcended in the form of sacrifice.

Differently categorized beings also enter the pūjā, the discriminations being segmentary and hierarchical. There are the goddess and the other deities, deities and demons, demons and avatars, avatars and ritualists, saints and men. On the lowest level are the demons, ghosts, and other spirits.

Debīpūjā itself includes new elements in addition to the general pūjā form. The temporary images (paintings, clay figures) are invested with life. Synchronically this extends the symbolic series to new relationships and actions.

In the purifications water and flowers play the main role. These items are symbols of purity, and their association with other objects and mantras establishes relations of purity: locality (seat, four directions, pūjā area, place of the ghat); men in the performance (ritualist and participants); and the offerings (vessels, flowers, water). Separations occur in even greater detail than before: water is subdivided into ocean, river, lake, and so forth. Everyday objects are represented according to use and situation; for example, different kinds of oils and perfumes are used according to type and origin. Kinds of earth are distinguished according to the sources from which they were obtained.

The central act is the giving of life. We noticed how the elements of life are symbolized in all pūjās; but in the supreme gift to the gods, life is symbolically reconstituted and offered to a lifeless image. The elements of these categories within the person of the ritualist are separated (*bhed*) and arranged in a certain order to reveal the composition of energy, tej, the very breath of life.

Beyond constituting the life of men, pūjās refer to the actions of deities and demons. Deities themselves are symbols of fields of experience, and their worship within the pūjā as a whole establishes their role in creating and maintaining these fields. Relations among gods are hierarchical: all originate from the goddess, and in relation to her they encompass lesser fields of action. They straddle heaven and earth in their activities, and each deity is separate in terms of identity and certain characteristics (caritra and guṇ). Deities are also symbols of experience, states, or situations (creation, destruction, anger, war, fortune, wealth, peace, disease, welfare, and so on). Aligned with the goddess as well as the world of men, the deities govern different fields of experience.

The prānpratiśṭhā and cakkurdān rites complete the synchrony of pūjā, and the planting of life in the image activates a diachronic process: origins and development. The way of reconstituting tej, the primal energy, introduces further units into the scheme, through the "covering" deities. These act to elaborate aspects of the goddess yet to be defined, exhibiting the full range of the field she encompasses. These aspects are separated and reunified as "screens" around the goddess. The scheme is completed in the following manner.

In the beginning are brahman, *sabda* (word), and *barṇa* (appearance of the word). Creation issues from *matrikabarṇa*: the female aspect of the word. The three forms of this barṇa are the three forms of Caṇḍī or Durgā, Mahā Sarasvatī, Mahā Lakṣmī, Mahā Kālī, and *sattva, raja,* and *tama,* the three qualities. Concentrating on and defining the matrikabarṇa, the ritualist separates the elements that constitute barṇa, the five vital airs, activating them through imagination, gesture, and mantra. The five airs, vital to life, are joined through an utterance and fused with *ātmā,* the self, to *parmātmā,* the universal soul, brahman. Hence the life of man becomes the life of divinity: this symbolism constitutes the life of the image. By separating the units of the creative process, the ritualist becomes divine in order to give divinity to an image. There is divinity in men because the elements and energy of life are shared by all created things. One aspect of life, the soul or self, is brahman itself. Creation is the *icchāśakti* (power of desire) of brahman, the female aspect (*prakriti*) of the genderless, formless brahman, in play (*līlā*) with the male aspect (*puruṣa*). From this play the three qualities emerge, then in turn the five elements, and so the process is repeated till all things are encompassed.

Tej (energy) and śakti (power) are invoked in the pūjās preceding Debīpūjā, but in the pūjās of the seventh, tej and śakti become the central part of the action. Just as the power of words is meant to do something, so tej is required to act, not only to be expressed. The relation between ātmā and parmātmā on the one hand, and life, tej, and śakti on the other creates a reciprocity and correspondence between men and gods. Ātmā and life in men are aspects of that which is a share of brahman and hence present in all things. Parmātmā, tej, śakti are linked to gods and men through actions in the pūjā. The life a ritualist gives the image does not come from just anywhere: it is his own life.

Synchrony in the pūjās of the eighth (together with sandhi) includes a further step of abstraction. Just as the multiplicity of creation is explored, and the principles of energy and power are symbolized in the previous pūjās, so in the Aśṭamīpūjās the origin and primal function of these principles are displayed. Not only are tej and śakti symbolized, but their origin and continued action is revealed and reenacted. At a higher level of abstration, not only are prakriti and her works symbolized, but the male aspect of brahman is expressed as well. Thus the symbolism accounts for the very beginning of creation and the possibility of action, not just the results and elements of the creative process.

The covering deities of the goddess are represented in parts of the lotus yantra. The lotus is drawn with different colors, and pūjās are performed for a hierarchy of deities. These deities exhaust the relationships of the goddess: the different aspects of Śiva and his attendants; the manifestations of Debī as mother, creator, and lover; the attendants of Durgā, demonesses and spirits. These are symbolized as concepts in the colors of the yantra: black, yellow, red, white, and gray. The yantra itself is a deity; it is the place of the goddess, a particular divinity symbolized in a locality. The principles of creation, male and female, are also symbolized in the yantra: the bija in the center and the bijmantra (seed mantra) representing the male element. In the ritual the bija brings the yantra to life in the same way as the image was brought to life the day before.

The idea of yantra is union and joining, and the action takes place in the pūjā of the yantra by means of the bijmantra. By uttering the bijmantra and placing a red flower on the seed kernel of the diagram, the ritualist joins the male and female elements. This is the *karma* (duty) and *karja* (work) of the yantra. The symbolic union is achieved through jñān and kriyā (yogic practice).

Synchrony and Diachrony in the Gājan

The sacred thread makes the bhaktas equal to the gods. This illustrates well the Bengali saying that one must become a deity to serve the gods. The gotra of Śiva that the bhaktas assume accomplishes their link to him. The gotra is important in all pūjās; when a special offering is made, the priest recites a sacred formula with the name and gotra of the offerer. The merits of the pūjā redound on the offerer and his line; hence gotra defines a series of relationships. Gotra in pūjā draws certain boundaries that are demolished in the gājan. In this sense alone are social limitations transcended in the gājan. The gotra is an ideal model linking past and present and identifying synchronic ties in the present. But in the gājan Śiva's gotra is much more. Not only do the bhaktas become Śiva's *aṅga* (part), but they become related to each other: all bhaktas are one in Śiva, as the participants often say. So a "castekinship" notion is replaced by a different one: in the gājan the gotra emphasizes what is common to all men, a recognition of similarities through the *brahmajñān* (awareness of a totality, the knowledge of brahman). Whatever happens to one bhakta, all the devotees are affected. A small transgression of the rules may create trouble for all (if something goes wrong in the gājan and a bhakta dies or is injured by the wrath of Bhairab, then all the bhaktas can prepare for some inauspicious event in the future). This causes concern among the bhaktas, and so they help each other to do the gājan properly. The gotra, then, is part of brahman, a symbolic expression of oneness beyond the fragmentation of a caste society.

Categories for men and gods are also merged in the gājan, but the distinction is not obliterated: worshiper and worshiped remain separate (in the myths of the gājan the deities worship Śiva). Not only is the status of men raised, but Śiva himself is elevated by the performances of the gājan. The ritual therefore not only defines but creates experience: the symbolism of words, objects, and actions realigns the relationships among gods, gods and men, men and men. There is a recognition of similarities and differences in the gājan; the oneness of men is opposed to the elaboration of the nonhuman world, which itself is reintegrated into the symbolic scheme through pūjās, offerings, and the manifestations of the gods.

Let me restate this process in detail. The ritualist in the gājan is the bhakta himself. Just as a priest must separate himself from the everyday world in the initial rites of pūjā, so the bhakta must go through a rite of separation. The bhakta marks parts of his body with red sandalwood paste and white clay, symbols of the goddess in her powerful and her benign aspects. Red is a symbol of the creative energy that is the cause of all things and events, in partnership with the male principle. This basic concern of the gājan is symbolized in the person of the bhakta (unlike the ordinary pūjās, where there is a dialectical relation between the priest and the manifestations of the deity in objects and concepts). The person here symbolizes Śiva himself (together with śakti: the red dress, red sandalwood marks). Many oblations must be performed by the bhaktas, just as in the ordinary pūjās the priest offers water to the gods. Even though the bhaktas are in a state of purity (*śuddhatā*), they go through numerous purifications. The towel has a central role in these actions, as it does in the pūjās, where it is used to dry the gods after the ceremonial bath. The cold food offering (fruits and milk, coconut water, sweets) is eaten by the bhaktas themselves; in the pūjās these items are offered to the gods (in turn the bhaktas offer the same items to the gods in the gājan during the day when they themselves are fasting). The parallels could be pursued further, but the point is clear: there is a link between servant and served, the relationship being symbolized through a series of parallel actions that align men and gods.

There is good reason for the appearance of the goddess as the first special act of the gājan. No act of bhakti can occur before the coming of the goddess. When Śiva and Durgā are together, not only is creation symbolized, but the precondition of being is fulfilled. On a different level the relation of Śiva and Durgā stands for the relation of puruṣa and prakriti (the male and the female principles). The former does not exhaust the latter. Just as Śiva symbolizes puruṣa, Bhairab, Viṣṇu, and Kṛṣna may express the same principle in different contexts, in different ways. The combination of these two elements is the union of Śiva and Durgā in the gājan (and in other pūjās as well, especially in the Durgā-pūjā), the creation of the world (out of brahman's icchāśakti), human reproduction, and the power of action in any activity. These are on different levels that should not be confused (and are not collapsed by the people).

The thread is also a symbol of the goddess; we note that a red suta is used in other Debīpūjās, in which the wearer is brought under the protection of the goddess. In other contexts it is associated with women; on bhratriditiya (second lunar day of the brother), girls tie the suta on the arms of their brothers as a sign of close, protective relationship. But, as I noted above, the yellow suta is important in the marriage ceremony. The same thread is tied around the gāmār tree with some durba grass. The tree symbolizes Śiva; the goddess and the god are again brought together, this time not separately, as on the previous day, but as a couple, in the context of all the bhaktas' relation to them. Though these pūjās are not regarded as a "marriage" between Śiva and Durgā, on one level there is a life-cycle component to these rites. The central concern is clear:

not only are Śiva and Durgā brought together in relation to the gājan, but bhaktas are also brought into a relation with Śiva, then Durgā, thus participating in the encounter between the two deities. The purpose is clear: the bhaktas share in the śakti generated by the Śiva-Durgā union. The full implication of these rituals is reaped on Rātgājan and Dingājan days, when the bhaktas' actions are a direct consequence of what was achieved during the first three days of the gājan.

The implications of the above discussion are as follows: first, the bhaktas form a corporate group through their relation to Śiva. In this they seemingly transcend all jāti principles. The idiom of everyday jāti relationships no longer differentiates them. There is a link among several categories normally kept sharply separate: bhakta, Brāhmaṇ, renouncer, deity. Yet these categories are not confused or merged into a single all-inclusive unit; rather, the distinctions are elevated to a higher level and expressed through vehicles other than those of everyday life. Third, the relation of Śiva and Durgā affects the bhaktas in a special way. The situation among the deities, however, inverts that among men: at one level the Śiva-Durgā relation has to do with marriage. Bhaktas are drawn into this relationship through the meaning of the suta and through participating in the appropriate rites. Fourth, we are led to believe that these differences occur because relationships in the gājan are expressed through principles different from those in everyday life. It is difficult to agree with this suggestion, since, after all, the reversals and the collapsing of roles are never complete. The principles determining ordinary nongājan relationships seem to reassert themselves every now and again. But does the analysis of these peculiar situations reveal whether the principles change, the form and relationship of categories remaining the same, or whether a change among categorical relationships (such as suggested above) results in a change of principles expressing the very same thing?

At first it seems that the third category of the deity-ritualist-worshiper schema disappears and that only the bhaktas, as ritualists, are left to face the Lord Śiva. Yet the three roles are distinct in the gājan, even though the offices of priest and participant are collapsed. The bhaktas are ritualists in the gājan, and, although the roles are distinct, they reside in the same person. The rite of separation at the beginning of the gājan enables the bhaktas to act out two distinct roles: the ritualist (*jajak*) who offers pūjā and the sacrificer (*jajmān*) on whose behalf the pūjā is offered. Elsewhere I have argued that groups of worshipers, caste and line, and locality act as replaceable categories of the jajmāni role in the structure of the pūjā. In the gājan the category of ritualist is replaceable. The situation in the gājan thus becomes the reverse of that in other pūjās.

Hierarchy is not obliterated in the gājan but is expressed in a different way. The jāti principle of hierarchy is reasserted through the categories of bhaktas. The separation among the bhaktas is no mere stratification; the pāṭbhakta is hierarchically superior to the other bhaktas. Hierarchy is more limited here than in the case of jāti society. The reason is that the principles of jāti separation do not express division among bhaktas: the pure/impure rules for the separation of groups and division of labor are, if not entirely absent, downplayed in the definition of groups in the gājan. In the gājan the bhakti of the chief bhakta must differentiate him from the other devotees. Hence the principle of hierarchy reasserts itself in the gājan, paradoxically enough, through the bhakti principle. Further, the segmentary system of groups in the gājan and the replaceable set of bhakta categories themselves form a hierarchy (see fig. 10).

This, however, does not entirely correspond to the jāti system of hierarchy. There is no absolute separation among bhaktas in terms of bhakti. The principle of bhakti is complemented by the śakti principle, also variable in the way it can be attained. Bhakti is related to śakti, since the former leads to the latter. We have to view the gājan against ordinary life, not in terms of parallel, corresponding hierarchies. In view of the seemingly egalitarian nature of the gājan, the reassertion of a limited

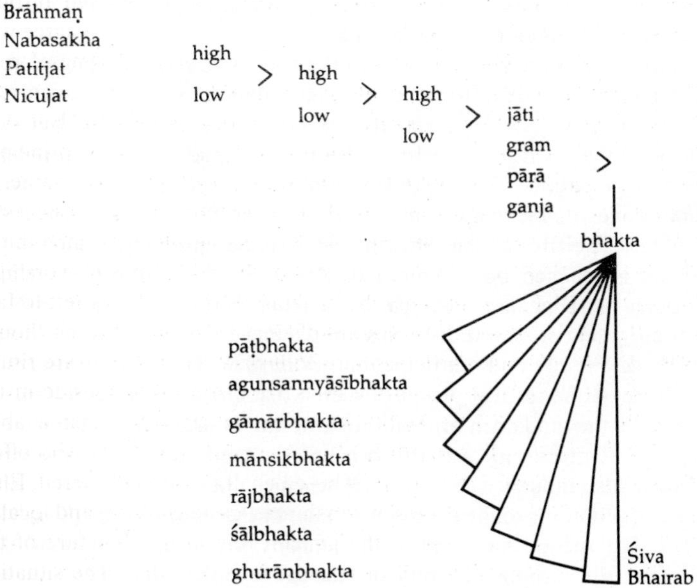

Figure 10. Hierarchies in the gājan.

hierarchy is remarkable enough. Bhakti and śakti create limited, not absolute separations in a set of relationships (not entities and substances), and their effect is seen in what a bhakta can do rather than in what he is forbidden to do.

Despite our expectations of simplicity, the gājan presents us with an elaborate series of classification and division, not only in the daily rituals that change from day to day but also in the scheme of each day's action. The line of development in the Rātgājan, the highest moment in the festival, is repeated in the pūjās of any one day in the gājan and, indeed, within each of the pūjās that make up a full day in the festival. The highest point in each of these schemes is given by a different act. The mānsik (votive) pūjā, the simplest form of pūjā, is itself no different once we break down the single act of offering into its constituent roles and offices. The bhakta as the servant of Śiva invokes the god, addresses him, and offers him honor and respect.

The sequential scheme is even clearer in the gājan than in other major festivals, the additional daily rites being sharply defined. Each additional rite and each day in the festival is a step in the preparation for the union of Śiva and Durgā, in which the unity of a single deity is expressed. Śiva in the gājan is a unity that is not explored in the multiplicity of its manifestations (see below). Śiva represents a principle, in different guises, in relation to the goddess (see fig. 11).

The gājan is a totality in its own right. It has a recognizable form and distinguishing content from the indigenous point of view. Its form is given by diachrony. Each day's activity can be seen as an additional building block of the festival as a whole. But there is much more involved than mere aggregation. The additional rituals complete a system: a system that derives its meaning from the effect of the Śiva-Durgā union on the bhaktas. The rites of the different days have a cumulative effect till the climax is reached on the night of Rātgājan. The tension is sustained through the Dingājan procession, but from then on the additional rites diminish, acts of bhakti disappear, and the last rite of reversal is quickly reached. The rise and fall in the developmental scheme is no conjecture: the logic of the festival promises such a diachronic dimension. Once we recognize the fundamental significance of the Śiva-Durgā union, we notice at once the diachronic way this principle is acted out. The actions of the bhaktas also influence the temporal scheme. The gājan of the day is less intense, according to the exegesis, because of the assurance of the previous night that the power (śakti) of the gods is active. The fire walking momentarily sustains the action on the same level as that of the previous night. With the last offering the devotees are relieved of potential danger, and only the immersion of the sacred thread is left for the next day.

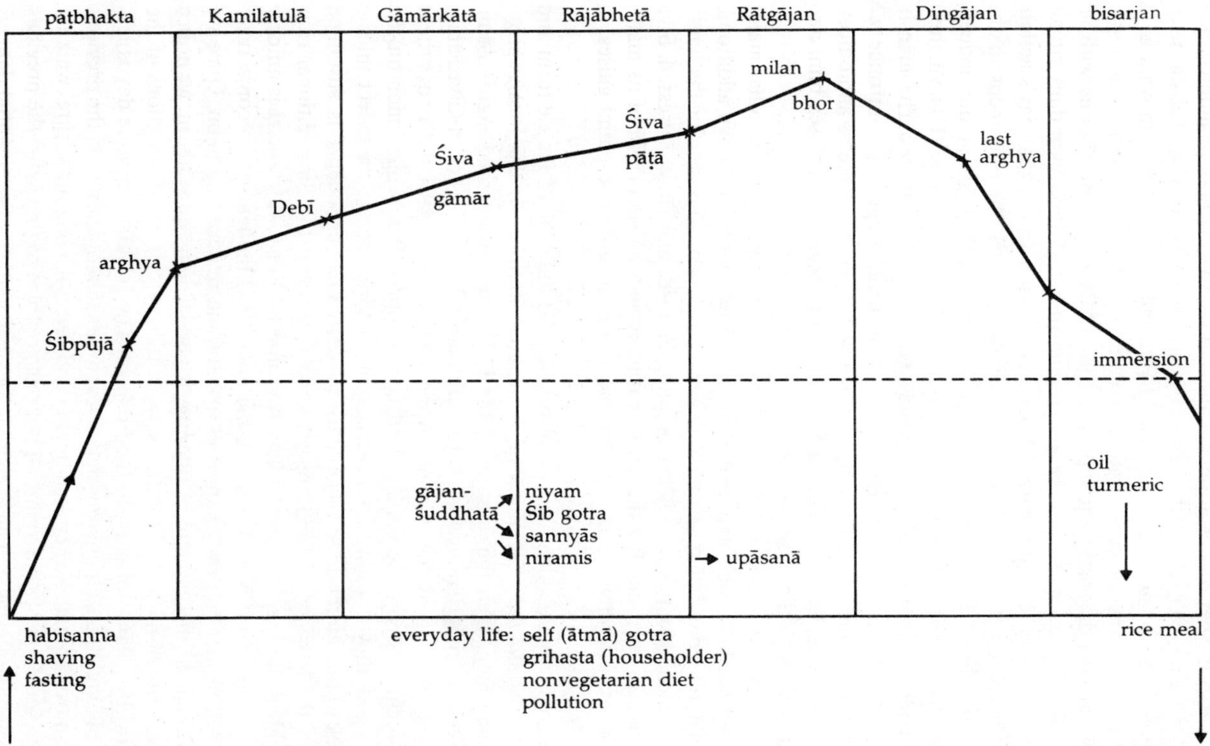

Figure 11. The sequential scheme of gājan.

The principle of development and cumulative, temporal action not only is characteristic of the festival as a whole, but is also true of the events of each individual day. Daily rites culminate in the offerings to the sun; the major days' activities culminate in some highly specific ritual. In the diagrammatic representation of development, the apexes of the different forms within the gājan seem to have little relation to each other. This is far from true. Closer examination shows that each high point has something to do with the relation between the offerer-ritualist and the deity. In all developmental schemes, each point of departure toward a higher plateau has to do with the same thing. The whole festival and indeed all pūjās designate a relation between deity and offerer. It is significant, however, that there is a particular stage in the unfolding of this relationship. In these high moments the nature of the relationship becomes specific: a personal tie of service is established. Each climax has to do with the most intimate encounter of deity and offerer. In most cases this is the moment of food offering. Giving and receiving food is a highly symbolic act, expressing, as we know, not only the systems of social relations but also of ideologies. Underlying this symbolism are fundamental oppositions such as pure/impure, high/low, sacred/non-sacred. In everyday life the act of eating is hedged about with all kinds of rules, interdictions and prohibitions. Eating holds potential danger for the eater. The preparation of food, the place where food is eaten, the company in which food is consumed, and the state of the eater must be pure (*śuddha*) because food is sacred (*pabittra*). If this is the case among men, then the feasting of the gods must be guarded even more closely. In other contexts a prayer cloth is held up to prevent worshipers from watching at the moment when food is offered to the gods, the moment of divine acceptance and consumption. When men offer food to a god, they share with a hierarchically superior being: the food comes back to the offerer doubly sacred for the deity's having touched it. Among men the leavings of food are polluting (*ēto*), but the greater the hierarchical distance the more likely it is that inferiors will take the ēto of a superior. So it is in offering to the gods: that the leavings of gods are sacred to men not only expresses an intimate relationship between men and gods in the moment of offering, it also demonstrates the permanent inferiority of men.

In the gājan, not only do food offerings by bhaktas express the status of bhakta, the culminating act of each ritual sequence also designates the most intimate tie between bhakta and deity. Among the various forms represented in my diagrams, all but one conform to this pattern. There is always an offering and an acceptance, except in the case of *milan* (union) and *bhor* (trance), the actions of Rātgājan. This is not surprising, since all actions of the gājan culminate in the celebration of "action" itself, which is made possible by the union of Śiva and Durgā. Hence the deity himself here comes to dwell in the body of the bhakta. The effect of mānsik pūjā is the same, only in this case the union of deity and man is "in the mind," *moner mānsik.*

Hierarchy, Time, and Locality

Symbolic units are related in synchronic as well as diachronic dimensions. In both cases the result is the same, a set of relationships forming a structure. Process is just as much the property of symbols in a structure as are relationships. There are some differences, as we shall see, but not in terms of history and system, or temporal versus structural form of time; rather, the contrast is to be understood in terms of the axes along which relationships are expressed. We found that we can analyze relationships among symbols synchronically and then move to an analysis of developmental forms with no trouble because in the pūjās synchronic relationships are also arranged syntagmatically, in the form of narrative and of sequential action. In both festivals we have had to study sequence and development, as well as visual, actional, verbal, or textual narratives. My account of the order in Saptamīpūjā came from one of the ways of worship, the text of an Upapurāṇa. The textual narrative complements the visual sequence, exegesis, and verbal narrative. The forms vary, but the structure is the same.

In the relationships among symbols, the kinds of narrative complement each other, both synchronically and diachronically. One kind of narrative (especially verbal exegesis) reveals mostly synchronic relations, another narrative (visual, textual) elaborates diachronic relationships. The central concern remains constant: relationships in space and time. If we can analyze relations within a field, then the boundaries may be set in terms of either space or sequence. In one case the axis of expression is synchrony, in the other it is diachrony. The differences are only in the contrast of reversible relationships in each case. In synchronic relations the processual aspects of time are reversible and the spatial ones are not; in diachronic relations the sequence is determined, whereas relations in space are reversible. In my synchronic analysis of the yantra, for example, the elements of time remained constant while the links among symbols were established by necessary relationships. The yantra, the puruṣa/prakriti principles, the goddess and Śiva, all participate in one dimension of time, the structural. However the links between puruṣa and prakriti, god and goddess, yantra and bijmantra are determined and necessary, the pairs of relationships being subject to transformations before their significance can be understood. In either direction certain mediations must be considered before the synchronic relationships are established. We proceed from yantra to puruṣa/prakriti in the rite, from male/female principles to yantra/bija in the myths. Time is reversible; the series of transformations are not. The opposite is true of narrative and the developmental scheme in the festivals; the necessary mediations being sequential, each step is replaceable by other categories from the synchronic scheme. Relations in diachrony are determined: purification must come before the giving of life, honorific service must be performed before food offerings, and so on. But any one of a synchronic series (e.g., the replaceable categories of divinities) may be unified.

There are constraints, however, because both kinds of relationships are linked together and dependent on each other. Once one unit has changed in the synchronic scheme, similar changes must be made at all other levels of the diachronic scheme. The differences therefore are relative and, advisedly, have to do only with the axis on which the relationships among symbols are expressed. In both cases the analysis is the same, though the boundaries of the field are set in different ways. Together the two kinds of relationships achieve a higher level of unity.

From this point of view we need not contrast the dimensions of time in a fundamentally irreconcilable way: after all, there is the primary division between the festival and the ordinary days in the year; both are recognized in opposition to each other. (Not only is time recognized through passage from one festival to another, being calculated according to lunar or solar schedules, both of which are typologies of divinities, but festivals are also recognized through their marked differences from ordinary time.) Once we consider the time in which ritual and myth are set, we have to do with reversible time (one festival partakes of time, the same way as any other, year after year, reiterating the same elements of time). There are levels within this notion of time, but these are not separate and opposed. Levels are separable in relational terms only: all levels partake of the same time, cosmology, life cycle of the gods, the gods' entry into the human cycle of life, the repeated annual calendar rites, the avatars' cycle of time, and so on. In a single pūjā the whole festival and event, the calendar year's rites are revealed in a microcosm, just as the cosmological and divine cycles are also enacted in the symbolic scheme of the pūjā. All pūjās participate in this cosmic time; hence the transformations in each pūjā from one level of time to another, from the most immediate and particular to the most general and abstract.

One consequence of this discussion is that relationships among units on diachronic and synchronic axes may be structured; but beyond that they also participate in given and determinate forms. The structure of all pūjās may be the same, yet not all pūjās are the same, nor do they mean the same. Once we find the structural underpinning of a system, we are still left the task of interpreting the structure in given contexts. Elements of structure that replace each other in relationships, and transformations of relationships from one level to another, are not superfluous but are significant in creating indigenous recognized forms. As I noted above, time and space are aspects of the same totality, and separations along those axes yield the ascending and descending sequences of the festivals as well as particular forms of synchronic and spatial elaboration within those sequences. The two processes are linked: the elements of structure are also situated within indigenous forms. This is the burden of the opening sections in this chapter: Durgāpūjā and Śiva's gājan are different, and the pūjās within the festivals are also different, in that these constituent units combine into forms through named stages and cumulative actions themselves providing meaning. Within each pūjā we can discern a particular form beginning with a separation, progressing to a climax, and ending in a disengagement. Together these forms yield a hierarchy of forms encompassed within the festivals, which are also recognized as a totality in themselves.

The same results can be realized through one particular festival form that combines space with sequence and thus has a special place in our account: processions. I noted that processions and circumambulations are an integral part of both festivals, but I have not discussed the levels of meaning involved in processions: processions not only connect the different localities, temples, and deities of the town, but they render the festivals visible to the population of the whole town and express the hierarchical segmentation and encompassment of localities, temples, deities, persons, and groups of persons. Beyond verifying these divisions, processions (and circumambulations) also define a deity in a locality, expressing at the same time the domain or provenance of a divinity.

Symbolic actions are not only images of cosmology and mythology; they are meant to bring about what they express. In the action of kriyā and yoga the intent is equivalent to accomplishment. Kriyā also means "magic" or power in the sense that the principles expressed in the mantras and symbolized in objects, drawings, food items, and colors are in dialectical relation to what has happened and continues to happen in the universe.

Each discrete unit, each pūjā within the festival, is a whole with definable boundaries. Each complete unit has both a developmental and a synchronic form. Each pūjā starts with purifications and invocations, progressing through various offerings to the worship of the "root" deities.

This particular pūjā within the pūjā consists of several stages, reaching a high point in offering cooked food to the deity.

Synchronically, the elements of pūjā are linked together to constitute a system—one that classifies items, concepts, and gestures in the ritual, thus giving the latter a position in the developmental and synchronic schemes.

The position of each unit is significant in both the synchronic and the sequential schemes. The ghat (vessel of invocation) is related to water, earth, and the twenty-five elements. It is also meaningful in the developmental scheme: once it is established it stands for the deity, is given offerings, and becomes the dwelling of gods as the action unfolds. The ghat, as the house of the gods, participates in the classification of the universe into units and relationships: the "house," as a locality, is in the center of the pūjā. It consists of water, earth, plants (mango), and fruit (coconut). By its position in one or another scheme, the ghat is either a microcosm of the world (in terms of the sacred) or one in a series of manifestations in the progress of the goddess from the elements of creation to her own form. Hence the meaning of the ghat is defined synchronically and sequentially, the two being aspects of the same thing.

It would be a mistake to contrast the developmental meaning of symbols with the synchronic. Together they constitute a hierarchical, relational field. Relations in space and time are images of each other. The two are complementary rather than contrasting. The developmental line of the festival as a whole is matched by the lines of constituent pūjās. The high points are provided by different events, yet all these events have something in common: the direct manifestation of a deity. In the festival the moment of sandhi signifies the "on-the-ground" appearance of the goddess. In the Debīpūjā or Śaktipūjā the moment of equal significance is the prānpratiṣṭhā, the act of giving life. The highest point of everyday pūjās is the moment of cooked food offering, bhog, when the deity actually partakes of what is given to her, signifying her presence in the particular locality of the pūjā.

There is a symmetry in the ascending and descending parts of the pūjā. The contrast can be seen in pairs of oppositions: being and manifestation, coming and going, giving and taking. The oppositions are mediated by men, in the image of their relationship to the gods. Men bring the gods and bid them farewell. They make offerings and receive blessings in return. The mediation takes place through the threefold structure of the pūjā performance involving the Debī, jajak, and jajmān.

Repetition and restatement are not redundant here. In addition to completing the structural universe (the total system of relationships), they tell something about time, both synchronically and diachronically. In either case, time is no mere lapse from one moment to another. Passage and sequence are recognizable only because sets of relationships are brought together within the ritual. Superimposed on the ghat as a dwelling fit for the gods is the new feature of the invocation of the goddess, immediately exhibiting another field of relationships: the goddess among myriad deities.

The festival as a whole represents a complete process: the coming and going of the goddess. Her emergence from and dissolution into water are meaningful on different levels of time in the structure of the rite. One of these is the relation of goddess to men through the year, the repetition of Durgāpūjās year after year, the cosmological process and the creation of the gods, the reenactment of the principles of action without which nothing can take place. In the person of the ritualist these fundamental principles of action are united: the process of creation is reiterated in the service of the goddess. The chronology of creation unfolds from the emergence of the goddess, to the creation of heavens and earth, mountains, rivers, men, plants, and animals, to the character and quality of created things. In the ritual, however, the process is reversed; actions proceed in the opposite direction from that indicated in the myths. Rites reverse the myths. In the ritual the goddess is reached through series of elements representing multiplicity in the world. Original oneness is reconstituted through the arrangement of numerous parts. In the myths the multiplicity comes forth from the creative energy, the goddess. Life is given back to the goddess, tracing back the steps through which it arrived.

The goddess mediates between heaven and earth. Deities serve the goddess as much as men do. Durgā is reached both from heaven and from earth, sharing in both worlds without belonging exclusively to either. Divisions and mediations through the goddess occur in different ways, in different classes. These are not exclusive oppositions: boundaries overlap once we recognize the significance of concomitant categories and symbols. There are divisions within the encompassing symbol of the goddess: her own manifestations and the relations among the deities as the primary parts of her own pūjās. The major contrast is between heaven and earth, but there is no dividing line; an overlapping area is governed by the goddess herself in her manifestations among gods and men.

Divisions appear in a similarly overlapping way when we view the same categories from different points of view. In her specific relations, though not in her origin, the goddess links different spheres of experience, categories of cosmos and society. Her relations include those of husband and wife (where Śiva is considered), creator and truth (in her relation to the puruṣa principle, divinity and rule (in relation to the king), queen, mother, and daughter (in relation to the people).

Finally, groups of worshipers among men and gods are drawn into clusters of relationships around the goddess, the one revealing the mediating role of avatars (incarnate gods on earth) in relation to brahman, the other showing the groups of participants in the pūjās of the goddess (in myth and in the performance of pūjās in Vishnupur).

The three main deities are Śiva, Durgā, and the sun. They are also represented in the five-god group of deities without which no pūjā can be celebrated. Why the sun? The sun is not worshiped in any image nowadays, yet it is regarded as a separate deity. The sun is incarnate, a visible being for everyone to appreciate. In the origin myths the sun is also a part of creation; hence it is also the result of the play, līlā, between puruṣa and prakriti. But the sun has an additional role: it is witness to this creative play. Līlā is related to *māyā,* the creation of the illusory world, the world of multiplicity that veils the essential oneness of all things in brahman. We come full circle: the sun is a symbol of brahmajñān, because by shedding its light on all discrete elements of the world it gives a glimpse of brahman—a way of experiencing a very difficult principle, the sharing of all things in the original word or principle that is brahman. The sun is a witness to the līlā of Śiva and Durgā. It is also a witness to the action of the bhaktas and their līlā. The sun mediates between the goddess, her consort, and the bhaktas, though it does not intercede: in the arghya oblations līlā is recognized through the unifying role of the sun. The sun is a condition of life—it regulates living (*niyantrita*)—and therefore "everyone wants the sun."

The role of the sun reiterates the tripartite structure of the pūjā: the sun is worshiped by the bhaktas, whose action also symbolizes the relation between Śiva and Durgā. The sun is in the position of receiving service from other deities in the gājan; Śiva in his "mobile" form (Bhairab) is the active ritualist, whereas Durgā is the One at Rest, a situation that is the reverse of the pūjās of the goddess. There Debī is the "active" element, and though in the scheme of the puruṣa/prakriti principles the goddess still represents action, in the gājan she is the one who comes to Śiva; she is the offerer. Bhairab, through his movements and manifestations (as pāṭā for example) aids the coming together of Śiva and Durgā. In the Suryaarghya the sun is the witness and the adored deity, while Bhairab, through the bhaktas, is the ritualist. Several transformations take place when we place the offering to the sun into the developmental scheme of the gājan (see fig. 12).

Śiva is meaningless and helpless without Durgā. All action in the gājan is made possible by the union (*milan*) of Śiva and Durgā. The bhaktas are the means by which the two deities are brought together. Milan is

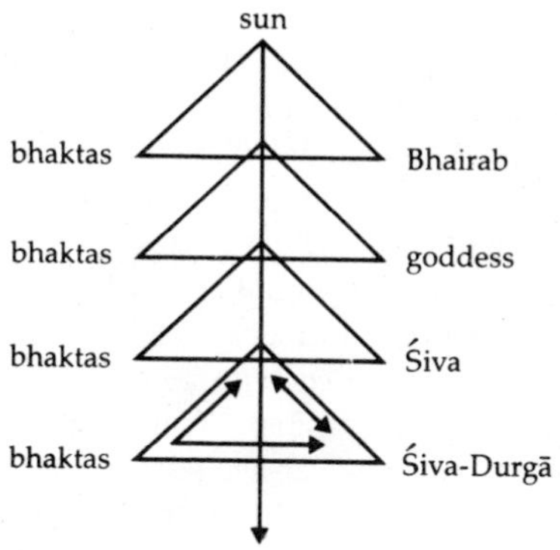

Figure 12. Relationships of the sun in the gājan.

necessary for men to act in the world. Men must be filled with the creative energy that emanates from the union of Śiva and Durgā. This energy is variable; different deities have unequal shares of it, and even the different manifestations of Śiva and Durgā produce widely varying kinds of energy. Hence the most *śaktigoti ṭhākur* (powerful lords) are brought together in the gājan. The influence and power (māhātmā) of Śiva-Durgā fills the bhaktas. This gives the context of the gājan, the paradoxical joy when the whole festival is regarded as painful for men; but in these circumstances men do not mind it—everything is done for their own benefit.

Milan śakti (the power of union), then, is the basic principle of the gājan. The image of Śiva is itself the symbol of milan śakti. The upright stone is the liṅga, the circle is the *gouri pīth* (the place of the goddess) or the *śaktipīth* (the place of creative power). These two elements are necessary for creation. Just as this happens in the world, so it holds true in the human sphere: the union of man and woman results in birth, and the original act of creation produces the world of men. The same is true of trees, fields, animals, and everything alive. In the same way, all inanimate things issue from the gods. These worlds are separate and different, but they share a parallel origin, the principle of creation. Bhaktas do not say that human sexual intercourse is symbolic of the basic principle that animates the universe as they know it. Rather, the direction is reversed: the creative principle acts in the world; there are different worlds parallel to each other in that the same structural principles are at work in them all.

The same principles are expressed in various ways on different levels. On the level of the One Truth, brahman, they are the personification of brahman's aspects having to do with desire: puruṣa and prakriti are the creative play, līlā, of Śiva and Durgā. The latter is already twice removed from the original word (*tattva* or *sabda*): brahman. Among the gods the principle is expressed by śakti, milan śakti, and the play of Śiva-Durgā (parallel to the encounter between the gods and goddesses). This itself is made possible by the categories unified in brahman. Among the gods, then, the principle is symbolized by Śiva-Durgā milan (union). Śakti and līlā extend not only to the world of gods but to all the created worlds, the world of men included. The śakti of the gods affects men, and the śakti of men is not distinguishable from that of the gods except for the contexts, the situations in which the power is manifest. In nature (the world of plants, trees, and earth), the principle is symbolized by seed and field; among men, by the union of man and woman. For the bhaktas these are separable spheres, the action being distinct in each case; only the principle remains the same. However, there is no primacy in these acts. Sexual intercourse in itself is not the symbol but the effect of the principle *among men,* a particular world of experience. The same principle accounts for all action; hence any claim that intercourse is the referent of the symbol would restrict the symbolic process to too narrow a field. Creation among men is a variation on a basic principle, and the sexual connotation is one among many. Different symbols express the relationships in different ways according to time, situation, and context.

In the most general sense the gājan symbolizes the origin and creation of the world. In another sense it enacts the continuing process of creation and contributes to the repetition and maintenance of that process. It symbolizes the repetitions within this cycle in ever-narrowing worlds, from cosmos to human experience (birth, marriage, and death). It inaugurates the new year, a beginning, which is merely a process already known, simultaneously happening on different levels of reality. The gājan affirms the role of men in this process. Without them the scheme would not work in the way men know it. The ritual is man's recognition of the law reflecting upon what happens in the world. Men can experience the effects of the principles from the events happening around them.

The exegesis shows the clustering of symbols around Śiva and Durgā. The explanatory principle is that of the encounter between puruṣa and prakriti, which can be recognized not only in the gājan as a whole but also in the individual rituals (where the symbols of the two principles are ordered into a narrative). The elements and items of everyday experience are arranged into a total scheme of relationships. There are different deities, and different objects and actions symbolize these deities. There are divisions in the nonhuman world of pūjās. Offerings (items of food, clothing, water, and items of honorific nature) are arranged in relation to the manifestations of the deities; thus these items themselves become powerful (and are regarded as potent, capable of removing barrenness in women, trees, and fields). Connections are established among the gods and their representations on earth, the images in the temples. Locality and the power of the god in a particular manifestation together define divinity. Divisions among men are also rearranged; the caste divisions are superseded by classes of bhaktas, giving way to a unity and a rudimentary hierarchy in terms of very different principles, bhakti and śakti. The rituals of the different days stress the various aspects of the integration that is celebrated in the gājan. Different actions take place in different localities, symbolizing the territorial units of everyday life. The actions themselves take place in a process: the intensity of the gājan rises through stages (each stage meaningful in itself but also essential to the next) till the full importance of the principle of union is achieved. Yet each action is in itself symbolic of aspects of the gājan as a whole; we saw that there are relations not only among the different parts of the gājan, but also between the parts and the complete festival—the idea of the gājan itself.

Prakriti is represented by the symbols of śakti, milan, and the goddesses Kamila, Caṇḍī, and Bhavanī. Puruṣa is symbolized by Śiva, the sun, and fire. Similarly, the deities themselves participate in, and result from, cyclical symbolic processes. Both the image and the idea of the deity are represented.

On Śiva's side the symbols share Śiva and Bhairab, both being aspects of the same thing: Śiva is rest, Bhairab is motion. Trident and gāmār tree represent Śiva encompassing Bhairab, and the cane, board, and basket symbolize Bhairab as a specific aspect of Śiva.

Parallel to the above are processes involving the goddess: the ghat and the suta represent aspects of the goddess. The bhaktas not only represent a relationship between Śiva and Durgā but are themselves related to the divine pair in different ways in specific contexts. In some ways they are like Śiva to Durgā, in others they are like Durgā to Śiva. These reversals are not a quaint play on the shared elements of puruṣa and prakriti as these would occur in all categories. Rather, they represent the encompassing nature of the puruṣa/prakriti principle in a segmentary hierarchy. All the elaboration of classes and divisions takes place within the categories encompassed by prakriti: what is representative of the puruṣa principle at a lower level in the hierarchy becomes prakriti on a higher level of abstraction. This system of segmentary oppositions does not end until brahman itself reached: prakiti is all, and brahman itself, in one of its aspects, is puruṣa.

Segmentation and the Transformations of Deity, Ritualist, and Worshiper

It is a property of hierarchically segmentary systems that as we reach higher levels of abstraction, encompassment is extended. As we reach the limits of a hierarchical system, from offering to pūjā sequence, to festival and the rites of the year, so the symbolism of pūjā becomes more encompassing and directly relevant to other spheres of experience. There are pūjās at all times of the year, not just a single unique performance. Time is marked and recognized by shifts from one pūjā to another. Different pūjās emphasize different aspects of the year, which in turn express different aspects of living. Divisions of time are themselves hierarchical, in marking units of social process and of the inclusiveness or exclusiveness of pūjās. In other words, there may be single performances: pūjās appropriate to the days of the year, smaller divisions of *prahar* (three hours), *muhurta* (moment), the moment at which a particular pūjā within a pūjā is to be performed or the full annual cycle. Each division being complete in itself, the incompleteness appearing on a higher level is transcended when another division of time enters to restore the balance. Hence time as a cycle of seasons defined by festivals integrates one half of the year in Durgāpūjā, the other half in gājan. The smaller divisions between the day and the year corresponds to other pūjās, sequences of pūjās, and festivals, referring to the life cycle of the gods, the different cults of different deities at different times in different places.

In the gājan Śiva is father, and men are recruited into a relationship with him (kinship, gotra relation), merging society into a totality through the gotra principle of relationships. Castes are merged in the play (līlā) of Śiva and Durgā, and men as individuals are engulfed in the energy created by the divine couple in union.

In Durgāpūjā the goddess is the mother of the world, the daughter of the house and line, an authoritative royal figure. In association with the male god she is responsible for the varied aspects of creation. Differences in the fields of experience are elaborated and defined to reveal the varied series and classes of things issuing from the goddess. Multiplicity is the core of Durgāpūjā.

What is sufficient and necessary on one level in each of the festivals becomes inadequate in terms of a system on another level. The two festivals complement each other in their detail and elaboration of basic principles; the sharing of units through male and female elements. Durgā must be understood as revealing divisions and parts in the universe, society, home, kinship, living, and experiential, existential situations, giving a total scheme in which all parts are related to each other and to the whole. Śiva's gājan, on the other hand, reintegrates these different classes and series of creation into an ongoing cycle of time, the oneness of the male principle. Puruṣa is hierarchically above prakriti even though the latter is the plural, multiple, and dangerous element. The gājan unifies in the body of the bhakta the separations of the Debī's creation by affirming the link between all created things and the male principle. All that is created is opposed to a single puruṣa expressed by male deities, Śiva, Viṣṇu, Kṛṣṇa.

Looking beyond gājan and Durgāpūjā, we find Śiva and Durgā complementing each other in the rituals of the year. In Śibrātri (night of Śiva), marriage and the love of husband are emphasized. In the other Durgā bratas the role of women as protectors of the family, givers of śakti, is marked. On this level the male element is not superior, the primacy of the female is apparent; the goddess here appears as the unifying principle of all variations and multiplicities.

Durgāpūjā starts with unity in multiplicity. The aspects of the world are to be comprehended through the goddess: she is the hierarchically foremost, encompassing category and symbol. Multiplicity is seen in opposition to the single concept of female divinity. As the rites develop and diversity increases, different duties and characteristics are separated in the manifestations of the Debī as well as the groups of people in a locality. Different pūjās also elaborate various classificatory series in the world. The performances proliferate, dividing society into smaller and smaller units, down to the sentient being. All differences are revealed as creations of the goddess; she brings variations and difference into the world. Nevertheless, the fundamental principle underlying Durgāpūjā is the same as that in the gājan. The interplay of the puruṣa/prakriti principle is the key to all action, and variations may be understood in terms of this basic relationship. The multiplicity of the Debī's creation is reintegrated in the rituals, into the single unity of god and goddess. Even Śiva and Durgā are subject to these principles. If Durgāpūjā starts with a unity (the idea of the Debī, the annual festival of the Debī as the summation of all goddess rites) and proceeds through diversity to unity at a higher level of integration (in the union of god and goddess), the gājan starts with multiplicity, the different castes and participants, the different forms of Śiva, and proceeds to equalize and merge diversity into union. Puruṣa/prakriti ultimately link the bhaktas to the divine consort, the dividing line between men and gods being crossed once again. In gājan all rites come back to Śiva, Durgā, and the sun with increasing reiteration and simplification on the level of ritual action. In Durgāpūjā there is increasing diversity and elaboration of goddesses. The gājan simplifies diversity but reiterates the basic principles of union and creation at increasingly complex levels of integration as the rites progress from day to day. In the Durgāpūjā the same principles are seen in detail— separation, multiplicity, and momentary union.

Oppositions emerge on the level of structure in each of the festivals, only to be reintegrated in higher-level relationships. The basic structure of pūjā is shared by both festivals: Durgāpūjā and Śiva's gājan form aspects of the field, necessarily participating in the same structure. However, the replacement of categories within the structure affects different elements in the two festivals. In Durgāpūjā the category jajmān (worshiper) is segmented in a hierarchical way; in the gājan the category of ritualist (*jajak*) is similarly segmented. This opposition is further clarified when we realize that the basic difference between the two festivals is that while in Durgāpūjā the ritualist is a separate person, in the gājan the worshiper acts on his own behalf. Alternatively, though the two roles are distinct, they are collapsed within the same person. In Durgāpūjā men participate in the offering through the category of jajmān, in accordance with a segmentary system: king, ṣolaānā, ganja, jāti ṣolaānā, pāṛā ṣolaānā, line, and so on. In the gājan the bhaktas participate in the role and category of ritualist, the distinction being merged in one category through the crossing of the line between deities and men. We have seen how the ritualist "becomes" divine in the Durgāpūjā. In the gājan the category of ritualist is replaced by the participants in accordance with another segmentary principle: that of divine gotra unifying people in relation to a divinity. The situation in the gājan is the exact reverse of that in Durgāpūjā. The divisions of society in the festival are brought into a relation with the Brāhmaṇ ritualist and with the Debī on the model of the relation between king, priest, and goddess. These divisions enter into the gājan also but are transcended at a higher level in the rite of the sacred thread aligning men with Śiva. The divisions disappear, only to reappear in the replacement of the ritualist category: the structure of society as it appears in Durgāpūjā is paralleled by the classes of bhaktas. Divisions within the gājan are just as hierarchical as in Durgāpūjā: the structure is once again pyramidal, with the relations of the pāṭbhakta to Śiva being the most encompassing. The relationship is repeated through the ranks of participant ritualists. Not only is the pāṭbhakta the chief of the gājan, but his relation to the deity encompasses those of other classes of bhaktas. The pattern is repeated in the relations of gāmārbhakta, rājbhakta, śālbhakta, and mānsikbhakta to the deity. That there are two offices in one category with the different classes of bhaktas replacing the pāṭbhakta as the ritualist in relation to Śiva and the sun is clarified further by the roles of Brāhmaṇ and king in the gājan. First we note that the two categories of ritualist and offerer are always in the background of gājan, precisely because gājan is also a unit within a hierarchical system. King and priest are both significant in the gājan. But the bhakta stands for both: he makes offerings to the deities on his own behalf. Nevertheless, he is related to the king, the owner of the land. The king's role is paralleled by the ṣolaānā, the totality that is itself expressed by the whole group of bhaktas (after all, the town-ṣolaānā is responsible for the gājan). Similarly, the bhakta is related to the Brāhmaṇ and to the agradhānī ritualist (whose role is particularly significant in the offering to the pāṭā, Bhairab, which enables the wooden board to act as divinity). The roles are distinct even though they are collapsed in the same person, only to be divided in the further relations between priest and king, ṣolaānā and agradhānī.

In the gājan the bhaktas themselves achieve what is solely the Brāhmaṇ's privilege in the Durgāpūjā. There is no prānpratiśṭhā in the gājan, since Śiva's liṅga and the sun are both incarnate deities. The liṅga is not parallel to the image of the goddess in the Durgāpūjā; rather, it is to be understood in opposition to the yantra, the sacred diagram. The liṅga is reproduced in the offerings to the sun at the edge of the river (often with fruit placed inside it) in the same way that yantra is drawn in the different Durgāpūjās within the festival (the representation itself being efficacious in the world of pūjā without the necessity of *prānpratiśṭhā,* the yantra coming alive merely through an object and a word). In the gājan, however, men become gods not through a dissection of creation into myriad parts, and the ensuing demonstration of equivalence in the structure of all things and events, but rather in the direct transformation of the life of ordinary men into the play of the gods, the transformation of the Śiva-Durgā līlā (cosmic play) into experience in the world of men. Men are thus involved in the līlā of the gods as units of equal value. Trance, initiation through paitā, and the merging of the ritualist and worshiper categories are all aspects of this process of becoming, a passage from men to gods. It must be remembered that the office of Brāhmaṇ is to be understood exactly in these structural terms: the Brāhmaṇ is the one who can become a deity through the ritual, hence bhaktas act as Brāhmaṇs in the gājan, achieving the same result in different ways.

Durgā is not only daughter, mother, and goddess to the king, she is also partner and ally. The duty of the king is to maintain *dharma,* proper order, which is also to be comprehended through the action of the goddess (and through the results of that action). Durgā exhibits the *rajasik* quality in this relationship of alliance, the quality of power and rule. The king serves the goddess, and in return Durgā bestows on him ability to wield power and to rule in the proper manner. This amounts to maintaining the systems of hierarchy surrounding the goddess in locality, society, and ideology. King and goddess are allies in rule.

But the king is also a devotee of Durgā, a bhakta who offers bhakti to the goddess. Bhakti and alliance are not exclusive; they are linked extremes on a continuum: through his bhakti the king can force the goddess to make him more powerful (*śaktigoti*). Some legends of the royal house describe fights between king and goddess in which the king emerges victorious and forces the goddess to do his bidding. Thus the king appears carrying a sword (and in full battle paraphernalia, according to legends about Durgāpūjās of the old days) at the crucial moment of assertion of kingship in his relation to the goddess. In one of these encounters a Malla king exclaimed: I will not eat your polluted food (*ucchista khaddo*). I will come to you as a rājā! The ability of the king to command was acquired through *sādhana* (disciplined practice) and bhakti.

Beyond political alliance (rule) the king has a marriage relation to an aspect of goddess. This interpretation is suggested by the rituals of Choṭoṭhākurānī in the rājā's Durgāpūjā. We already mentioned the possibility of analyzing the king's dharma as the Four Goddesses. But beyond this the significance of the Youngest Queen points to marriage alliance. First there is the small, temporary temple of the goddess. Then there is the no longer observed practice of the rājā's wearing the sāri that was used to dress the Kala Bou (the banana wife of Gaṇeś) or the nabapatrika (the Nine Durgās) of the Youngest Queen.

Thus the king is brought into a marriage relation with the goddess, in a symbolic expression of the "magic" powers of kingship: the king's role in preserving the world and time. Every year the process is repeated: the king renders visible his fourfold functions and his dharma for his subjects. Beyond mere expression, we see here a structuring of the universe in many of its aspects, as not only in recognition of categorical roles but in assurance of maintenance and continuance of structures and functions on all levels of a complex system.

The king does not "marry" the goddess in the way he married his bride. The two events are on different levels and are not confused The marriage symbolism is used, indirectly to suggest the functions and powers of kingship, expressing symbolically the difference between rājā and people and constituting royal power shared by deities and kings. The levels are hierarchically segmented, and the rituals accomplish the transformation from one to the other: the symbols may be the same, but they mean different things on different levels. Yet there are no absolute exclusions in this system. The people may also be brought into a similar relationship with the goddess.

In this line of inquiry, however, we leave the local ideologies and follow the logic of the relationships so far uncovered. What should we mean by king and bhaktas "marrying" the goddess? We note the marriage symbolism of yellow suta, sāri, Durgā's ghat, and Śiva's trident all in a relationship, and we also note the task of uniting god and goddess. Further, we recognize the transformations of the person into bhakta, renouncer, deity, and ally of the goddess. But the series would not be symbolic if it were to be a mere marriage (in the human sense) between two partners. Just as the gods are invited to witness and sacralize marriages between men and women, so in the case of Śiva and Durgā men share in the results of divine power and action. But we can go further: in the marriage rite bride aṇd groom become and are treated as divinities, in the case of Durgāpūjā and Śiva's gājan king and bhaktas are Śiva in relation to Durgā, and Durgā in relation to Śiva. Hence the king wears Durgā's sāri and parades around the town as a goddess, and hence also men as bhaktas and renouncers may represent the female principle in relation to the single puruṣa ideology. Here Vaiṣṇava and Tantrik influence may be combined and expressed as a unity in Vishnupur: the whole created world is female in relation to the male principle, Kṛṣṇa or Śiva. In the same vein we can argue that in the gājan the bhaktas are brought into a marriage relation with Durgā, through Śiva, and reciprocally with Śiva through the goddess. But these are all mediated relations: the king's through kingship, śakti, and bhakti (alliance, power, as well as devotion); the bhaktas', through their relation with Śiva, again in terms of śakti and bhakti, the creation of energy, ability, and power, and the fruits of devotion. I say mediated relationships advisedly, for one could easily slip into substantivist, monistic language and thinking by stating a direct relationship with marriage between bride and groom. Whereas the marriage of men and women has to do with saving the line (*baṇgśa rokkha*), the nurturing of the fruit that issues from seed and earth, the encounter of bhaktas, the marriage of Śiva and Durgā has to do with śakti and the maintenance of the world. The partial marriage symbolism is noted and abstracted by the anthropologist from three different cycles of relationships: kinship-caste-marriage, royalty and divinity, gods and men.

We may be permitted a note of speculation: What happens when even the category of king disappears from these systems of transformations? Will the ṣolaānā, the collectivity, replace the rājā in his alliance to the goddess and arrogate to itself the tasks of kingship? To some extent this is already happening. That the momentary transcendence of bhaktas in the gājan achieves at one stroke renununciation, "magic," fertility, and power suggests that the collectivity can carry out the tasks of the rājā in the scheme of the world. But here we must leave the immediate context and take note of other signals. Parallel to the above process are those that abstract from kingship into government and from the holistic universe we discussed into religion in the Western sense. Once the principles of śakti and bhakti, dharma and rajas, puruṣa and prakriti no longer hold sway over the whole society, they become encompassed details and eventually become dominated as "religion," by "economics" and "politics." The growth of individualistic pietism in Bengal (different from bhakti) suggests that the process of differentiation and separation between domains is advancing.

Particular gods are not in exclusive relations with the other categories in the structure. As we saw, Durgā parallels the relations of Viṣṇu and Śiva to jajmān and jajak, but even beyond that Śiva and Viṣṇu may replace each other in relation to Durgā, while remaining within the "deity" category. This does not happen in haphazard ways but is worked out in the puruṣa/prakriti relation between deities. Bhairab, Viṣṇu, Śiva, and Kṛṣṇa may express this in relation to Durgā in different contexts.

Participation, replacement, and correspondence as well as segmentation, autonomy, and exclusion are characteristic of the systems I have discussed. Yet units and elements are subject to unification, inclusion, and hierarchy as well in the multidirectional relationships they exhibit. None of these processes are merely indigenous or merely analytic. The terms in which I comprehend these circumstances are a part of the transformation of indigenous categories not only within the subject of this study but in the emergence of indigenous principles as explanatory principles. Let us take the symbolism of ghat and liṅga as a case in point.

The ghat (earthenware pot of worship) always appears in association with the goddess. Śiva is worshiped in the liṅga form (on several occasions the liṅga is built from sand), and although on occasion he may be invoked in a ghat the goddess worship is inconceivable without the ghat. Śiva and Durgā are thus opposed in the festivals: whenever Durgā is brought to the locality of the worship a ghat appears, but this is not so with Śiva. Going further, the ghat represents a dwelling, the temple of the gods, but both temple and ghat are like the human body, which also becomes a receptacle for the gods in the pūjā context and in the trance of gājan. If body and ghat are equivalent in one moment, the difference of Śiva and Durgā is also maintained in ghat and liṅga and in the person of the bhakta (in the gājan) and of the offerer (the jajmān in Durgāpūjā). In the latter case the person, not the body, variously stands for Śiva, for father, daughter, son, ally, and partner of Durgā, and, finally, for both the female and the male principles (severally and together) in respective relations to puruṣa, Durgā, and brahman.

The container and the contained is a variation on the encompassing and encompassed relationship. In a hierarchy the relations are reversible on different levels: *patri* and *patra* (container/contained; bride/groom) are parallel to Durgā ghat and Śiva liṅga and are not linked in one direction alone. In one sense the bride encompasses the groom (in holding his seed in her womb), but the groom encompasses the bride in another sense (in assuming the bride into his father's line, baṅgśa). In Durgāpūjā the ghat and yantra encompass seed and Śiva, but in the gājan Durgā is brought to Śiva, is placed in his temple, and is encompassed by Śiva. The idea that puruṣa and prakriti are mere abstractions unrelated to the world of action is also dispelled by the construction of the yantra of Durgāpūjā. At first sight yantras call to mind the esoteric knowledge of the Tantras, but more immediately they activate the processes of power (śakti). They do not merely represent something: something has to be done to a yantra, a mantra recited over it, a seed placed in the middle of it; in either case Śiva is introduced into the diagram representing the goddess. The dual performance and reciprocal relationship activate the ritual. Now let us compare this with the bringing together of Durgā and Śiva in the gājan, with the generation of power (śakti), and of trance (bhor). But this is not all: in the ideology, the same dual relations recur with great frequency: action and the ability or power to act, fire and the ability or power to burn, sunlight and the energy of the sun. The union of Śiva and Durgā is not a mere representation of śakti—after all, Durgā is śakti; rather, it is an accomplishment of the power of action, the ability to act.

Beyond Vishnupur

The categories of the festival system not only form a structure in terms of a logic of classification, they also define an idea and boundary for the sacred. Further, they give us the Bengali derivation of divinity, and they define the relation between men and gods. This relation is quite different from the opposition of human and divine in the West. There is no basic opposition in the Bengali scheme, only different levels within a domain. It has nothing to do with a fundamental contrast between "supernatural" and "natural," "sacred" and "profane."

The derivation of the idea of divinity is clear in the festivals we discussed. Two aspects are of primary significance: locality and situation. These define different deities and different images of the same deity. Models for divinity are to be found in the experience of the worshiper. The case of the ritualist is no different, he "becomes god" through experience in order to serve the gods. The worshiper is not identified with divinity; the roles are separate. But the link is established through action and belief—the various forms and kinds of ritual in which relationships of men and gods are often reversed or even collapsed, both being symbolic processes that cannot be understood without an abstract separation of roles and a primary division of the categories. I do not claim an identity in substance or effect: men are not gods, but in their relationships the categories are reversible and shared among the units. These circumstances ought to lead us to an understanding of divinity and to the relation between constructs and action.

Divinity is recognized and comprehended through imagination (*kalpana*), discipline (*sādhana*), interpretation of discrete intervention (*upasthīt haoya,* manifestation), knowledge (*jñān,* awareness of the classes of creation, the fundamental principles giving unity to surface diversity in the world), devotion (reaching a deity through bhakti), and following the precepts of a guru, the renouncer.

There are transformations from one level to another through rites and symbols in pūjā and through the processes of yoga, sādhana, and kriyā. Continued action in the world is governed by these transformations. The levels in the scheme clearly indicate the grades and classes dividing the continuum between things and brahman (the Supreme Spirit). Men and gods are only two of many possibilities. The list could be extended and the levels exchanged in the hierarchy in terms of different ideologies. It should be stated that men are further distinguished from special kinds of men, leaders, artists, and other great men, just as these are in turn distinguishable from a yet higher class, saints and renouncers. Classes of divinities may be inferior to these, or, alternatively, *sādhaks* (adepts) may reach a higher level of classification, a part avatars (such as Rāmakṛṣṇa). Oppositions are in terms of relational categories within a hierarchical system and the levels are many, not just a basic dual division (see fig. 13).

The scheme tells us the nature and character of the deities themselves. Multiplicity and oneness are the keynotes of these characteristics. It is now possible to answer the question: Why necessarily so?

We meet the notion of oneness in both the gājan and the Durgāpūjā. Durgā and all her manifestations are encompassed, as categories, by the category of Debī. The hierarchy of goddesses encompassed by Durgā is to be understood in terms of relationships. The units standing in relationships are defined in the ideology as well as the structure. In the ideology there are discontinuity, identity, substance; in structure there are relationships that exhaust the categories. The separations on the levels of ideology allow us to construct the structure and explain the significance of repetitions. Were it not for the ideology, we would have to say that all units in the hierarchy are in one-to-one relation with the Goddess

Brahmā
Bhagavan
avatar
Isvara—god
Ṭhākur—lord
part-incarnations
Deb-debī
saints, gurus, reformers
deities of the people—Bhūmidebatā
mahāpuruṣ—leaders, great men
men and women
living things
created things

Figure 13. Levels of divinity.

Durgā, the multiplicity being resolved in terms of oneness. This is not the case, however. We can assign each goddess or divinity a position in the structure in terms of its unique relationship to the most encompassing category. The units themselves are more or less inclusive, hence they belong to different levels. Locality and situation define each deity and give it relative inclusiveness or exclusiveness. The multiplicity of divinities can be comprehended in terms of locality and situation, which in turn are transformable into social relations and social structure. Different deities, or the same deity, may stand in a certain kind of relationship to a locality, a social group, a social experience, and a situation. The hierarchy of deities separated from oneness in terms of localities and situations is to be found in the structure of society, time, and cosmology. Situation and locality define discrete deities that are regarded as substantive and affective in the ideology.

These characteristics allow us to analyze the gods in terms of their relationships. In the pūjā the aspects of the goddess are to be found in positions that the goddess as a symbol occupies in the rite, the locality with which she is in alignment, and the situation to which the myth refers. These two components define all deities and place them at a certain level of the mythic-ritual scheme. The same logic applies to symbols of the goddess, the concepts to which symbols refer. Durgā as mother encompasses the aspects of the goddess as wife, lover, and daughter. As a symbol the goddess encompasses the other female deities in their relationships to each other. All female deities share in the relation to the whole, the notion of the goddess itself. The town is one and the goddess is one in the same terms—through their relations to each other and to the people. Together they form another kind of unity.

Deities have particular identities, but at the same time they participate in a structure. We saw, however, that elements are shared in categories; there are no exhaustive oppositions among deities in terms of their characteristics. The principle of sharing is clear in the concept of *brahma-jñān*: all things share in brahman. Directly, only a renouncer can strive to realize brahman, true knowledge. But the deities themselves, the avatars, the leaders (*mahāpuruṣ*) may achieve in some ways a glimpse of that knowledge. This realization itself creates a hierarchy.

The indigenous concept of knowledge may resolve another paradox in the gājan, the role of the sun. On one level we saw the sun participate in a tripartite structure similar to the ones we found within the pūjā system, among the gods and in society. On another level the sun not only represents the male principle (as Śiva is related to bhaktas, the sun is related to Śiva), but it represents brahman in relation to the created world (including Śiva and Durgā). The tripartite structure is resolved in a fundamental opposition. The sun is related to the world as brahman is, only the sun is incarnate and visible whereas brahman is not. The metaphor is clear when we consider the logic behind it: brahman is true knowledge, the world without māyā and līlā (in terms of which alone can men classify the universe). The sun makes things visible and turns darkness into light, reflecting the true nature of things that men see through a veil of illusion. The sun is brahman in a particular relation and in a limited sense. As the above is to the below, as the sky is to earth, the sun is to the nature of things. In this the sun acts as a reminder of the brahman, truth, the true knowledge. We can state further that this understanding of the sun is at the highest level of abstraction in the gājan. At that level there are no male or female elements, hence the sun is opposed to both Śiva and Durgā in the gājan. At lower levels of abstraction the duality of male and female is realized in a segmentary way. What is male at one level becomes female at another. Hence men and women are distinguished at one level, only to be merged into prakriti and opposed to puruṣa at a higher level.

The derivation of divinity and the role of the renouncer complete and enhance the dynamism of the model implicit in our discussion so far. The model can be used to approach the equally dynamic reality of Bengali beliefs and actions. New processes in the cultural field (beyond the mere reaffirmation of beliefs and actions owing to the interplay of units in a structure and in an ideology) are introduced by a renouncer who rearranges the parts of a previous system and initiates changes within a set or a system. There is a dialectic in the model, in reality as well as in the processes of fieldwork and analysis.

The ritual mythic field is constantly changing, renewing itself by rearranging and recombining its elements in different ideologies, giving rise to new forms and to new meanings of the old categories and practices. In this way new classificatory units are created in society. The new meanings and rites may be introduced by reformers, ritualists, gurus who also have a crucial role in the whole scheme: that of the renouncer who is, paradoxically, free to affect society because he is outside it. In the ritual scheme one way of deriving divinity comes from the renouncer himself, who gives the model for divinity with which men can identify in ritual action and which they can reenact symbolically through the priest or bhakta.

The domain defined by performance and symbols in action cannot appear as a static, balanced equilibrium system; it appears rather as a process of communication through symbolic actions, concepts, and objects that coalesce into a system that has implications for the whole of Bengali society: festivals may form and express other domains of action.[1]

The claims made here relate to classification and order in Bengali festivals as a system of symbols. In simple terms, the theory states that concepts and categories culturally defined act in two ways: one, to form a structure of abstract sets of relations in a system of logic; two, to form ideologies in relation to social groups and values, beliefs held by these groups. The meaning of categories is given by their logical, systemic, and structural characteristics. Their ideological role is given by their structural meaning in relation to specific ends in human experience. I use the word ideology in two senses; first it pertains to the particular sets of ideas, concepts, categories—the representations of persons in groups within a hierarchical universe. Second, it refers to the total set of concepts and representations in a society, pertaining to the whole of the hierarchical social universe. The two senses are linked, but the separation highlights the mediating role of the anthropologist in the processes of analysis.

In this study I have relied almost exclusively on indigenous models in a dialectical relation to action and to my own observations. Ideology, model, idiom, and exegesis stress aspects of the same phenomena. In discussing myths and rituals we are dealing with accepted forms of action and norm, preferred and prescribed action. All these are a part of the self-awareness of the local people. Analytically, we may distinguish between the ways of action, together with indigenous interpretations, and the abstractions the anthropologist makes from those materials. The latter is also a model, an abstract order, and without being extraneous to the reality it remains ordered because the reality itself is grasped and interpreted by the social actors in terms of an assumed order. That the anthropologist's construct of an abstract order is structural, relational, and logical is possible because the construct is relevant to the concrete reality. Reality does not have a one-to-one correspondence to the abstract order. Rather, the imperfection of daily life and the looseness of experience themselves depend on the assumption of a higher-level order. It is therefore not surprising that we can construct an abstract, ordered world out of the discontinuous fields of living, everyday experience. The striving toward order is within that experience. Its systematization and unification from discontinuous series is the work of the social scientist.

Everyday life is comprehensible to the actor and to the anthropologist only through assumption and abstraction: the difference between the two is often deemed too important. To the actors the fields may be separate, the order may be established through cultural assumptions and presuppositions in broken-up parts, applicable to separate, discrete fields. To the anthropologist, who tries to unravel the implications of these presuppositions of order by looking at several fields at once, it may appear that there are more fundamental similarities among the fields than the people themselves assume. From a broader perspective, different boundaries may appear to be significant: the anthropologist's view may stress similarities, variations, and differences other than those emphasized by the people themselves. Neither of these views is better or more correct than the other, but they differ in some ways. However, the difference is not an opposition; the two models are complementary and shared at every level of fieldwork and analysis; only the proportions change. We noted that there is no single "native" model. Nor can we postulate in opposition a single "anthropologist's" model. Multiplicity is true not only of the phenomena, but of the ways we try to comprehend reality. Indigenous models and ideologies of social groups are primary data for the anthropologist. The internal ideological models participate in the analytical and presentational models of the anthropologist at every level of abstraction.

In observing ritual action, and the moving to abstraction from exegesis, indigenous models are almost equivalent to the anthropologist's models. At higher levels of abstraction the participation is still present, though the proportions and degrees change. The analytical model is still recognizably indigenous, though it is no longer equivalent to any of the ideologies; rather, the latter can be approached and comprehended in terms of the former. The two classes of models overlap and share in elements and composition: pristineness is illusory at all levels, and the opposition is neither fundamental nor clear in the dual relationship of actor's and scientist's models. The dialectic takes place at all levels of analysis, not only in the mind but also in the field, and in the encounter between Bengali experience as formulated in ideologies and the anthropologist's attempt to find the principles that determine the form and structure of that experience.

The abstract order, based on indigenous experience, is revealed through a full narrative of actions and interpretations. Hence the crucial significance of fieldwork, which proceeds in a continuously self-correcting way. Work in the field is concerned with pointers to a systemic, relational scheme, testing assumptions about relationships in a holistic universe against each new piece of evidence. At the same time, the emerging scheme is questioned in the light of each new day's experience. In this way a dialectic is developed, a confrontation with experience in one's own mind. There is a constant dialogue within the fieldworker between the experiencing self and the abstracting self, fitting the parts together as the links become evident.

If we were to pursue, and locate, dialectic as a truth (as some people advocate), then we would indeed reduce anthropology to the study of lineal development and change. Such a dialectic would also limit the direction (and single-mindedness) of the processes we study. There is no single process of change transforming societies from one stage of development to another. Structural studies have revealed the multiple directions of relationships in societies through time. Dialectic and indeed structure cannot be objectified as truth, the end result of our study. Both are processes in need of further interpretation and explication. A dialectical relationship adequately expresses the encounter between fieldworker and other societies as well as that between the fieldworker's society and other people. Similarly, the interplays between subject and object, category and action, structure and history, are dialectical in human societies.

In the same vein, structure need not be the rigid, objectified construction it becomes in some hands. Rather, as Jakobson has said, structures are processes on synchronic and diachronic axes, in constant flux. We do not have to travel far from this conception of structure to realize that structure and dialectic are not exclusive but are different aspects of the same thing: the continuities and changes designated by these processes are inevitably linked. Dialectical relations yield structures that exist in time and in turn set domains and boundaries for the former. The festivals we studied exhibit regularities set up within certain forms in particular contexts yielded by the reciprocity of the ideas and actions of people. But these relationships are necessary and determinate to the extent that structures through time are formed dialectically in action: ideologies affirm structures, the latter giving regularity, continuity, and meaning to the former.[2]

It has been customary to oppose, separate, and realign religion and society, great tradition and little tradition, text and context, Sanskritic or Brāhmaṇic and local-level Hinduisms. The way these oppositions are used seems to refer to sacred books and recital of texts (where rituals are discussed at all, they are secondary to considerations of the Sanskritic vs. the local calendar, purāṇic or other blueprints of performance, the enactment of myths as referable to some tradition or another). These oppositions do not refer to living reality: they put together performance with a blueprint the investigator knows to be true independently and a priori. Yet my evidence and procedure suggest that there are no master keys to the puzzles and no correct versions to the variations of myth, rite, narrative, and action.[3]

No such distinctions emerge from my analyses and interpretations. Following Ramanujan, however, I posit a separate and autonomous significance for the analysis of texts (if only to establish an initial and heuristic difference between anthropology on the one hand and history, theology, literary criticism, and other disciplines on the other). The meanings discovered in textual studies cannot be assumed to be the same as those in the rites I have discussed. These meanings are not opposed, however, in the sense of two orders or levels of reality communicating with each other. The texts (though not textual study and its resultant meanings) are encapsulated within the festivals. Purāṇa, pūjā, and gājan together form a totality. To select a level of textual data within this totality would be equivalent to separating out the behavioral elements for independent analysis. The meaning of a text in relation to others in a textual study will of necessity be different from the meaning of the same text in the study of festivals. As I have noted in the provisional analysis of Durgāpūjā, the difference is provided by the sociological apperception of man: we study myths, legends, rites, narratives, and sacred books within the contexts of action in the world.

The more familiar triad of Brahmā, Viṣṇu, and Maheśvār changes to Durgā, Viṣṇu, and Śiva in particular contexts. Durgā assumes the royal characteristics of both Viṣṇu and Brahmā, displacing Brahmā altogether and leaving Viṣṇu entirely to the sattvik category. Kṛṣṇa, on the other hand, is a royal deity in his journeys through the year, thus assuming some of Durgā's characteristics not only in the cycle of Vaiṣṇava rituals but in his relation to the town and in his significance within the total mythic-ritual domain. Similar transformations occur in the myths and legends about the relation between Durgā and Kṛṣṇa.

Śiva, on the other hand, the renouncer par excellence, is firmly tamasik in certain ways. Śiva may also be royal (in his role as king's kuladebatā) and sattvik in his renunciation (in the gājan myths and rites). But he achieves these in a tamasik way, the path through death and the burning grounds. In this respect Śiva is Tantrik in the judgment of both the anthropologist and the townspeople. Yet, again, Durgā may accomplish all these in herself: creating and destroying, renouncing and living in the world of everyday life. Thus Durgā becomes, through Śiva and Viṣṇu, both a participant in other categories and an autonomous actor in any or all categories, with a series of identities.

In participation and separation, unity and identity, structural segmentation and replacement, Durgā is both a very local and a transcendent divinity. In Durgāpūjā the goddess is elaborated in her relationships on many levels clearly as a locality deity, immediately involved in the minutiae of everyday life. Although the purāṇic myths are a part of the festival, the emphasis is placed on the relation between Durgā, people, and town (and the segmentary subdivisions within all these categories).

Śiva, on the contrary, is the least local deity in the festivals: few myths and legends connect him to Vishnupur (with the significant exception of the Bhaskor Paṇḍit narratives in relation to the Ṣāṛeśvar temples). Although Śiva is of the town, as we noted above, this structural relation itself needs to be interpreted, for it differs from the way Durgā encompasses the town.[4] The Bhaskor Paṇḍit legends refer to an outsider, a Marattha invader, and the related myths of Bhaskor Paṇḍit's defeat have Kṛṣṇa and Śiva agree about the deliverance of Vishnupur. Bhaskor Paṇḍit, a devotee of Śiva, is repulsed by Madan Mahan (a form of Kṛṣṇa) wielding the huge Dalmadal cannons (one of which stands enshrined and worshiped today, some way out of town). Śiva consents to this eventuality, and Kṛṣṇa's ascendancy is firmly established. Śiva is aloof and distant, a renouncer of the tamasik way. His energy, śakti, and power are necessary to make the universe and the world of men work, but he is not called upon for the myriad details of everyday life. None of the other major Śiva temples in the town have local myths and legends associated with them. In stark contrast are the series of śāstras, purāṇas, mahātmās, maṅgals, pāṇcalis, and other sacred narratives of Durgā and Kṛṣṇa. Even in the gājan Śiva deputes Bhairab to act on his behalf.

Bhakti is not opened to hierarchy in absolute terms, and it is not an alternative value (as it would be were we to oppose, in society, the inequality of hierarchy to the equality of bhakti). There are reversals within the hierarchical universe, and both gājan and Durgāpūjā include aspects of ritual reversal. In this, bhakti is opposed to hierarchy, only to be encompassed in hierarchy even more securely. Bhakti here is not the same as bhakti in the sects or in the devotional literature. There is a relationship between these levels, yet it should also be clear that bhakti can be subordinated in some way to other principles; if not always a way to transcendence, it may be parallel and not superior to these principles.

Bhakti and bhakta are a part of the festival system not only because Śiva's devotees in the gājan are bhaktas and the attitude to the goddess in Durgāpūjā is one of bhakti, but also because bhakti is a category within the system denoting a particular relation between deity and offerer, between offerer and sacrificer, and between sacrificer and deity.

Bhakti places the personal god, whether it be Durgā, Śiva, or Kṛṣṇa, above all other gods, even above the universal spirit (brahman). But dissolution and merging are not incompatible with bhakti, nor is bhakti opposed to śakti. The former results in the latter, and the latter reaffirms, restates, and reestablishes the former. On the other hand, bhakti is not a feature of individualism reminiscent of renunciation. Rather, it is yet another way of arriving at hierarchy in the world. A bhakti orientation elicits either śakti in the rajasik relation or (sacred) love (*prem*) in the sattvik relation, or *sneho* (affection for an inferior) in the tamasik relation. These also correspond to the public world of action, power, and rule (politics, not coincidentally, is *rājniti*), to the aspect of transcendence and renunciation (both in the sects and in the bhakti rituals of everyday life) and to the world of everyday life (kinship, caste, and marriage; *jāti-bhed* or *jāti-pratha,* the system of castes; *sommondhi-pratha,* the system of relationships; *mā-bābā somporko,* relations through mothers and fathers; *sangsār,* everyday life). Let us note, however, that we are not setting up hard and fast boundaries. Bhakti yields śakti in kinship, caste, and marriage, and it suggest transcendence, to a degree, even in that domain. Śakti in turn requires bhakti, and both may be rewarded by affection (sneho) on the levels of everyday life, rule, as well as renunciation.

Śakti and bhakti do not denote opposing sectarian traditions in my account: the two combine happily, elegantly, experientially, and meaningfully. Nor would the position of the puruṣa/prakriti relationships be enhanced in the contexts we have studied by reference to the systems of Indian philosophy. A definite parallel may be there, but are they the same? Just by virtue of its significance in a local system, I am justified in asserting that the strictly philosophical meaning of puruṣa and prakriti is of no direct consequence for this study.[5]

Although both festivals end in rituals of reversal, far more is going on than the anthropological category of "reversal" would allow. The reversal aspects allow us to highlight the extent to which society is "expressed" in the festivals. But beyond that is the question of transcendence. Durgāpūjā brings the goddess into the world of men. From this encounter a series of classifications and transformations of levels are generated. The gājan bhaktas parallel the Brāhmaṇ priest in transcendence, but they also parallel the renouncer and Śiva himself. In Durgāpūjā most household rites celebrate Durgā on certain days as the daughter or mother of the house. The community pūjās serve her as the mother of Bengal, the rājā worships her as partner and ally. At moments the goddess is revered as the female principle and as creation itself. We have already noted above how all these levels are separated and transformed in Durgāpūjā. Similarly, we noted the levels of gājan symbolism, where all bhaktas achieve transcendence during the festival.[6]

In the course of this study we have examined variant regional performances of the gājan to a much greater extent than those of Durgāpūjā, mainly because there is a fuller series of myths, mahātmās, and purāṇas of Durgā than of Śiva. Several conclusions can be drawn from this. The most immediate is a forceful realization of the locality of Durgā and the alocality of Śiva. In the two festivals the goddess represents the manifold nature of creation (including the world of social relations), whereas the lord consistently represents a more distant and general, though equally necessary, element. Even in the day-to-day affairs of the gājan Śiva remains distant, and Bhairab is the *mālik* (chief) of the rites. Thus Śiva is also represented in motion, close to the bhaktas, but even Bhairab does not attain the multiplicity encompassed by the goddess.

More particularly, there is no opposition between pūjās and sacred narratives. In this sense then there is no opposition (complementary or otherwise) between myth and ritual. Myths, in indigenous terms purāṇas, māhīmās, pāncalis, and so forth, are a part of the festivals: certain actions evoke or refer to well-known narratives, and some of the latter form moments of performance (as, for example, the recitation of the Caṇḍī legend). The relative absence of specific stories about Śiva in the gājan is a function of his alocality in this system; yet it appears from a consideration of other gājanlike performances in Bengal and Bihar that other male deities may take over the roles of Śiva and of the sun in other contexts. This is most spectacularly true of Dharma's gājan, where the surviving regional texts could easily be used for a performance of Śiva's gājan. In this case Śiva replaces Dharma (or vice versa) in a local complex without too much else changing from the one set of rituals to the other. The general form of the ritual sequence holds true in either case, with some necessary changes allowing for locality and for some characteristics of the deities involved. Our task here is not to disentangle the variations among regional performances, though with more reliable and more complete accounts of action and ideology this would be a fascinating and attractive prospect. For the present we shall have to remain content with the general conclusions about myth and ritual presented above and with the limited comparisons among variant performances given in chapter 3. Our discussion so far resolves the question, Why more myths of the goddess than of Śiva, and why more texts of Dharma than of Śiva? The locality/alocality contrast may be seen in other rituals and other deities elsewhere in Bengal and in India. Variant performances of Durgāpūjā would have to be considered for more binding generalizations about Bengal as a whole, yet the data we have from Vishnupur are sufficient to generalize within a case.[7]

Yet locality versus alocality is not an exclusive opposition. Although it situates the contrast between Durgā and Śiva, it does not vitiate the most general expressiveness of Durgā as a vehicle for more abstract concepts. Despite the locality of Mrinmoyī Debī, we have already noted the varied significance of prakriti as goddess. Within the specificity of Mrinmoyī is also the most general meaning of the goddess in Vishnupur, in Bengal, and indeed in all India—the female principle.

Deities and men, concepts and actions, things and abstractions participate in a relational structure, yet they retain their individual identity in ideology and dialectic. They are repeatedly placed in systematic relationships, yet there is no confusion about their separate meanings. They participate in each other's relationships, they replace each other, they merge in a higher unity and separate yet again into autonomous units. The system of relationships, the extension and contraction of boundaries constitute a domain in which all these units and elements participate in accordance with the principles I have enumerated. There are varying degrees of inclusion and exclusion in this domain, in keeping with hierarchical and segmentary characteristics.[8] On the different levels of relationships in festival, rite, myth, and ideology we find units encompassing each other or segmenting into more exclusive elements. The relationships of units exhibit correspondence as well as opposition, combination and assimilation as well as separation and repetition. Segmentation and separation may mean autonomy and identity, but not isolation. Identity, divergence, exclusion, and difference may mean the independence of levels on which these processes and formations are recognized, but it does not mean their exclusiveness and isolation. The concepts and processess we referred to are situated in and take place within a hierarchical universe, not in separate worlds. Here we find the dialectically related levels accommodating unity and identity as well as structural replacement and segmentation. Inclusion and exclusion, separation and merging, encompassment and segmentation, participation and autonomy, transformation and assimilation, hierarchy and transcendence, correspondence and divergence, are elements of this relational universe. In combination and often in parallel with the indigenous concepts of *śakti* and *bhakti, māyā* and *līla, puruṣa* and *prakriti, jāti* and *varna, suddha* and *asuddha, pabittra* and *apabittra, pūjā* and *parab, yogā* and *kriyā, mantra* and *mudra,* they enable us to construct analyses, to perform interpretations, and to strive toward comparative understanding. In this quest my aim is the comparison of societies to reveal both the uniqueness and the universality of social experience.

Appendix One

A Note on Locality

The boundaries of this study correspond, in a sense, to the geographical area of the ancient kingdom of Mallabhum.[1] The small kingdom (of the past) or the administrative region (of the present) is the area, the social and physical space, in which the total system is acted out. We may expect significant variations in neighboring regions or kingdoms. The region with Vishnupur as its center is surrounded by similar regions and centers. There are ties among the people of a region not only through marriage and descent, jajmāṇi, jāti, and other relations, but also through ritual, myth, and legend. In this region, for example, the pūjā of Mrinmoyī Debī (the Earthern One, the Goddess Durgā) of Vishnupur is regarded as the pūjā of Mallabhum. In other ways as well, Vishnupur is a ritual center: Durgāpūjās of various castes involve "caste brothers" from all over the region. Vaiṣṇava preceptors living in the town have disciples in the district and beyond. In Śaiva cults the Śaivite sāddhus of the town are similarly related to the region. The same is true of the low-caste ritual complex and its ritualists, cults, and medicine men (*ojha*s). Taking kingdom, region, and the present district as defined through these ties as forming separate levels, we may imagine a set of concentric circles around the town: some of these circles would overlap with those drawn around other centers.

The town is in the District of Bankura in the western reaches of West Bengal. It is the administrative center of one of two subdivisions in the district. The district lies between the hills of Choṭo-Nagpur and the alluvial Gangetic Plain of Bengal. In area the district has not changed much during the past ninety years. It contains about 7.7 percent of the area and 4.7 percent of the population of West Bengal. Vishnupur *thana* (police station) contains 5.5 percent of the area and 6.1 percent of the population of the district. The town has been a municipal, urban area for the past hundred years or so.

The soil is much poorer here than in the alluvial flats of the delta. Much of the area is covered by scrub jungle. Several major rivers flow through the district, each of them playing a role in the ritual life of the people. The seasons are well marked, most noticeable being the difference between the hot and the wet seasons. The dry riverbeds of the summer suddenly become torrents in the rainy season.

The present district enters the early history of Bengal as part of one kingdom or another, and as the core of various more or less independent kingdoms. The area was affected by the Islamic invasion of the twelfth century A.D., but the Hindu principality of Vishnupur began to flower after this period. The Malla kings created an independent kingdom and pursued a discreet diplomacy, allying themselves to the Mughal emperors from time to time. They ruled over a number of tributary kings but rarely paid tribute themselves. Up to the early eighteenth century the kingdom prospered, being famous for its temples, bazaars, arts and crafts, silk weaving, schools of music, and traditional learning.

A combination of famines, Marattha invasions, and the expansion of the East India Company saw to it that the kingdom was well on the decline by the end of the century. During the nineteenth century the kings lost most of their revenue lands and administrative powers. Much of the land was acquired by the neighboring Burdwan rāj.

Parts of the Malla estates were added to other districts as a result of administrative changes in the nineteenth century. In the twentieth century the district played a part in the noncorporation and revolutionary movements of the 1940s.

The 1950s saw the greatest change in population; there was a 37 percent increase in Vishnupur thana alone (during the previous fifty years the decade variation in population was 20 percent within the limits of ± 10 percent). The density of population per square mile has generally been constant (between 400 and 500), but it increased to 700 in the 1950s. At 4,500 per square mile, Vishnupur town has the densest population. The municipal area is about eight square miles.

Most people of the town speak a dialect of Bengali. Most houses are built of mud with thatched roofs, but about one-third are brick or cement. Fifty-seven percent of the town's male population and 26 percent of the females are literate.

About 25 percent of the residents are designated "scheduled" or "low" castes. The major part of the population, almost 50 percent, is made up of the Nabasakha group of castes. The high castes, Brāhmaṇ, Kāyastha, and Baida, constitute about 20 percent. In the late 1960s the town's population was about 35,000.

Although the site of this study is a town, very different in scale from the usual South Asian ethnographies of villages numbering not more than a few hundred people, I would not make a special case for "urban anthropology." My approach is anthropological in the holistic sense. Following Pocock (1960), I do not separate "urban" and "rural" into opposing analytical universes. Nevertheless, there is a difference—if not in epistemology and in method, then in the very scale of the study—that allows greater opportunity for analysis and understanding.

Given the size and morphology of the town, the observation and performance of rituals and festivals is also more varied and fuller than in a smaller unit. The annual calendar of cyclical rituals is also more complete, allowing the observer several chances to observe the same ritual sequence in different contexts (allowing even for a revision of the initial impression of "sameness"). Thus I was able to follow the gājan performance more than a dozen times and to participate in dozens of Durgāpūjās, not to speak of hundreds of other pūjā performances. At the very least the data are more complete and varied for my having worked in a town. Then also, Vishnupur's being the center of a region allowed us to make specific trips, with the townspeople, to temples and festivals in villages up to twenty or thirty miles away, a set of journeys that revealed a system of processions, pilgrimages, and festivals in a wider locality, thus defining the reality of the region in terms of pūjās and festivals with Vishnupur as its center. It would not be difficult to insist that working in a town yielded historical, literary, and oral as well as written materials and at the same time to reflect on how the "centerness" on "centrality" of the town allowed me to encounter more, and more varied, people than in a smaller social unit. On the other hand, the very scale of the study took away the kind of the detail we have grown accustomed to from smaller-scale ethnographies. There are hidden virtues in this circumstance, since it makes us realize that interactional and behavioristic approaches are more a property of a system's scale than of its meaning. The jāti system is not a face-to-face system in Vishnupur, and the almost forty thousand people in the town do not all encounter each other within the year, let alone every day. Nevertheless, there is a *jāti-pratha* (system of castes) in the town, and there is significant and effective categorization of people as persons and as members of groups. Hence relations among people are mediated, expressed, and defined as well as interpreted by categories, not by mere behavioral interaction. In this way the richness of detail is yielded back to us in a larger context, with the added realization that the smaller-scale, avowedly empiricist studies of our discipline may have to be reexamined in the light of these findings.[2]

Appendix Two

Fieldwork

The month of our arrival in Bengal—Agrahayan—saw the celebration of Ītu, the sun god, and later of Ṭusu, the husk of the newly harvested rice. People discussed these rituals spontaneously as public or private activities, observed in different ways by different people. The celebration of the sun led straight to the festival of the new rice at the end of the following month (a solar festival), with more varied and marked public activity. Since people talked about these festivals in the context of social divisions and localities as well as myths and ideologies (what ought to be done and what is meant), I began to question everyone I met about them. They all knew about these events and could offer some personal account. The whole town was involved in these two months of festivities. It became clear that included were feasts of gods, harvests, and social groups as well as celebrations of birth and death anniversaries of great men, saints, leaders, and incarnations of the gods. Thus the birthday festivities of Gandhi, Netaji, Tagore, Vivekananda, Rāmakṛṣṇa, and Buddha were observed. These too were part of a field that at first seemed to belong to the gods alone. Yet to me all of them were unknown qualities. Similar actions could also be observed at life-cycle celebrations: birth, puberty, marriage, death, and the remembrance of ancestors.

On many of these different occasions I met the same people: ritualists, leading townsmen, and general participants. Local ties began to be differentiated, and the smaller and larger segments of the town separated. Social divisions began to take shape through recurring celebrations involving some of the same people and conspicuously excluding others.

At the beginning, the study was defined for me by people and words. Words described events that everyone knew about and everyone participated in. It seemed to me that these actions changed from season to season: each part of the year had its set of festivals. People often designate major public rituals by the season in which these take place. This, however, was just one of many possible classificatory schemes, and I began to explore others, for example, the social group performing the actions. The same group celebrates many different occasions and may form part of a larger whole in other festivals. But if all social divisions observe the same type of occasion (in larger or smaller segments) time after time, and if they exhibit a bewildering array of variations in the performance, then in addition to social ties something else must be involved. If not, why so many celebrations and so many variations?

I soon realized that seasons, social divisions, and individual beings were classified, in an overlapping rather than exclusive way, by the pūjās appropriate to them. People coalesce around pūjās, in kinship, caste, corporate, and voluntary groups. Taking the rituals themselves, it seemed that pūjā actions and the deities, symbols, and objects involved defined other aspects of society as well. But this did not lead to any understanding of the system, since the same people served different deities on different occasions. Sectarian ideologies do not define society except for the sects themselves. Yet there were so many parallels and correspondences that there was some sense in the above correlations. Objects also tended to recur from occasion to occasion, thus giving the first glimpse of a classification of things, activities, and time. The outlines of a holistic system began to emerge. In themselves parts and features mean nothing, but in relation to other elements they began to show some regularity and predictability.

Having made some acquaintance with what was going on during the year, I could embark on the observation of pūjās—their contexts, paraphernalia, and participation—as well as concentrating on classification and meaning. In witnessing festivals, I found that not everyone offered extensive descriptions of all events and actions. Thus I would test what I saw and start a dialectic between what I noted and thought and what people said and did. I could verify my understanding of recurrent concepts with chance acquaintances as well as with people I sought out for specific purposes. These initial sets of statements were invariably couched in terms of what one ought to do, now one should act, and who ought to do what.

In visiting the different areas of the town and observing different kinds of action, I found that many pūjās and related events centered on certain temples. Temples were linked to residential localities. But caste groups, temples, pūjās, and locality groups were not in a one-to-one correspondence. Caste groups clustered in certain areas, around certain rituals, in relation to certain temples and markets. I decided to concentrate on these clusters and to study all ritual activity in the chosen localities defined by these variables. This way I could study the town as a whole (in townwide public performances) and also limit the study in terms of locality, ritual action, and social segment. I soon found that caste alone was not definitive or derivative of ritual and belief; what people of different jātis could say about pūjās did not vary significantly. Later, differences and variations emerged in many ways, caste being only one of several.

Observation of pūjās creates complexity, the event being more varied than its description. The social and spatial boundaries did not become clear for several months, nor did I realize till later that many different cycles (family, line, caste, locality, season, sect) of rituals were linked. Gods, ritual action, belief, objects, and offerings participate in this system together with people, locality, and ideology. Often the same pūjā was performed in different parts of the town, in different social contexts. This made the work more difficult but at the same time more rewarding, since after a while variations led to greater consistency as well as diversity. Times of performance tended to vary, thus allowing wider observation, and this in turn led to a typology of pūjās in terms of several factors.

At the performances themselves there was ample opportunity to discuss the rites with the participants and to question onlookers in detail. The connection between rite, locality, and social group could be recognized in this way. Townsmen often spent time watching festivals, discussing rituals while the action was going on; hence I could raise problems without strain and interference.

Later on I followed up initial contacts systematically and made use of photographs, slides, and tapes in making a full record of ritual action. Taking these materials back to the performers after some time, I could enter into long, detailed discussions of specific items, ideas, and actions. Again, I encountered many people in each locality and found all types of commentary useful, in groups or individually, each context having advantages that could be used to test the results. Such encounters led to lasting ties with people, and to insights into what people were about, what made them volunteer interpretations and stress certain things. Some of these ties became warm friendships, and then collecting data was no longer of primary significance, since the experience of living brought more immediate obligations. Such experience is fraught with sadness as well as joy. Paradoxically, such open relationships deepened my understanding even without the motivation of wanting it to happen that way. Too much preoccupation with research methods and objectification rather than living experience may destroy a cultural understanding of existential situations.

Specific discussions led to more specific explanations and to a greater reliance on ideology than is normally the case in fieldwork. But beyond these regular, more structured settings, I continued random discussions with new acquaintances in all kinds of situations. These were helpful in verifying the meaning of categories, collecting a range of meanings, and finding variations of meaning and use in different contexts.

In time I was able to discriminate between statements and to evaluate information. This did not mean discarding data; it meant classifying them, since most statements and events were important and relevant, even when redundant, regardless of source. I took into account all I heard and all I saw: within a large enough universe of discourse, it is possible to classify data according to source, situation, knowledge, speaker, receiver, and other contexts. There is no "correct" exegesis and explanation, only variations on themes. Collecting a full range of variations leaves room for verification and testing: the idiosyncratic is soon distinguishable from the systemic. But even individualistic interpretations must be taken into account, because "mistakes," "contradictions," and "idiosyncrasies" may also occur in terms of a larger system, at least through the use of the same categories. Meanings in a culturally defined system do not just emerge: a relational assumption and willingness to pursue connections and an unwillingness to put a stop to the limit of exegetical meaning contribute to the possibility of analysis. Paradox and contradiction may be resolved in a wider set of variations: a symbol may have many meanings with different people stressing different aspects in different contexts.

The literacy rate in the town was high, so another kind of information came from printed sources. Several local newspapers carried reports on festivals, dissertations on the meaning of rituals, and poems addressed to deities. Legends of major temples were given in printed booklets extolling the power and influence of local deities. Townsmen had written histories of the Malla kingdom, descriptions of the pūjā system of the district, and accounts of local customs. I discussed many of these matters with the authors themselves. Thus it was possible to compare the structural features of ideal models of the past with the relationships among categories in the present.

The town has geographical, social, temporal, and ideal structures, and these have their image in the ideologies of the people. Divisions were established by links among people, rites, ideologies, and localities. Social structure therefore had room for many kinds of groups, not only corporate but shifting and nonconcrete ones—a system hierarchical and segmentary in relation to particular activities, purposes, and meanings. I could test the various classificatory schemes by taking them to different people and could thus see how associations as well as firm links worked out in action, ideology, and discussion. In the later stages of my stay I asked leading questions to highlight contradiction, paradox, and inconsistency: in this way I learned more and gave proof of my commitment to those who would teach me. There are different systems of knowledge in action: categories remain the same, but their contents become more abstract as the number of knowers becomes smaller. Indigenous models also have powers of abstraction with widening distance from actual performance and event.

Finally, initial oppositions and relationships are either confirmed or rejected in the research process: public and private spheres of ritual, community, and life-cycle festivals, social, sectarian, and ideological dimensions take a firmer shape. There was a whole field of belief and action to be explored in terms of indigenous categories.

Appendix Three

The System of Time

The Bengali year begins with the month of Boiśakh (April-May). It is a solar year, each solar month ending with the passing of the sun into a new house of the zodiac. Divisions within the month are lunar. There are two halves to each month according to the waxing and waning of the moon: the bright and the dark. These cut across the solar month. Each day within these halves is a lunar unit called the *tithi* (which does not correspond to the solar day). Tithis are numbered from one to fourteen, beginning with the day after full moon and new moon. Taken inclusively, one cycle consists of sixteen tithis. The discrepancy between tithi and day is reconciled by adding a number of tithis in the appropriate months.

The lunar months are counted within the solar year by equalizing them, by the addition of tithis, with solar months as defined by the passage of the sun from *rasi* to *rasi* (houses of the zodiac). The 1968–69 Bengali year happened to begin with the first day of the solar month and the first tithi of the lunar month. As the lunar calendar falls behind the solar, an extra full day/night tithi is added, beyond the regular addition of a tithi (when the difference between tithi and day reaches a full tithi).

The lunar month has thirty tithis (twenty-eight days) and one or two additional tithis; an extra "full-day" tithi makes up the solar month when the lunar month is thirty-two days, one "day" extra when thirty-one, and one tithi extra when thirty (with additions up to four days).

Each solar month has a full and a new moon in it: hence the months are both solar and lunar, though the number of tithis and days fluctuate within them. If we take the solar count as constant, then the full moon would fall on any solar day within the month, varying eleven days in the year.

The fourteen days preceding the new moon or Amābassā are called the dark half, Kṛṣṇa Pakkha. The fourteen tithis preceding full moon, or Purnimā, are called the bright, or Śukla Pakkha. The pakkhas also mark months, depending on which pakkha begins the month. The lunar month consists of two pakkhas and two tithis for Amābassā and Purnimā. The solar month to which the lunar month gives its name cuts across the pakkhas, yet part of each half would appear in the solar month (parts of pakkhas may form one month). Since the lunar and solar months do not synchronize, and since the festivals and pūjās follow the lunar schedule (because all pūjās occur on a particular tithi and are known by the name of the tithi), often there is great variation in the solar days on which the pūjās fall each month. The fourteen tithis are the first, Pratipada; second, Ditīyā; third, Tritīyā; fourth, Caturthī; fifth, Paṇcamī; sixth, Saṣṭhī; seventh, Saptamī; eighth, Aśṭamī; ninth, Navamī; tenth, Dasamī; eleventh, Ekādasī; twelfth, Dādasī; thirteenth, Trayadasī; and the fourteenth, Caturdasī. These terms are important because pūjā days are often referred to by the tithi number alone. There is a very close connection between the calendar, the categories of the calendar, and pūjās. The smaller time divisions of *prahar* (about three hours), *daṇḍa,* and *muhurta* are all significant units of ritual. Certain actions must take place at certain moments (muhurta) within a certain prahar (the first, second, third, or fourth part of the night) or within a certain tithi. The major units are all associated with pūjās. The Purnimā of each month is always the occasion for some special worship (Dol Purnimā of the God Kṛṣṇa; Kojagari Purnimā of the Goddess Lakṣmī. Amābassā is devoted to the worship of the Goddess Kālī. The bright half usually contains the pūjās of Viṣṇu, the dark half the pūjās of Kālī, Śiva, and Bhairab. Saṇkraṇti ends the solar month and occasions celebrations as in the harvest festival of Pouś Saṇkraṇti (January-February). Caitra Saṇkraṇti is the end of the Bengali year, and it is also marked by a series of rituals. The lunar tithis are also significant: there are certain pūjās for each tithi (general acts of worship appropriate to each day), and certain major pūjās fall on particular tithis. The name (number) of the tithi is also the name of the pūjā. So the worship of Sarasvatī must take place on the fifth tithi in the bright half of the month of Māgh (January-February), and the celebration is known as Scrīpaṇcamī. The fifth in the dark half of Jaiṣṭha (May-June) is Nāgpaṇcamī, the feast of Manasā, goddess of snakes. The birthday feast of Kṛṣṇa falls on the eighth of the dark half in Bhādra (August-September).

The major days of the Durgā festival, for example, fall on the sixth (Ṣaṣṭhī), seventh (Saptamī), eighth (Aśṭamī), ninth (Navamī), and tenth (Dasamī). Debī worship proper begins on the seventh (the sixth is the night of invocation). This being the major pūjā of the year, the tithis are called mahā, or the great, so Mahāsaptamī, Mahāaśṭamī, and so on (the great seventh, the great eighth).

The gājan festival of Śiva generally follows the solar schedule. There are variations, however. The main gājans take place around the end of the solar year; the ābārgājans, usually smaller celebrations, may occur in the first or second month of the new year. The days within the festival are solar, but they are named after the distinguishing characteristics of the pūjās that take place.

Appendix Four

Durgāpūjās in Vishnupur: Line and Caste Variations

Baṇgśa and jāti rituals of the goddess depart from some of the rites described in the text. The form and procedure of the pūjās are much the same; the significant differences come, as we may expect, precisely where the sacrificer, the jajmān, enters the worship.

In line worship the goddess acts as the *kuladebatā* (ancestral deity). This need not be an ancestral cult; it may be instituted by a person or a group, but the worship then becomes the responsibility of the line issuing from those persons. Not all kuladebatās go back many generations, and not all lines have such deities. When extended families split up, the deity follows one of the new lines, responsibility for the pūjā being divided among all agnatic relatives. This may involve the actual shifting of the deity from locality to locality. Just as the deity is shared by those on whose behalf the sacrifice is performed, so the service is shared among priestly lines. Priests may inherit pūjās and temples, and these are divided equally among the baṇgśa heads in case of temple worship and passed on to offspring in case of individual kuladebatā service. The priest becomes a *kulapurohit*. But there is no new line deity with each segmentary split; rather, the original pūjā is divided and shared. New deities are installed as the result of devotion and the desire of a male *kartā* (head of household) to perpetuate the object of his devotion in his own baṇgśa.

The kuladebatā always stays in the ancestral locality, the line's place of origin. When segmentation occurs, the line closest to the original locality assumes full responsibility for the deity, shares being sent in from the other segments. Often, however, these obligations are not fulfilled, and a new line deity may appear. In other cases some may be excluded from the pūjā of the kuladebatā and may set up their own deity. These groups become visible only at the time of Durgāpūjā.

Household worship can also be preceded by rites resembling those of the three Ṭhākurānī. On the day the rājā's worship begins, some lines also take a ghat from the tank and invoke the goddess. Daily worship then takes place with offerings of cooked rice and *payās* (rice cooked with milk and sugar). On the night of the sixth, *kalparambha* is performed. These major rites are preceded by the gathering of relatives from all over the region, the state, and even the nation. In several cases the "ancestral house" is an ideal construct, having been replaced long ago by a number of houses covering large pāṛās. Yet those who have moved to other parts of the town or beyond return for the annual pūjās.

The segment worshiping the original kuladebatā is under the direction of the eldest male, who also performs the rituals. Here the legends are more carefully followed: not those specific to the royal house, but those with a general, countrywide currency. The goddess's temple is regarded as her father's house. The temple in which she stays the rest of the year is her father-in-law's house. On the sixth the Durgā temple is decorated for the triumphant return of the goddess. Bhairab accompanies her to her father's house.

Baṇgśa pūjās are exclusive; fewer castes participate, and only members of the line are directly involved. The drummers are Doms, playing the large ḍhāks, not the small drums of the rājā's pūjā. Before breaking fast, the women of the house worship the goddess with flower offerings. The Brāhmaṇ recites three times, repeating each time the women throw flowers on the image.

The final day of the pūjā marks the greatest difference from the rājā's worship: all relatives including women and children participate. This day all gods and goddesses, Durgā, Śiva, Lakṣmī, Sarasvatī, Gaṇeś, Kārtik, and Bhairab, are worshiped, and then they depart to their own homes. Durgā goes back to her husband and Bhairab to his own temple. The distinctive feature of the worship is the rite bidding farewell to the goddess, performed by the women of the household. Women worship the goddess in the nabapatrika by waving the maṅgal patra around her, touching all the items to her—the same rite women perform for the bride at weddings, both in her father's house and later in her father-in-law's house. The rite is performed only by women of the house related by marriage or blood.

The most magnificently celebrated caste pūjā is that of the Jele (fishermen). By common consent this Durgā is the most beautiful of all the temporary images in the town. The pūjā is celebrated in the main Jele locality, but men of the caste live in six different pāṛās scattered around the town. Three localities join the main pāṛā in the annual worship for three consecutive years, then the other two pāṛās take over the responsibility for the pūjā. The headman of the main pāṛā looks after finances, and other headmen and *paricalok* (local leaders) help him with the preparations. Jele of the whole region contribute to the pūjā: representatives of fisherman groups come from more distant places. According to caste legends, all fishermen originate from Durgā. Part of the cost is covered by a practice that links mythology and social organization. The headman collects five rupees from bridegrooms who take women from the Jele settlements in the town. Since Durgāpūjā is the time when married daughters return home to their father's house, it is fitting that prospective grooms should contribute to the pūjā. Relatives by marriage may also participate. The pūjā connects locality and caste: for the Jele, the goddess and her people are inseparable. There were no fishermen before the pūjā was established, nor did the goddess arrive after the Jele settled. Durgā is the mother of all fishermen.

The five major days of the pūjā are observed in much the same way as in the rājā's temple. The differences are in the jāti character of the pūjā. The men of the caste, as jajmāns, welcome the ritualist at the beginning of the festival, offering gifts of food and clothing. The women of the caste bid farewell to the goddess on Dasamī day. Both rites are called baraṇ. The feasting involves only caste brothers of the locality. Since this is a non-Brāhmaṇ caste, no cooked rice can be offered; bhog therefore consists of uncooked rice, fruits, and an array of sweets. The bhog is divided among the people belonging to the jajak category: garland maker, purohit, Dom-musician, and image maker. The practice is similar in pūjās: bhog is divided among the jajaks as well as line members (in the case of the Brāhmaṇs described above, the array of jajak castes is wider: Dom, potter, garland maker, barber, and low castes who provide flowers for the worship). Flower offerings may be performed by all castes during the pūjā. In ṣolaānā pūjās food offerings are sent to the rājbaṛi (palace), demonstrating the link between king and pāṛā pūjās.

Similarly, Kāmārs (blacksmiths) of the town do a ṣolaānā pūjā in their caste area within the Āṭpāṛā division. Here only the Kāmārs of this locality worship together. Here too women make flower offerings, and they bid farewell to the goddess on the tenth day. Individual and caste worship are parallel; despite the fact that the Kāmārs organize the pūjā, other castes are not excluded from participation. Money offerings are accepted from all castes, and the prasad is also distributed. One unique feature of this caste worship is the recitation of songs welcoming the goddess. These *āgamuni,* welcome or "arrival" songs, are performed on the night of the seventh day by a group of pāṛā people, high and low castes singing together.

Finally, there are two more types of ṣolaānā pūjās: the first is the neighborhood festival of Egāropāṛā. Most castes of the town are represented here. The men who look after this pūjā are members of the Kṛṣṇa temple committee. At this public performance the differences from household worship are striking. The goddess is not just a daughter returning home, though that element is also present. The emphasis is on royalty: the queen, the mother is honored in these townwide rites. Correspondingly, the kinship aspects are played down and flower offerings by devotees are minimal. The other is the pūjā of the Hindu Satkar Samity established by a Kāmār devotee. This is a charitable institution that also maintains one of the public burning grounds (*sosan*) in the center of the town. Here the goddess is worshiped as the universal mother. The festival is designed to involve the whole town; it is also called a *sarbamaṅgalapūjā*: for the welfare of all. The worship takes place in the *āśram* (retreat) itself, and subscriptions are solicited from all over the town. On Nabamī day a general feast is given to poorer townsmen and to invited dignitaries and leaders. Both high- and low-caste people participate.

Notes

Chapter 1

1. For baṅgśa and kula in relation to Bengali kinship see Fruzzetti and Östör (1976*b*).

2. See the general accounts of Durgāpūjā in Ray (1950) and Chakrabarti (B.S. 1377), but anthropological analyses of Bengali festivals are few and far between.

3. Many of these interpretations are put forward in a pluralistic and overlapping manner in the representative examples of the anthropological literature. But, though a single work cannot be characterized by a single phrase, the reader will find examples of any or all of these approaches in the works of Hutton (1963), Srinivas (1952), Douglas (1966), Turner (1967, 1969), Marriott (1955, 1966), Singer (1972), and Leach (1965, 1968). On the other hand, Bengali scholarship has concentrated on evolutionary, historical, and folkloristic studies: Banerjea (1966), Bhattacharja (1964, 1968), Dasgupta (1958, 1962), Palit (B.S. 1319), and so forth.

4. Again, for representative examples see the works of Srinivas (1966), Singer (1972), Marriott (1955, 1966), Harper (1964), Mathur (1964), Mayer (1960), and so on.

5. Several scholars have noted this phenomenon in recent years, but it was most succinctly put by Cohn (1967).

6. There is a vast literature on these topics: the problem of "kinship" can be illustrated by reference to Murdock (1965), Fox (1967), and Keesing (1975); the problem of "economics" by reference to Belshaw (1965) and Nash (1966). See also Fruzzetti and Östör (1976*a*), Östör, n.d.

7. For example, we do not question the application of the concept to Western societies and histories.

8. A common assumption is that religion can be accounted for by something else: economic or political power, social integration or conflict, and the like. Attempts to go beyond this are easily transformed into theology. Being concerned with ontology and ideological truth, theology cannot answer sociological problems, and, lacking a societal apperception, it does not encounter socially constituted reality. A compromise approach would divide the two spheres into sacred and profane; but in whose terms are these boundaries set out? Is there something to our festivals themselves beyond economics, politics, and kinship?

9. Lévi-Strauss has shown how the distortions of a "sociological" language have created the problems of totemism and has demonstrated how ethnographic categories may form the grounds of anthropological analysis. To him we owe a more rigorous concept of structure and a discovery of the logic of classificatory systems. From here, however, his analysis took a turn toward considering myths as bounded texts exhibiting underlying structures as ends in themselves, ultimately attributable to the basic properties of the mind. In this pursuit Lévi-Strauss is no longer concerned with the meaning of categories and the analysis of social relations in terms of them.

Dumont carried the task further: relying on ethnographic categories (which in some cases were also those of Indian civilization), he noted a determinate structure within the relations among the categories of jāti (caste) and varna (the classical fourfold division). The notions of purity and pollution, ethnographic to begin with, were found to be structural principles. The resulting theory of hierarchy is perhaps the single most important contribution to the sociology of India. But Dumont's focus was the jāti system, and his concern with beliefs and rituals was meant to elucidate fundamental relations in the hierarchical universe of caste relations. We may go beyond this to examine festivals as a totality in their own right, allowing the discovery of indigenous domains different from social scientific conceptions.

Turner came to the study of symbolism with a concern for social tensions; yet he proceeded to study ritual sequences for the symbolic meaning they generate. His insistence on the significance of exegesis for anthropological analysis brought a new departure to our discipline; yet we may extend this approach beyond the mere symbolic expression of social processes.

Geertz, coming from another direction, recognized indigenous categories as meanings constructed in and for everyday life. In interpreting cultures, he insisted on relating logic and structure to people and on viewing symbols as meanings both of and for actions. Although inevitable problems of vantage point arise from the interpretive approach, I shall follow Geertz in studying symbolization as both defining and interpreting experience.

Schneider's work has already served me as a point of departure. Although my study is less concerned with ideology, I recognize the fundamental significance of his symbolic and cultural studies for my own endeavors.

10. I witnessed the gājan twelve times, but other gājanlike performances would multiply this figure. I followed the autumn festival four times, but other Durgāpūjās would push this figure well beyond thirty.

11. The theory was first developed in a course of lectures at the University of Chicago in fall 1969.

12. For example, recent contributions by Beck (1972), Babb (1975), and Wadley (1975) retain the dichotomies noted above (caste and ritual, religion and society, text and practice, and so forth). In addition, many other regional studies are necessary before a comparative analysis of pūjās and festivals can be undertaken on an all-India scale.

13. I shall speak of Durgā, Debī, and the goddess interchangeably and generally. When more specific meanings are called for, I shall identify the particular form by a particular name.

14. See the later discussion of the relation between indology and anthropology. "Myth" is used here descriptively, but when greater precision is called for the specific Bengali terms and narrative forms are identified.

15. Literally, smaller Purānas, words of auspiciousness and vows: they are often used to refer to the same thing—locally composed narratives about the exploits of particular deities.

16. I collected these legends in the course of fieldwork, but several versions have appeared also in publications about the town: Mullick (1921), Mitra (1940), Ray (1954), Karmakar (1967/68), Hunter (1868, 1876), and Banerji (1968).

17. These stories are not told of the Malla kings alone: several "frontier" kingdoms of Bengal, Bihar, and Orissa share the legends of royal origins. There are close similarities with stories of the Buddha's life as well.

18. Given by the late Vishnupur Sanskritist Sri Girija Sankar Ghor.

19. Beglar (1879), Bloch (1906), Spooner (1911), and other archaeological writings of British surveyors, but also Banddapadhyay (B.S. 1371).

20. The Dharma Ṭhākur literature is extensive, but it often isolates the narratives from the social contexts, making it hazardous to use for comparative purposes. Some claim that the cult is a remnant of Buddhism, others link it to "tribal" practices, yet others see it as folk literature, and some are content with summaries of the rituals: Sastri (1894), Bhattacharja (1952, 1953, 1964), Sarkar (1917), Chattopadhya (1961), Sen (1833), and Chattopadhyay (1935, 1942).

Chapter 2

1. For kula and baṇgśa see Fruzzetti and Östör (1976*b*), and for an elaboration of the argument see chapter 4 below and Östör, n.d.

2. *Ṣolaānā* refers to the community as a whole (a neighborhood, a caste, or a town). *Ṣola* means sixteen and *ānā* is the old division of money (one-sixteenth of a rupee); so sixteen annas designates a whole, a totality.

3. *Ghat*, the vessel of worship, is not to be confused with *ghāt*, the edge of an open body of water where some of the rituals take place.

4. Dry and hard items are more sacred than boiled and soft things: the latter have been "mediated," as it were.

5. The phrase refers to special celebrations even if these are regular—thus Durgāpūjā in the autumn is *akāl* (out of time, season) because the Durgā festival used to be held in the spring (now Bāsaṇtipūjā) until Rāma was forced to perform the autumn worship in order to defeat Rāvan.

6. Magic is used here not in its anthropological sense, but in reference to *kriyā* (action), a pattern of transformation.

7. Karma, dharma-artha-kama-moksa, sattva-raja-tama are categories well

known from the literature of Hinduism, but they are also ethnographic categories in local systems and contexts. See the discussion below.

8. Mantras and mudras (and their performance) are described in various publications that are locally available.

9. The text referred to is the Brihatnandikeśvar Durgāpūjā rules of procedure, widely available in the town. The prescribed stages leave much room for local variations. The exegesis given below is that of the participants.

10. *Pān* refers to the betel leaf (used in rituals) and to the preparation made of betel leaf, areca nuts, and other spices (eaten after meals).

11. Low-caste participation is not allowed in some line pūjās, but in other ways too Durgāpūjā is not a festival of the lowest jātis, even though the latter have pūjā functions and take part in aspects of the worship. With the direction the public festivals are taking, this participation will be more significant in the future.

12. Note the parallel with the Manasā stories (Dimock and Ramanujan 1964).

13. In household pūjās the image is often kept for seven days before immersion.

14. Here we are dealing not with entities and substances, but rather with relationships; so hierarchical segmentation differs from a requirement of full participation.

Chapter 3

1. For a cultural study of the bazaar, see Östör, n.d.

2. This, as we shall see, is not absolute, and the gājan is not simply a ritual of reversal.

3. Boiṣṇab or Bostom is the caste reference of Vaiṣṇava. Originally a devotional movement, today, in addition to its sectarian meaning, Bostom/Boiṣṇab also denotes a caste. Bostoms of the town are often found reciting songs of Kṛṣṇa's līlā (cosmic play). See note 8 below.

4. For jāti categorization see Östör (1978*b*). As noted above, gājan is not merely an egalitarian foil to enduring hierarchy.

5. Temples and images are described at length in various publications: Beglar (1879), Banddapadhyay (B.S. 1371), Bloch (1906), and Sanyal (1972).

6. Doms are a low jāti of basket makers who are also musicians playing drums and flutes at various festivals.

7. For a general discussion of pūjā see Östör (1978*a*, *b*) and chapter 2 above.

8. Śiva is the characteristic and usual transcription, but the Bengali pronunciation would be Śib (thus also Biṣṇu and Boiṣṇab and Biṣṇupur).

9. This story is widely known and told in the town, but it is also a purāṇic account appearing in several classes of narrative.

10. Gāmār is the decorative tree *Gmelina arborea;* śāl is the forest tree *Shorea robusta,* nim is the margosa tree, and bel is the wood apple tree.

11. The Ṣāṛeśvar gājan dominates the whole region: it includes a wider range of variant rituals than any other gājan, and its aspect of reversal is also more pronounced because of the larger percentage of lower castes participating in it in preference to other gājans.

12. Palit (B.S. 1319) and Sarkar (1917). Sarkar translated large sections of Palit's work verbatim and supplemented it from other sources.

13. For pūraṇic texts see Sarkar (1917), and for references to Caitra parab in the Upapurāṇas, see Hazra (1963).

14. Ramaipaṇḍit's *Sunyapurāṇ,* p. 79; but see also the Dharmapūjā Bidhan. Note in this connection the jhāpbhanga incident in the Lausen story.

15. Ramaipaṇḍit's *Sunyapurāṇ,* pp. 80–81.

16. Palit (B.S. 1319), part 1, section 1, chap. 3; Sarkar (1917), chap. 2.

Chapter 4

1. Festivals yield a system and a structure beyond other systems and structures. I also noted that they seem to participate in other systems such as "caste," "marriage," "politics," and "economics," but I have not analyzed these as I have done for pūjās and festivals.

Pūjās lead us to a domain in indigenous terms, not through the opposition of general sociological categories but through the recognition of a thing both in itself and in combination with other things, defined through history and through present practice in Bengal. Far from cultural uniqueness delivering us to some kind of solipsism, we are able to situate the problematics of our discipline in the middle of subject-object relationships, relying on mediation, indigenous construction of categories, and the processes of structure and dialectics within and between ourselves, our society, Bengalis, and Bengali society. This line of thought, if pursued further, would recognize that "religion," "economics," and so forth have become indigenous to India to a degree, revealing the extent to which Indian society has come to approximate the West.

2. The deity/ritualist/offerer triad may be found on different levels of abstraction: brahman/purusa/prakriti, goddess/rāvan/avatar (or goddess/divine ritualist/divine offerer), Durgā/priest/king, Durgā/priest/community; on each level the categories stand in the same relationship to each other. There are gifts, intercession, alliance, sharing, and exchange. The relationships are passive or active, corresponding to the basic binary principles of male/female. The ritualist mediates, intercedes; the deity and offerer share and exchange. But sharing extends to all three categories; the principle of puruṣa/prakriti is not an opposition, but a way of merging units in a hierarchical, segmentary system; the structures are never in a steady state; rather, they are dynamic and circular. Relations also are not static, since there is always an imbalance that ensures further restatement; prakriti issues from brahman, and purusa is dialectically opposed to prakriti, the creation of elements through prakriti ensues, and so on to the hierarchical segmentary divisions in society. In the king/priest/goddess triad the deity issues a command, an alliance ensues, and the priest mediates.

The deity is related to other segments of society (jajmān); so once again we regain a hierarchical system with relationships between encompassing and encompassed. In the sequential schemes the arrival and departure of deities climax in food offerings, life-giving, and the presence of divinity. Again the basic principle of the triad is expressed through sharing among categories and by the dual direction of the process creating an imbalance only to be restored by a dialectic (departure results in arrival, annual rites return, the whole scheme is repeated within each pūjā).

3. Tambiah (1972) is right to question Dumont and Pocock's (1959) dichotomy of Brāhmaṇic and popular levels in Hinduism. Nevertheless, Tambiah (1972) and Leach (1968) both retain dichotomies—if not this-worldly/otherworldly, then doctrinal and practical religion. In India, at least, doctrinal, sectarian, practical, local, all-India, popular, and other aspects are distinguishable, case by case, in the same locality; yet, generalizing within our case, the are related structurally, functionally, historically, dialectically, and so forth.

4. The king's "marriage" alliance to the goddess also brings the principle of action into the locality (of worship).

5. Nevertheless, the specialized systems of philosophy, sectarian theology, medicine, and astrology are related to some extent to the anthropology of the town, if only in a sociologically encapsulated way. In this regard we note the recent work of O'Flaherty (1973) on the myths of Śiva, where she argues that the Great Lord's asceticism and eroticism are linked in a necessary oscillation resulting in the creation, accumulation, and release of power and energy. Some of the terms used in this original study should be familiar to us: *sannyāsa, tapas, tej, līlā,* and so forth. These do not mean the same thing everywhere; yet it is significant that, although O'Flaherty is decidedly concerned with a universe of myths in texts (hence contents play an overwhelming role), she does not oppose a Brāhmaṇic or Sanskritic level to local levels. On the contrary, local narratives find themselves side by side with Purāṇas and Epics. O'Flaherty's account suggests a parallel to my discussion: her findings are relevant to these festivals not because they would solve some of our puzzles, but because the position of some principles and categories in the two accounts are similar.

6. Transcendence is not the property of the renouncer alone: the gājan bhaktas attain this threefold (as Brāhmaṇs, sannyāsīs, debatās); in Durgāpūjā the king is similarly related to priest and goddess (and, by structural replacement, so are the householder, community, and so forth); cf. Dumont, Heesterman, and others.

7. Cf. Dumont (1970 *b*), "The Structual Definition of a Folk Deity." Note, however, that in our case there is an explict relationship between goddess and lord. I hasten to add here that I have considered the problem of Dharma-Śiva relations not because Śiva's gājan is somehow incomplete, but because we have such rich, centuries-old local data on Dharma Ṭhākur only a few miles away from Vishnupur. Bhaktas are not at all puzzled by the relative absence of local stories relating to Śiva and Bhairab: the divine model for the performance ("the gods did it before us") is quite adequate. In spite of its extraordinary detail, Durgāpūjā has the same rationale: Rāma's pūjā, Surat Rājā's pūjā, but there is much more to the shared properties of both festivals (the history of the town; the alliance between king and goddess; the creation of the qualities, castes, and the world of action; goddess as mother, daughter, and creator; the relation of Śiva and Durgā).

8. Hierarchies are variously arranged in the festivals: they are not static, permanent, or unchanging. Śiva, Durgā, Bhairab, and the sun alternate in their relationships throughout (and within each performance), transforming, reversing, exchanging positions and relations vis-à-vis each other. Pure and

impure (Dumont 1970*a*) gives the form of hierarchy; yet the relationship itself is encountered at every turn. Hierarchy dominates the relations among deities, among the categories of the threefold structure, even among bhaktas. The forms are the same, parallel to the instance of pure and impure, though they are not derived from the latter. The encompassing element is also found in all these instances. This, however, does not mean that elements in a hierarchy are identical and that substances or entities are confused and merged: Kāmakkā, Satī, Caṇḍī are separate and yet are encompassed by Durgā (here the synchronic and diachronic perspectives combine to define the structure of hierarchy at different moments in a cycle of development).

Appendix 1

1. This section is based on indigenous estimates, my own observations, and information culled from Chatterjee, Gupta, and Mukhopadhyay (1970), Mitra (1953), and Banerji (1968).

2. In this regard refer to my forthcoming volume (n.d.) on legendary history, festivals, and folk theater, bazaar and trade, revolution and change in Vishnupur as parallel though different approaches to the same reality.

Glossary

Ābārgājan	"Gājan-again"; repetition of the gājan
Adhikār	Responsibility; authority
Agradhānī	Ritualist; offerer of arghya
Āltā	Red lac
Aṅga	Part
Añjali	Offering of flowers
Ārati	Evening devotion
Arghya	Offering of lights
Āsura	Demon
Ātmā	Self; soul
Avatar	Incarnate deity; incarnation
Bali	Sacrifice
Baṇgśa	Line (descent)
Barṇa	Appearance; color
Bedī	Altar platform
Bel	Wood apple tree
Belbaraṇ	Invocation in the wood apple tree
Beṭ	Cane or sapling carried by bhaktas
Bhakta	Devotee

Bhakti	Devotion
Bhattacharya	A ritualist in pūjā
Bhog	Cooked food offering
Bhor	Trance
Bhuta	Spirit; ghost
Bij	Seed
Bijmantra	Seed mantra
Brata	Vow in women's ritual
Darśan	Sight; taking sight of
Dharma	Law; duty
Dhotī	Man's garment worn wrapped around the waist and legs
Dhunaporan	Burning of incense
Dhyen	Meditation; description
Durgāpaṭ	Painted representation of Durgā
Gaṅgājal	Water from the Ganges
Ganja	Marketplace
Ghat	Vessel of invocation
Ghāt	Edge of open water used for washing and bathing
Ghī	Clarified butter
Ghurānbhakta	Devotees who roll on the ground
Gotra	Maximal descent label
Guṇ	Quality
Habisanna	Rice cooked with ghī
Homa	Fire sacrifice
Jajak	Sacrificer; one who performs pūjā
Jajmān	Offerer; one on whose behalf pūjā is performed
Jalājog	Gift of water
Jāti	Caste; kind; sort
Jogkriyā	Yogic action
Kalpa	Period; time
Kalparambha	Beginning of kalpa
Kamandala	Water jug used in pūjā
Kosakusi	Vessels used in pūjā
Kriyā	Action
Kuladebatā	Deity of the line
Kusa	Sacred grass
Līlā	Divine (cosmic) play
Liṅga	Stylized phallic symbol used to represent Śiva
Mahātmā (mahitta)	Power of divinity
Mandap	Open-sided temple
Maṅgal	Auspiciousness

Maṅgalghat	Auspicious vessel
Maṅgal patra	Plate with twenty-four offerings
Mānsik	Vow; resolution
Mantra	Sacred incantation
Mat	Way; kind; opinion
Māyā	Illusion
Mela	Fair
Milan	Union
Mudra	Yogic gesture used in pūjā
Nabapatrika	Group of nine plants used in pūjā
Namaskār	Greeting consisting of word and gesture
Nāmgotra	Name and descent categories
Nāthmandir	Open temple pavilion
Niyam	Rule; observance
Noibedda	Cold food offering
Pabritta	Sacred
Paitā	Sacred thread
Paṇḍal	Temporary place of worship
Paṛā	Neighborhood
Pāṛā solaānā	Neighborhood community
Parmātmā	Universal self or soul
Paṭ	Painting on canvas
Pāṭā	Board studded with nails; sign of Bhairab
Pāṭbhakta	Chief or leading devotee
Pīthasthān	The fifty-one places of goddess worship
Prajā	Subject (to jajmān)
Prakriti	The created world
Praṇām	Salutation; prostration
Pranayan	Yogic breathing in pūjā
Prānpratiśṭhā	Giving life to an image
Prasad	Sacred leftovers of deities
Purohit	Ritualist; priest
Puruṣa	Male principle
Puspañjali	Flower offering
Rajasik	The second quality, passion
Rūp	Appearance; form
Sabda	Sound
Sāddhu	Ascetic
Sādhak	One who preaches ascetic practice
Sādhana	Ascetic practice
Śakti	Power of the goddess
Śāl	Jungle tree

Saṅkalpa	Declaration of intent
Śaṅkha	Shell
Sāri	Woman's garment
Śāstra	Sacred texts
Sattvik	The first quality, truth
Sebā	Service of deities
Snānjal	Water of a deity's bath
Ṣolaānā	Community
Śrāddha	Funerary rites
Srenī	Order; line
Śuddha	Pure
Suta	Bracelet made of threads
Svastik	Sign of peace
Tamasik	The third quality, inertia
Tantrik	Ritualist in puja
Tapassā	Practice of austerities
Tattva	Truth
Tej (teja)	Force
Trisur	Trident of Śiva
Tulsī	Sacred basil plant
Yantra	Sacred diagram
Yoni	Symbol of Durgā
Yuga	Age; time

References

Agrawala, S. 1963. *Devimahatmya.* Benares: Ramkrishna Math.

Babb, Lawrence A. 1975. *The divine hierarchy: Popular Hinduism in central India.* New York: Columbia University Press.

Bagchi, P. C. 1939. *Studies in the Tantras.* Calcutta: University of Calcutta.

Banddapadhyay, A. K. B.S. 1371. *Bankurar Mandir.* Calcutta: Sahittya Saṅgsad.

Banerjea, J. N. 1966. *Puranic and Tantric religion.* Calcutta: University of Calcutta.

Banerji, Amiya Kumar. 1968. *Bankura, West Bengal district gazetteers.* Calcutta: Government of West Bengal Press.

Barnett, Steve; Fruzzetti, Lina; and Östör, Ákos. 1976. Hierarchy purified: Notes on Dumont and his critics. *Journal of Asian Studies* 35:4.

Beck, Brenda E. F. 1972. *Peasant society in Konku: A study of right and left subcastes in south India.* Vancouver: University of British Columbia Press.

Beglar, J. D. 1879. *Archaeological survey of India,* vol. 8. Calcutta: Government of India Press.

Belshaw, Cyril S. 1965. *Traditional exchange and modern markets.* Englewood Cliffs, N.J.: Prentice-Hall.

Bhattacharja, Asutosh. 1952. The Dharma cult. *Bulletin of the Department of Anthropology* (Government of India), vol. 1, no. 1.

———. 1953. Dharma worship in West Bengal. In *The tribes and castes of West Bengal,* ed. A. Mitra. Census of India, 1951. Calcutta: Government of West Bengal Press.

———. 1964. *Baṅgal Maṅgalkāyyer Itihās.* 4th ed. Calcutta: A. Mukherjee.

———. 1968. Dharma and serpent worship in Bankura District. In *Bankura, West Bengal district gazetters.* Calcutta: Government of West Bengal Press.

Bhattacharya, S. 1970. *The Indian theogony.* Cambridge: Cambridge University Press.

Bloch, T. 1906. The temples at Vishnupur. In *Archaeological survey of India, Annual report, 1903/4.* Calcutta: Government of India Press.

Bose, D. N. 1956. *Tantras: Their philosophy and occult secrets.* Calcutta: University of Calcutta.

Chakrabarti, Cintaharan. B.S. 1377. *Hindur Acar—Anusthan.* Calcutta: Lekhak Sambāy Samiti.

Chakravarti, Chintaharan. 1935. The cult of Kalarkarudra (Cadak pūjā). *Journal of the Asiatic Society of Bengal,* 3d ser., 1:430–37.

———. 1963. *The Tantras: Studies on their religion and literature.* Calcutta: University of Calcutta.

Chatterjee, A. B.; Gupta, A.; and Mukhopadhyay, P. K., eds. 1970. *District census handbook, Bankura.* Census of India, 1961. Calcutta: Government Printing, West Bengal.

Chattopadhya, Gauranga. 1961. Carak festival in a village in West Bengal: Its socio-religious implication. In *Aspects of religion in Indian society,* ed. L. P. Vidyarthi. Meerut.

Chattopadhyay, K. P. 1935. The *Cadak* festival in Bengal. *Journal of the Asiatic Society of Bengal,* 3d ser., 1: 402–5.

———. 1942. Dharma worship. *Journal of the Asiatic Society of Bengal* 8: 101–37.

Chattopadhyay, K. P., and Bose, N. K. 1934. The *Manda* festival of Chota Nagpur. *Journal of the Asiatic Society of Bengal,* n.s., vol. 30.

Chaudhury, M. N. 1945. The cult of Vana-Durga, a tree deity. *Journal of the Royal Asiatic Society (Letters),* vol. 11.

Cohn, W. 1967. "Religion" in non-Western cultures? *American Anthropologist* 69:73–76.

Dalton, E. T. 1872. *Descriptive ethnology of Bengal.* Calcutta: Government of Bengal.

Dasgupta, Shashi-bhushan. 1958. *An introduction to Tantric Buddhism.* Calcutta: University of Calcutta.

———. 1962. *Obscure religious cults of India.* 2d ed. Calcutta: University of Calcutta.

Dimock, Edward C. 1966*a*. Doctrine and practice among the Vaisnavas of Bengal. In *Krishna: Myths, rites, and attitudes,* ed. Milton Singer. Honolulu: Eastwest Center.

———. 1966*b*. *The place of the hidden moon.* Chicago: University of Chicago Press.

Dimock, Edward C., and Ramanujan, A. K. 1961. The goddess of snakes in medieval Bengali literature. *History of Religions* 1, no. 1:307–21.

———. 1964. The goddess of snakes in medieval Bengali literature, part 2. *History of Religions* 3, no. 2:300–322.

Douglas, Mary. 1966. *Purity and danger.* London: Routledge.

Dumont, Louis. 1970*a*. *Homo hierarchicus: The caste system and its implications.* Chicago: University of Chicago Press.

———. 1970*b*. *Religion, politics and history in India: Collected papers in Indian sociology.* The Hague: Mouton.

Dumont, Louis, and Pocock, David. 1959. Religion. *Contributions to Indian Sociology,* no. 3.

Fox, Robin. 1967. *Kinship and marriage: An anthropological perspective.* Baltimore: Penguin.

Fruzzetti, Lina M. 1975. Conch shell bangles, iron bangles: An analysis of women, marriage, and ritual in Bengal. Ph.D. diss., University of Minnesota.

Fruzzetti, Lina M., and Östör, Ákos. 1976*a*. Is there a structure to north Indian kinship terminology? *Contributions to Indian Sociology,* n.s., 10, no.1:63–95.

———. 1976*b*. Seed and earth: A cultural analysis of kinship in a Bengali town. *Contributions to Indian Sociology,* n.s., 10, no.1:97–132.

Geertz, Clifford. 1973. *The interpretation of cultures.* New York: Basic Books.

Ghosh, Benoy. 1957. *Pascim Baṅger Saṃskṛiti.* Calcutta.

Harper, Edward B. 1964. Ritual pollution as an integrator of caste and religion. In *Religion in South Asia,* ed. E. B. Harper. Seattle: University of Washington Press.

Hazra, R. C. *Studies in the Upapuranas.* Vols. 1–11. Calcutta: University of Calcutta.

Heesterman, J. C. 1964. Brahmin, ritual, and renouncer. *Wiener Zeitschrift für die Kunde Sud- und Ost-Asiens* 8:1–34.

Hunter, W. W. 1868. *Annals of rural Bengal.* Vol 1. London: Smith, Elder.

———. 1876. *A statistical account of Bengal.* Vol. 4. *Birbhum, Bankura, and Burdwan.* London: Trübner.

Hutton, John Henry. 1963. *Caste in India.* 4th ed. New York: Oxford University Press.

Jakobson, Roman. 1960. Concluding statement: Linguistics and Poetics. In *Style in language,* ed. Thomas A. Seboek. Cambridge: MIT Press.

Karmakar, Phakirnārāyan. 1967/68. *Bisṇupurer Amor Kahini.* Calcutta: Publishers Only.

Keesing, Roger M. 1975. *Kin groups and social structure*. New York: Holt, Rinehart and Winston.

Langer, Susan. 1964. *Philosophy in a new key*. New York: Mentor.

Leach, E. R. 1965. *Political systems of highland Burma*. Boston: Beacon Press.

———, ed. 1968. *Dialectic in practical religion*. Cambridge: Cambridge University Press.

Lévi-Strauss, Claude. 1963. *Totemism*. Boston: Beacon Press.

———. 1967*a*. *The savage mind*. London: Weidenfeld and Nicolson.

———. 1967*b*. *Structural anthropology*. New York: Doubleday.

———. 1967*c*. The story of Asdiwal. In *The structural study of myth and totemism*, ed. E. Leach. London: Tavistock.

Marriott, McKim. 1955. Little communities in an indigenous civilization. In *Village India: Studies in the little community*, ed. McKim Marriott. Chicago: University of Chicago Press.

———. 1966. The feast of love. In *Krishna: Myths, rites, and attitudes*, ed. Milton Singer. Honolulu. Eastwest Center.

Mathur, K. S. 1964. *Caste and ritual in a Malwa village*. Bombay: Asia Publishing House.

Mayer, Adrian C. 1960. *Caste and kinship in central India*. Berkeley: University of California Press.

Mazumdar, R. C. 1943. *History of Bengal*. Vol. 1. Dacca: University of Dacca.

Mitra, A. 1953. *The tribes and castes of West Bengal*. Census of India, 1951. Calcutta: West Bengal Government Press.

Mitra, J. N. 1940. *The ruins of Vishnupur*. Calcutta: Newman's Printing Press.

Mullick, A. P. 1921. *A history of the Bishnupur Raj*. Calcutta.

Murdock, George P. 1965. *Social structure in Southeast Asia*. New York: Quadrangle Books.

Myrdal, Gunnar. 1967. *Asian drama*. 3 vols. New York: Pantheon.

Nash, Manning. 1966. *Primitive and peasant economic systems*. San Francisco: Chandler.

Nicholas, R. W. 1967. Ritual hierarchy and social relations in rural Bengal. *Contributions to Indian Sociology*, n.s., 1:56–83.

O'Flaherty, Wendy D. 1973. *Asceticism and eroticism in the mythology of Siva*. New York: Oxford University Press.

O'Malley, L. S. S. 1908. *Bankura: Bengal district gazetteers*. Calcutta: Bengal Secretariat Book Depot.

Östör, Ákos, 1971. The play of gods among men: Society, locality, time and ideology in symbolism of myths and rituals in a Bengali town. Ph.D. diss., University of Chicago.

———. 1978*a*. On the ethnographic study of complex Bengali pūjās and festivals. Part 1. Durgāpūjā in Bishnupur; Part 2. Siva's gājan in

Bishnupur. *Journal of the Indian Anthropological Society,* vol. 13, no. 3; vol. 14, no. 1.

———. 1978*b*. Pūjā in society: A methodological and analytical essay on an ethnographic category. Part 1. Ideology; Part 2. Structure. *Eastern Anthropologist* 31:119–76.

———. N.d. *Deities, ritualists, merchants, and revolutionaries: Essays in the anthropology of a Bengali town.* Forthcoming.

Palit, Haridas. B.S. 1319. *Adyer Gambhira.* Calcutta.

Pañjikā (almanac and calendar). 1966/67 to 1973/74. Gupta Press. Calcutta.

Parsons, Talcott. 1964. *The social system.* Glencoe, Ill.: Free Press.

———. 1965. An outline of the social system (and various introductions). In *Theories of society,* ed. Talcott Parsons et al. Glencoe, Ill.: Free Press.

Pocock, David. 1960. Sociologies, rural and urban. *Contributions to Indian Sociology,* no. 4, pp. 63–81.

Rāmāipaṇḍit. B.S. 1314. *Sunyapurān,* ed. N. Basu. Calcutta: Baṅgiya Sahitya Parisad.

———. B.S. 1323. *Dharma Pūjābidhān,* ed. N. Banddopadhyay. Calcutta: Baṅgiya Sahitya Parisad.

Ramanujan, A. K. 1973. *Speaking of Śiva.* Trans. with an introduction by A. K. Ramanujan. New York: Penguin Books.

Ray, Amarendranath. 1950. *Baṅgalīr Pūjā Parban.* Calcutta: University of Calcutta.

Ray, B. G. 1964. *Religious movements in modern Bengal.* Santiniketan: Visva-Bharati Press.

Ray, Gangagobinda. 1954. *Mallabhum Kahini.* Bishnupur.

Ray, Niharranjan. B.S. 1359. *Baṅgalīr Itihās.* Calcutta: Book Emporium.

Roy, S. N. 1927. The festivities in honor of Śiva in the month of Chaitra. *Journal of the Anthropological Society of Bombay* 14, no. 1:181–85.

Sanyal, Hitesh. 1972. Religious architecture in Bengal. In *Aspects of Indian culture and society,* ed. Surajit Sinha. Calcutta.

Sarkar, Benoy Kumar. 1917. *The folk element in Hindu cultures.* London: Longmans, Green.

Sarkar, J. N., ed. 1948. *History of Bengal.* Vol. 2. Dacca: University of Dacca.

Sarma, Jyotirmoye. 1969. Pūjā associations in West Bengal. *Journal of Asian Studies* 28, no. 3:579–94.

Sastri, M. M. Haraprasad. B.S. 1363. Baṅge Bouddhadharma. In *Haraprasad Racanābali,* ed. S. K. Chattopadhyay. Calcutta: Eastern Trading Company.

———. 1894. Discovery of the remnants of Buddhism in Bengal. *Proceedings of the Asiatic Society of Bengal,* 135–38.

Scheftelowitz. 1929. *Die Zeit als Schicksalsgottheit in der Indischen und Iranischen Religion.* Stuttgart: W. Kohlhammer.

Schneider, D. M. 1965. Some muddles in the models; or, How the system really works. In *The relevance of models for social anthropology,* ed. Michael Banton. London: Tavistock.
———. 1968. *American kinship: A cultural account.* Englewood Cliffs, N.J.: Prentice-Hall.
———. 1972. What is kinship all about? In *Kinship studies in the Morgan centennial year,* ed. Priscilla Reining. Washington, D.C.: Anthropological Society of Washington.
Sen, R. K. 1833. Charak pūjā ceremonies. *Journal of the Asiatic Society of Bengal* 11:609–12.
Sen, Sukumar. 1945. Is the cult of Dharma a living relic of Buddhism in Bengal? In *B.C. law volume,* ed. D. R. Bhandarkar et al., part 1. Calcutta: Indian Research Institute.
Shastri, Ashokanath. 1949. Durgā pūjā. *Bharatiya Vidya* 10:241–62.
Singer, Milton. 1972. *When a great tradition modernizes.* New York: Praeger.
Sirkar, D. C., ed. 1967. *The Sakti cult and Tara.* Calcutta: University of Calcutta.
Spooner, D. B. 1911. Bankura District. *Archaeological survey of India, Annual report, Eastern Circle 1910/11.* Calcutta: Government of India Press.
Srinivas, M. N. 1952. *Religion and society among the Coorgs of South India.* London: Oxford University Press.
———. 1966. *Social change in modern India.* Berkeley: University of California Press.
Tambiah, S. J. 1972. *Spirit cults of north eastern Thailand.* Cambridge: Cambridge University Press.
Turner, Victor W. 1962. *Chihamba, the white spirit.* Rhodes-Livingstone Paper no. 33. Manchester: Manchester University Press.
———. 1967. *The forest of symbols.* Ithaca: Cornell University Press.
———. 1969. *The ritual process: Structure and anti-structure.* Chicago: Aldine.
Wadley, S. S. 1975. *Shakti: Power in the conceptual structure of Karimpur religion.* Chicago: University of Chicago Department of Anthropology.
Wagner, Roy. 1975. *The invention of culture.* Englewood Cliffs, N.J.: Prentice-Hall.

Index